THE CONFUCIAN WAY
OF
CONTEMPLATION

Plate I. *Chih-ts'ang,* "The Wisdom That Is Stored"
(calligraphy by Okada).

THE CONFUCIAN WAY

OF

CONTEMPLATION

Okada Takehiko and the Tradition of Quiet-Sitting

RODNEY L. TAYLOR

University of South Carolina Press

For my Mother and Father
who began my learning

BL
1857
.T39
1988

Copyright © University of South Carolina 1988

Published in Columbia, South Carolina, by the
University of South Carolina Press

Manufactured in the United States of America

Library of Congress Cataloging-in-Publication Data

Taylor, Rodney Leon, 1944–
    The Confucian way of contemplation: Okada Takehiko and the
tradition of quiet-sitting/Rodney L. Taylor.
        p.   cm.—(Studies in comparative religion)
    "Selected bibliography of Okada's works": p.
    Includes index.
    ISBN 0-87249-532-9
    1. Religious life—Confucianism. 2. Confucianism. 3. Okada,
Takehiko. I. Title. II. Series: Studies in comparative religion
(Columbia, S.C.)
BL1857.T39 1988
299'.51243—dc19   87-22940
                                                                         CIP

STUDIES IN COMPARATIVE RELIGION
Frederick M. Denny, Editor

The Holy Book in Comparative Perspective
Edited by Frederick M. Denny and Rodney L. Taylor

Dr. Strangegod: On the Symbolic Meaning of Nuclear Weapons
By Ira Chernus

*Native American Religious Action: A Performance Approach to
Religion*
By Sam Gill

*The Confucian Way of Contemplation: Okada Takehiko and the
Tradition of Quiet-Sitting*
By Rodney L. Taylor

CONTENTS

Editor's Preface   3
Acknowledgments   5
Introduction: Meeting with a Confucian 7
Part I. A Confucian Life of Contemplation
   1. The Confucian Quest   13
   2. Centering the Self in Quiet-Sitting   31
   3. Moral Action from a Contemplative Mode   56
Part II. Selected Translations from Okada Takehiko's *Zazen to Seiza*
   4. *Seiza:* A Prefatory Discussion   77
   5. A Critique of Zen   94
   6. A Discussion of *Seiza*   123
Part III. Okada Takehiko in Dialogue
   My Life   165
   Kotsuza—Just Sitting   179
   The Names of My Study   185
   On Prayer   189
   On Death   191
   On the Goodness of Human Nature   193
   Art and Religion   196
   Science and the Respect for Life   199
   The Threat of Nuclear War   207
   World Religions   210
Notes   213
Selected Bibliography of Okada's Works   222
Index   225

List of Plates

Plate I. *Chih-ts'ang,* The Wisdom That Is Stored (calligraphy by Okada) *Frontispiece*

Plate II. Okada in His Garden 32

Plate III. Okada in His Study 95

Plate IV. Poem and Calligraphy by Okada 166

THE CONFUCIAN WAY
of
CONTEMPLATION

EDITOR'S PREFACE

The comparative study of religion has been known by different names in the century of its existence as an independent field overlapping the social sciences and humanities. This series makes no special claim for the phrase "comparative religion" beyond viewing it as a widely used label for an equally wide range of scholarly interests and methods. We are committed to viewing religion as a universal dimension of human life and the study of religion as an enterprise that can and should be made intelligible beyond disciplinary, area studies, and confessional boundaries.

The books in the series, although written by specialists, are intended for a broad spectrum of educated readers. No particular school of religious studies is supported to the exclusion of others; instead, the aim is to be catholic and integrative, providing the results of a variety of approaches to different traditions, with the expectation that the quality and innovativeness of the projects will be sufficient to generate useful discussions of substantive, theoretical and methodological issues.

Rodney Taylor's *The Confucian Way of Contemplation: Okada Takehiko and the Tradition of Quiet-Sitting* is a groundbreaking study of the life and thought of a contemporary Japanese Confucian. Professor Taylor has for some time now been contributing valuable insights into the Neo-Confucian tradition, emphasizing its fundamental religious quality by careful analysis of the cultivation of sagehood. But most of Taylor's research has been on pre-modern texts from China. Not until his encounter with Okada Takehiko did the author begin to turn his research focus towards living Confucianism, and in the unexpected context of modern Japan.

The Confucian Way of Contemplation provides an excellent example of a type of comparative religion scholarship that is increasingly considered to be essential to the further development of the field: the taking account of both text and context in the interpretation of historical traditions that possess both extensive literary sources—scriptures, biographies, meditation guides, doctrinal treatises and other texts—and living devotional settings. Taylor's discussion of quiet-sitting within both the Zen and Confucian traditions comes compellingly alive when viewed in relation to the thought and example of Okada. This kind of study could not have been accomplished without traditional linguistic, historical, philosophical and phenomenology of religion preparation. But it probably never would have been conceived, let alone attempted, without a sense of the importance of checking the tradition with a live exponent, who, unlike written texts, *talks back,* and on topics never imagined by earlier thinkers.

We have in *The Confucian Way of Contemplation* an absorbing study of Confucian self-cultivation, together with a running comparison with Zen parallels. By means of extensive sections of a key Okada work in translation, and through a record of dialogue between Okada and Taylor, as well as the author's own authoritative interpretations, a successful balancing of text and context, past and present theory and practice in Confucian meditation has been achieved.

Frederick M. Denny
Series Editor

ACKNOWLEDGMENTS

I would like to acknowledge my deep gratitude for the support I have received that has brought this project to its present publication. That support began with an American Council of Learned Societies study grant to Japan (1976–77). It was this grant that permitted me to meet Okada Takehiko and begin my study of his writings. This, of course, was only possible because of the support of my teacher Wm. Theodore deBary at Columbia University. My teacher of Japanese in Japan, Nakamura Yoneo, was an invaluable source of early support and assistance in my first readings of Okada. In addition, the project would have taken a very different turn if I had not received a National Endowment for the Humanities summer stipend in 1983 to return to Japan to engage Okada in conversation for nearly a month. This conversation has become a critical link in presenting the story of Okada and, in turn, the religious life of a Confucian in contemporary Japan. I was helped tremendously in this dialogue with Okada by the excellent and faithful assistance of Okada's son Susumu. Clearly, the dialogue could never have taken place without his help with translation and the nuanced interpretation of his father's thought. The warmth and friendship of Okada's colleagues at Kyūshū University during my stay in Fukuoka was also a major support to me. I am also indebted to the University of Colorado at Boulder's Council on Research and Creative Work for additional financial support in the production of the manuscript as well as travel funds.

Permission has been granted by several sources for the use of some of the material contained in the present book. First and foremost, I want to thank

Okada Takehiko for allowing me to translate his book *Zazen to Seiza (Buddhist and Confucian Meditation)*, of which three chapters appear in this volume. I would also like to thank the *Journal of Chinese Religions* for granting me permission to use material that first appeared in an earlier form in *"Zazen to Seiza:* A Prefatory Discussion" (*Journal of Chinese Religions* 10 [1982]: 19–38) and Temple University Press for granting me permission to use parts of the dialogue with Okada on animals that first appeared in "Of Animals and Man: The Confucian Perspective," in *Animal Sacrifices: Religious Perspectives on the Use of Animals in Science,* ed. T. Regan (Philadelphia: Temple University Press, 1985), pp. 257–59.

Colleagues have played an invaluable role in reacting to my ideas and to the manuscript as it took shape. Foremost in this respect have been the contributions of Sam Gill, Paul W. Kroll, and Frederick Denny. Expert readers of the manuscript have also responded with extraordinary time and care and made a number of useful suggestions. For their efforts in this respect, I want to thank Bardwell Smith and Conrad Schirokauer. As my administrative assistant Gladys Bloedow knows all too well, a manuscript seems to go through an endless number of revisions. For her talent, thoroughness, and patience in dealing with a manuscript and its author, I express my thanks.

None of this, of course, would be possible without the support of my family. I am eternally grateful for that support even when the writing of the manuscript intruded upon family times. To Judith, Meghan, Annika, and Dylan I give my thanks.

Rodney L. Taylor
Boulder, Colorado

INTRODUCTION: MEETING WITH A CONFUCIAN

The story of my acquaintance with Okada Takehiko and in turn the story of the origin of this book began some years ago. I had received a grant to study in Japan for the academic year 1976–77. It was, as I recall, a spring weekend in 1976 that I was attending meetings of the Seminar on Neo-Confucian Studies at Columbia University and had the occasion to talk with my former teacher Wm. Theodore deBary about my forthcoming trip to Japan. I was planning to work at Kyoto University, and he was sharing some of his own experiences of living and working in Japan generally and the Kyoto area specifically. We were discussing several prominent scholars of Neo-Confucian studies, some of whom I might have the opportunity to meet. The subtleties of various areas of scholarship were discussed, particularly methodological strategies and approaches often used in Japanese studies of the Confucian tradition.

Suddenly Professor deBary paused for a moment, and said that if I had the occasion to meet Okada Takehiko, even though he lived far from Kyoto, I would be meeting someone who was very different, someone who did not approach the tradition with what he might describe as an intellectual model. Okada's concerns were at heart not merely addressing intellectual or historical questions. Professor deBary said that when you meet Okada Takehiko you are meeting the living tradition itself. It was not a disinterested intellectual model, but a personal quest from the living tradition.

Initially, a living example of the tradition seemed an interesting problem in terms of method and theory. There was, after all, nothing really remaining of the Confucian living tradition. There were no longer the Confucian ceremonies conducted on a twice-yearly calendar; the Confucian civil service examination system had long ceased to exist. It is undeniably the case that Confucian religious and moral values pervade East Asian cultures, but it was very different to think of a particular contemporary person as focusing and centering these values for his own worldview. Contact with such a person could be an interesting issue and one deserving the attention of a historian of religion. I left for Japan with this observation in the back of my mind.

I was not prepared, however, for meeting Okada Takehiko. I arranged to spend several days with him in Fukuoka to discuss his work on Confucian meditation. Within a few moments of our meeting as we drove from the Fukuoka train station in a taxi to my hotel, he turned to me and with no hesitation said, "I feel that the world is in tremendous moral and spiritual decline. What do you think can be done about it?" The question stunned me. In a sense it reminded me of Zen koans and the master's role in confronting the student with a situation or problem that had direct relevance to his own enlightenment. But this was no Zen master, this was a scholar of Confucianism. Yet I had also been told that he was different, he was not just a scholar of the tradition, he *was* the tradition. And here was my first clear perception of the tradition itself. It was no longer filtered through texts, or through historical reconstruction. I was meeting it.

My method became the interaction with and recording of a living tradition. The goal was to present Okada as he presented himself to me, to permit others to see Confucianism as more than textual hermeneutics. It was this intense interest to reveal a living point of view that was the beginning of this study.

My plan had originally been to translate major sections of Okada's work on Confucian meditation and to introduce this with a historical discussion of the practice itself, but I realized that to do this would be to undermine the very element I wished to explore, namely, the religious insight of a Confucian. I came to realize that Okada's written work was essential, particularly his study of Confucian meditation, but I also needed to talk with him at length. I needed to bring the questions posed in his *text* to the framework of his own *context*, to let him *speak* of the importance of what he had *written*.

After delays of several years, I was able to return to Japan during the summer of 1983, posing questions about the place of Okada's academic work in the framework of his own religious life. The result of these sessions provided an intimate sense of a living Confucian, of the way in which his academic work emerges directly out of his deeply felt religious concerns. I returned home with fifty hours of recorded conversations and have transcribed a number of sections of our conversations for the present volume.

As it has taken shape, the present book contains major sections of translation from Okada's volume dealing with Confucian meditation, *Buddhist and Confucian Meditation (Zazen to Seiza)*. Of the five chapters that make up *Zazen to Seiza*, three have been included here only slightly abridged, chapters 1, 3, and 4. These chapters present Okada's interpretation of quietude and quiet-sitting. The order of the chapters as they appear in translation is the same as they appear in the original. Chapters 2 and 5 have, however, been excluded. Chapter 2 was not included because it focused primarily upon introductory issues in the practice of meditation and included materials that took the discussion outside the context of the Neo-Confucian understanding of quietude and quiet-sitting. Chapter 5 was excluded because it is a translation into modern Japanese of sayings by Kusumoto Tanzan. I have referred to some of these in my own introductory chapters, but since the chapter is entirely Kusumoto Tanzan and does not present further perspectives of Okada, it seemed outside the purpose of the present study.

A word is in order about the style of *Zazen to Seiza*. The work is both polemical and technical. Its polemical dimension is seen primarily in Okada's critique of Buddhism, especially Zen Buddhism and its meditative practices. To some his tone may appear inappropriate, and for others the nature of the critique may seem superficial and repetitive. It is important to remember, however, that Okada is speaking as a Confucian himself, and as such he is expressing part of his own worldview, which considers Buddhism to a degree as a negative influence in the development of East Asian cultures. The nature of his critique, primarily a criticism of Buddhism's lack of concern for moral action in the world, is the major historical criticism of Buddhism by Confucians. To some this may appear shallow, particularly those demanding a philosophical critique, but this has remained the heart of the Confucian view of Buddhism. From the Confucian perspective, a Buddhist does not genuinely concern himself with issues of the world because Buddhism ultimately sees the world itself as having only a qualified existence. If its character is transitory and empty, then action on behalf of the world is of little meaning. Okada speaks of Buddhism in this way from his own faith in Confucianism and its affirmation of the world. His own Confucian worldview is incomplete without an understanding of his critique of Buddhism.

Zazen to Seiza also appears as a technical work. It is constructed of numerous historical sources, and its argument is at times subtle and complex. Okada intended the work, however, as a general statement about the Confucian way of contemplation to a Japanese audience more familiar with Buddhism than with Neo-Confucianism. In this spirit, it does not have the normal scholarly apparatus, identification of sources, discussion of complex terms, and so forth. In fact, it has no footnotes at all. When I first saw this, I told Okada that if this were ever to appear in English translation, the hundreds of quotations would have to be identified. It would have to be presented as a scholarly work. I asked if he could help, since many of the original Chinese sources had been translated into Japanese and I was not sure I could reconstruct all of the original Chinese texts. He laughed and said that he could not possibly remember where many of these passages came from, and besides many were from memory anyway. Initially, I was exasperated. How was it possible to quote sources and not identify them? It is quite clear, however, that to Okada the identification of these sources is not important. Rather, the importance lies in the statement of the role and nature of the Confucian way of contemplation and the effect this might have in the world today. One can easily lose oneself in the process of identifying sources, which would only prove one of Okada's major contentions, namely, that Confucianism is studied primarily as intellectual history. For most people it remains a scholarly pursuit, and is not allowed to present itself as a worldview experienced by Confucians. Okada's intention is to show Confucian experience, to focus upon the subjective structure of the tradition, and he intends *Zazen to Seiza* to reflect his own experience of Confucianism. For this reason, the text is presented in translation as he presented it in Japanese, and as such it becomes an intimate view of his own Confucian experience. A number of the passages Okada quotes can be readily found in works such as W. T. Chan, *A Source Book of Chinese Philosophy;* and W. T. deBary, *Sources of Chinese Tradition.*

The present volume also contains sustained sections of dialogue between Okada and myself, dialogue ranging over issues of specific aspects of Confucian religious thought and practice as well as topical issues responded to from a Confucian perspective. It is thus both what Okada has written and what he has said. And what he has said brings the Confucian perspective upon issues the modern world argues and debates. This is not a forced "relevancy," but a recognition that Confucians as a central component of their worldview have always responded to pressing issues of their own day. Okada is first and foremost a Confucian. Responding to issues of one's own generation as a Confucian is exercising a responsibility Confucians have always exercised. More important, such responses are themselves a vital part of one's religious life. They represent the quality of wholeness of human response for a religious person who sees all facets of existence as religious. The Confucian is no different from others in sharing this central feature of *homo religiosus,* religious man.

PART I
A CONFUCIAN LIFE OF
CONTEMPLATION

1. THE CONFUCIAN QUEST

For much of the later Confucian tradition, what is usually called Neo-Confucianism, the quest of the religious life was the goal of sagehood. The earlier tradition, Classical Confucianism, also spoke of sagehood, but it often did not have the immediacy to the religious life as a realizable goal that it comes to have for many schools of Neo-Confucianism. The Classical Confucian thinker Mencius (372–289 B.C.E.) made the goal more realizable in the eyes of the later Confucians by arguing that anyone could become a sage. He stated that all people have the capacity for sagehood within their nature.[1] For many Neo-Confucians, this quest for sagehood became the focus of learning and self-cultivation. There are, however, many different approaches to sagehood, different ideas of the learning and self-cultivation necessary to reach the goal, and different images of the role of the sage. The history of later Confucianism is in many ways a record of the centrality of sagehood and the diversity of dialogue about it.

Sagehood itself is seen as the development of one's full moral capacity, but it transcends the purely moral category, for the pursuit of sagehood places the individual in direct relation with what is judged to be Absolute Truth. For early Confucians, this state was described as Heaven, *T'ien,* and at times it appeared to have an almost theistic structure about it. For the Neo-Confucian, the meaning is expanded. It is most commonly tied to *li,* principle, understood as the underlying structure of humanity, the world, and the cosmos and is often referred to as *T'ien-li,* the Principle of Heaven. It is not generally theistic, but in many cases it is monistic and reflects the new philosophical sophistication of the Neo-Confucian. On the religious side, its role is essentially in continuity with the earlier use of *T'ien,* continuing to be viewed as that which is ultimate and the source of religious authority.

This realization of *T'ien-li* is, it appears, directly experienced by at least some Neo-Confucians. When experienced, it is even described as an enlightenment experience, characterized by a kind of shattering experience of oneness with all things. Such experiences are expressed in distinctly Confucian terms, seen in terms of moral virtues, but in this case such virtues are raised to the very structure of the Absolute itself. One experiences the universal goodness through commiseration with all things. One of the key expressions of this vision and one that remains a kind of *locus classicus* for all future generations of Confucians is found in the writing known as the *Western Inscription (Hsi-ming)* by the Sung dynasty Neo-Confucian Chang Tsai (1021–77).

> Heaven is my father and earth is my mother, and even such a small creature as I finds an intimate place in their midst. Therefore that which extends throughout the universe I regard as my body and that which directs the universe I consider as my nature. All people are my brothers and sisters, and all things are my companions. . . . Even those who are tired and infirm, crippled or sick, those who have no brothers or children, wives or husbands, are all my brothers who are in distress and have no one to turn to.[2]

The universe and I are one. The conclusion draws the individual into the moral implications of such a vision. If all things are one, then I share a moral relation with all things and have moral responsibilities to those less fortunate than myself. This is not simply a philosophical proposition, nor is it an intellectual schema of the world; it is first and foremost something that can be directly experienced. Granted the primacy of experience, how does one arrive at this realization? This is the role of learning and self-cultivation, which is in turn the departure point for a variety of opinions and positions on the nature of learning and self-cultivation.

Strategies of Learning and Self-Cultivation

One of the principal writings used by Neo-Confucians to discuss the process of learning and self-cultivation is the *Great Learning (Ta-hsüeh),* a text from the period of Classical Confucianism and originally a chapter from the ritual classic the *Book of Rites (Li Chi).*[3] The text offers a strategy of learning that is essentially steps of self-cultivation. The interpretation of these various steps, and even the ordering of the steps themselves, has played an important role in Neo-Confucian discussions of the religious life. In the *Great Learning,* the process of learning and self-cultivation is said to begin with *ko-wu,* the investigation of things. It goes on to *chih-chih,* the extension of knowledge, *ch'eng-i,* the sincerity of intention, *cheng-hsin,* the rectification of the mind or heart, and then *hsiu-shen,* cultivation of the person. From there it moves to more externally focused activities: the regulation of the family, ordering of the state, and finally peace in the world. The later steps require little explanation and are not stages of self-cultivation as much as they represent increasing spheres of influence that are the product of self-cultivation.

The first five stages represent interior stages of learning and self-cultivation, and these in turn have been the chief focus of discussion and debate. What does it mean to talk of the investigation of things, the extension of knowledge, or the sincerity of intention? The answers to these questions are directly related to the practice of the religious life, and they provide the basis for standard forms of discourse and interpretation that inform the worldview articulated by Okada himself.

The Learning of the School of Principle

The Ch'eng-Chu School, or the *Li-hsüeh,* School of Principle, was named after its two principal founders, Ch'eng I (1033–1107) and Chu Hsi (1130–1200). To the School of Principle, learning and self-cultivation could be interpreted as a broad-based gradual process that permitted the individual to move toward the development and realization of one's own nature, the nature described by Mencius as the mirror of the Way of Heaven. Learning was viewed as both book learning as well as practical applied learning. This was the investigation of things, and this was the beginning point of learning. Ch'eng I says, for example, of the investigation of things:

> One way is to read books and elucidate moral principles. Another way is to discuss people and events of the past and present, and to distinguish which are right and which are wrong. Still another way is to handle affairs and settle them in a proper way. All these are ways to investigate the principle of things exhaustively.[4]

In each of these cases, and in almost *any* context, what was sought in the investigation process was the *li,* or principle of the situation. This meant an ability to penetrate into the inner nature of whatever it happened to be, a book or the complexities of an interpersonal relation, to seek its principle.

For both Ch'eng I and Chu Hsi, principle is described as particular in the sense that each thing has a principle and yet is also universal, in the sense that principle underlies all things. Ch'eng I says, for example:

> Things and the self are governed by the same principle. If you understand one, you understand the other, for the truth within and the truth without are identical. In its magnitude it reaches the height of heaven and the depth of earth, but in its refinement it constitutes the reason for being of every single thing.[5]

To touch this principle is to touch the universal in each and every situation. This contributes to learning and self-cultivation by means of its ability to lead the individual gradually to appreciate and eventually to understand the principle within one's own nature, a principle no different from external principle. This process was what, from the Ch'eng-Chu point of view, the first five stages of the *Great Learning* were attempting to describe. Thus to investigate things meant to examine things broadly and thoroughly, investigating each thing for its specific principle. The extension of knowledge refers to the process of widening the sphere of this investigative procedure. Chu Hsi comments upon these two steps:

> If we wish to extend our knowledge to the utmost, we must investigate the principles of all things we come into contact with, for the intelligent mind of man is certainly formed to know, and there is not a single thing in which its principles do not inhere. It is only because all principles are not investigated that man's knowledge is incomplete.[6]

What is advocated is nothing short of the "exhaustion of principle," *ch'iung-li,* the point at which principle has been thoroughly and completely investigated. The result of this is a thorough understanding that encompasses both internal and external spheres just as principle itself encompasses these spheres. At this point the mind will be fully manifest, the mind of "total substance and great functioning" *ch'üan-t'i ta-yung.*[7]

Clearly, from the Ch'eng-Chu perspective, the primary focus of learning remained "things," that is, book learning and human activities and relations. This investigation was for the most part an outward-directed search for principle with the understanding that when principle is thoroughly studied, that is, thoroughly exhausted, through external things, the truth contained in the interior of the self thereby becomes fully manifest. The search was for a gradual accumulation of the knowledge of principle.

This search for principle was facilitated by the correct attitude of mind, *ching,* seriousness or reverence. This was referred to as the principle of "abiding in reverence," *chü-ching.* Chu Hsi incorporated this into his synthesis of the Ch'eng-Chu teachings, and it continued to play an important role in the School of Principle. If investigation and extension were to be carried out, then it was imperative that the proper frame of mind be cultivated and sustained. This was seen as the state of *ching.* Ch'eng I states: "Self-cultivation requires reverence (*ching*); the pursuit of learning depends upon the extension of knowledge."[8]

The term has been translated as both seriousness and reverence. Both are accurate, but it is clearly more difficult to sense the ultimate religious focus of the learning if the quality of reverence is left unspoken. Both suggest a level of attentiveness, but reverence has the advantage of suggesting, in addition to the level of attentiveness, the quality of religious response by an individual to that which is regarded as Absolute. In this sense, it is equivalent to one of Joachim Wach's criteria of religious experience, that it must be a *response* to what is regarded as Absolute.[9] What is expressed by this term is the attempt to place the individual in a relationship to that which is viewed as Absolute.

Chu Hsi, in his synthesis of Neo-Confucianism, which comes to define the character of the Ch'eng-Chu School, was highly selective in the particular ideas he chose to assemble.[10] Thus, while he readily accepts Ch'eng I's understanding of principle and his basic model for learning and self-cultivation, particularly the central role assigned to abiding in reverence, he is less favorably disposed to other prominent Sung Neo-Confucians' schemes for self-cultivation. One of these is Chou Tun-i (1017–73) whose metaphysical import he recognizes and utilizes, but whose focus of self-cultivation he criticizes. Chou Tun-i stressed the importance of quietude, *ching,* and the principle of *chu-ching,* "regarding quietude as fundamental," as primary components of self-cultivation. The difference in these models is evident in Ch'eng I's view of quietude. A question is posed to Ch'eng I of whether *ching,* seriousness or reverence, is not in fact identical to the state of quietude. The answer is a very direct one. Any discussion of quietude from Ch'eng I's point of view leads to Buddhism; only the word *ching,* seriousness or reverence, should be used, not the concept of quietude.[11] This view to a large degree reflects Chu Hsi's own perspective on quietude. Other Neo-Confucians, on the other hand, extended quietude to specific forms of practice including meditative and contemplative practice. Chu Hsi himself seems to have been influenced early by such ways and to have practiced meditation, *ching-tso* (Japanese: *seiza*), quiet-sitting. He eventually, however, qualifies the use of the practice and advocates a continuing role for meditation in balance with study, "a half-day quiet-sitting, a half-day study" (*pan-jih ching-tso pan-jih tu-shu*). In this way, he retains emphasis upon the process of "exhaustion of principle" with Ch'eng I's principle of "abiding in reverence" and sees meditative practice as supporting the strategy of Ch'eng-Chu learning.

The School of Mind's Model of Learning

The Lu-Wang School or, as it is often called, *Hsin-hsüeh* or School of Mind, drew together other personalities who interpreted the model for learning and self-cultivation in a different way. It is named for Lu Hsiang-shan (1139–92) and Wang Yang-ming (1472–1529). The differences posed by the School of Mind that make it appear to stand in opposition with the School of Principle can be illustrated by a passage from Mencius. It involves the story of a man who decided that his corn was not growing fast enough and determined that he would help it grow by pulling it all up![12] In the context of farming, the story suggests that there is a delicate balance that needs to be maintained. On the one hand, a certain level of nourishing and nurturing is necessary without which the corn would not grow at all. On the other hand, too much nurturing will kill the corn. So, too, with self-cultivation. Too little nurturing will not permit human nature to develop and mature; too much will kill it. What is too little cultivation? In turn, what is too much cultivation? For the School of Principle, the model of self-cultivation focuses upon the investigation of things and the extension of knowledge in a process of exhaustion of principle to develop human nature. From the point of view of the School of Mind this is too much nourishing and nurturing. This is what kills the spirit.

For the School of Principle, human nature as well as all things contain principle; and the person, through learning (that is, through the mind) is in need of coming to understand that principle. To accomplish this task requires broad learning and extensive self-cultivation. It requires the exhaustion of principle so that the nature will be properly developed. The School of Mind, however, begins with the position that principle is already contained in the mind, not simply human nature and things in general. The emphasis is upon preserving what is there and letting it grow through its own nourishment. Thus the steps of self-cultivation are themselves regarded as of less consequence. The broad and extensive process of investigating things, of an extensive searching process, becomes unnecessary.

For the School of Mind, the capacity for sagehood is already inherent within the mind; it is essentially a matter of letting it emerge. Of course, there will be subtle differences on how best to accomplish this task. The broadest distinctions, however, draw a line between this point of view and the general schema of learning as advocated by the School of Principle. The School of Mind accuses the School of Principle of being too strict and over-zealous in its nurturing of the nature. The School of Principle is "helping it grow," as it were. There is too much effort. On the other hand, the School of Principle accuses the School of Mind of being too lax in the necessary rigors of self-cultivation, giving too much freedom to the mind to grow and develop on its own. Something needs to be developed.

Ch'eng Hao (1032–85), the brother of Ch'eng I, illustrates this distinction by his own difference from his brother. Ch'eng I was frequently cited as strict and unbending, upholding the necessity of rigorous learning and self-cultivation in the model that became synonymous with the School of Principle. His brother, on the other hand, represented an ideal closer to the position of the Lu-Wang School.

> If one purposely uses reverence to straighten his internal life, it will not be straightened. . . . If one is "always doing something without expectation," one will be straight. For if one can practice reverence to straighten the internal life and righteousness to square the external life, one can be harmonious with things.[13]

The issue is a subtle but important one. Ch'eng Hao's comment calls into question the pursuit of learning and self-cultivation and stresses that a more spontaneous response will produce the desired results. The internal quotation from Mencius[14] emphasizes the need for lessening the quality of conscious and strenuous self-cultivation, substituting in its place a less consciously strict and rigorous model. In Ch'eng Hao's essay on the nature of *jen,* humaneness or goodness, we find the following passage:

> If one preserves it *(jen)* with this idea, what more is to be done? "Always be doing something without expectation. Let the mind not forget its objective, but let there be no artificial effort to help it grow." Not the slightest effort is exerted! This is the way to preserve *jen.* As *jen* is preserved, the self and the other are then identified.[15]

Again the reference is to the same story from Mencius. If one simply preserves what is already there, there is no need for anything else.

This creates a different model of learning and self-cultivation, one that is more concerned about the preservation and nourishment of what is already inherent. The greatest spokesman of this model is Wang Yang-ming. For Wang Yang-ming, this innate capacity is called *liang-chih*, or innate knowing; and learning and self-cultivation become activities focused upon the preservation, nourishment, and emergence of this innate capacity, the seeds of sagehood itself.

Since we have already used the example of the *Great Learning* to discuss the method of learning and self-cultivation advocated by the School of Principle, it is appropriate to return to it, but this time from the perspective of the School of Mind. Chu Hsi, in his work on the *Great Learning,* had reconstructed the text, placing *ko-wu* and *chih-chih,* the investigation of things and the extension of knowledge, as the first two steps of the learning process.[16] Others disputed this reconstruction. One of those who found himself in opposition to Chu Hsi was Wang Yang-ming, and in his own commentary to the *Great Learning* the difference in the interpretation becomes clear.[17] Instead of the investigation of things and the extension of knowledge being a broad-based learning process fundamentally oriented to external sources of principle, Yang-ming reverses this, turning it inward upon the self. The mind was viewed as the repository of principle, and thus the highest good, the seeds of sagehood, was already inherent in the mind. In this framework of interpretation the investigation process did not pursue external sources of principle, but returned to the chief seat of inherent principle, the mind itself. Thus Wang Yang-ming says of the investigation process, "To investigate is to rectify. It is to rectify that which is incorrect so it can return to its original correctness. To rectify that which is not correct is to get rid of evil, and to return to correctness is to do good. This is what is meant by investigation."[18]

Self-cultivation for Wang Yang-ming becomes an internal process of correcting that which is already there. We begin with the internal perspective and the rest of the process unfolds from it. Having rectified this innate knowledge, corrected its faults and shortcomings to permit it to emerge in full, we need to extend this innate knowledge of the good as one comes in contact with things. This is the extension of knowledge, namely the extension of the innate knowledge of the good. This is the command to do the good and to rid oneself and others of evil.

> If as we come into contact with the thing to which the will is directed, we really do the good and get rid of the evil to the utmost which is known by the innate faculty, then everything will be investigated and what is known by our innate faculty will not be deficient or obscured but will be extended to the utmost.[19]

Through this process the will is made sincere and in turn the mind is recti-fied.

While these are described in the commentary as the steps of learning, the sequence of steps for Wang Yang-ming and his followers played a much smaller role than it did for the School of Principle. In fact, Yang-ming states, "While the order of the tasks involves a sequence of first and last, in sub-stance they are one and cannot be so separated."[20] Their function can be differentiated, but their substance is one and the same. To the School of Principle the sequence of steps is important to the progression of self-cultivation; for the School of Mind all steps are contained in the initial real-ization of the innate knowledge of the good.

It seems ironic that the School of Mind was opposed to meditative practice. After all, it was the School of Mind that began with the premise that the mind itself is the repository of innate knowledge, the seeds of sagehood. It would appear appropriate for meditation to be used as a practical form of self-cultivation for the realization of this innate substance.[21] Yet, for the most part, the School of Mind was opposed to this practice. Why? The answer lies in the demand for moral action, *kung-fu*. The realization of innate knowledge went together with moral action. The process of rectification was for Wang Yang-ming a process of doing moral good; it was not an occasion for sitting in a perfectly still setting to produce an experience in the context of quietude. Realization was to be found within action itself.

There is, however, an exception. The stress was still upon the doing of moral good, but several followers of Wang Yang-ming felt there was a place for quietude in self-cultivation. These include Nieh Pao (1487–1563), who taught and practiced quiet-sitting, and Lo Hung-hsien (1504–64), a major influence in the development of a quietist branch of the School of Mind. Lo relied heavily upon the Sung Neo-Confucian Chou Tun-i and, as a result, stressed quietude. In turn, he taught and practiced quiet-sitting. For Lo, a model of contemplative practice became the means for realizing innate knowledge. With his acceptance of the Yang-ming theory of innate knowl-edge, Lo remained a disciple of Yang-ming learning, but in certain ways he drew very close to the Ch'eng-Chu followers of the late Ming.

The Late Ming School of Principle

It is difficult to understand Okada's own point of view and practice as a follower of Chu Hsi and the School of Principle without understanding the changes that the School of Principle underwent during the Ming dynasty (1368–1644). Without understanding this context, many of his points would seem to stand in contrast with the tradition he is said to represent. In fact, it is people such as Okada who have called attention to the need to understand thoroughly the Ming developments, particularly the late Ming developments after the time of Wang Yang-ming,[22] and have thus ushered in a great current of research that helps to explain the differences that exist between the Sung dynasty model of the School of Principle and what one finds in studying the Ch'eng-Chu orthodoxy during the Tokugawa period (1615–1867) in Japan.[23]

Most would agree that one of the most significant factors in the changing climate of Ming dynasty Ch'eng-Chu teaching is what W. T. deBary has referred to as the "burden of culture."[24] It is deBary's contention that we need to understand the Ch'eng-Chu focus upon the processes of the investigation of things and the extension of knowledge, first in the setting of the Sung period and then in a setting that differed by the geometric increase of books, encyclopedias, works of art—nearly every conceivable area of learning. The difference is a very simple one. For Ch'eng I and Chu Hsi the processes of investigation and extension could still be reasonably carried through to completion. In that sense, it was possible to engage in the exhaustion of principle, that is, to investigate things thoroughly. But the addition of several centuries of cultural artifacts, all of them sources of learning about principle, complicated this problem enormously. What then is one to do with the call for extensive and exhaustive investigation when there is no possibility that all things can be investigated?

This is not to say that Chu Hsi insisted that *all* things be investigated, but there was a generally understood approach, which suggested that the process of investigation was to be as broad as possible. It began with the Four Books and the Classics and spread from there. This principle becomes a more difficult directive to follow, and eventually the investigative process is simply buried under the sheer burden of culture. One possible effect of this is to change the process of investigation: to minimize the external directedness of the process and to focus upon the internal dimensions. In such a change, the aspects of preservation and nourishment can become more important than the exhaustion of principle understood in terms of external learning.

Even early Ming period followers of the Ch'eng-Chu teachings show tendencies toward a shift in the investigative process.[25] They are subtle changes, but nonetheless clear. For Hsüeh Hsüan (1392–1464) of the Ho-tung School, principles are not simply in things, but are in the mind as well, and his focus in the investigative process becomes far less "intellectual" than that of Chu Hsi.[26] In the case of Wu Yü-pi (1391–1469) and Hu Chü-jen (1434–84) of the Ts'ung-jen School, we find similar characteristics. The internal focus is clear. Mind becomes a major repository for principle. For Hu Chü-jen "the investigation of things should be done only in one's own personal life." This was because principle was recognized as within the individual. The investigation process shifts to one of preserving and nourishing what was already contained internally. "Since mind and principle are not separated, the preservation of the mind and the investigation of things must extend each other."[27] The same terminology will be used, but in this case, for example, investigation is defined in terms of preservation.

These differences may also be seen in the focus given to *ching,* reverence, by both Wu Yü-pi and Hu Chü-jen. While reverence is clearly of major importance as a state of mind that is to complement the process of investigation and extension, for these two Ming figures reverence is seen as more important than the extension of knowledge itself. Thus a mental attitude whose purpose is the attentiveness of the individual can be seen as a method proper to the interior-focused dimension of principle. Reverence was appropriate to the task of what Mencius called "preserving and nourishing the mind."

One of the effects of studying the Ch'eng-Chu School followers of the early Ming is to realize that Wang Yang-ming was not alone in his attempt to change the learning and self-cultivation of the Chu Hsi School. In fact, Yang-ming is often presented only in his complete break from the Ch'eng-Chu learning rather than as someone who struggled to make the Ch'eng-Chu teaching work in his own daily practice.[28] In many ways, his new strategy remained an attempt to give further meaning to Chu Hsi's teaching and practice. He, too, agonized with the burden of culture.

Late Ming figures fit into this emerging model of a different Ch'eng-Chu teaching and practice. Particularly important in this respect is the figure Kao P'an-lung (1562–1626), a member of the Tung-lin School and a follower of Chu Hsi. Like the early Ming Ch'eng-Chu followers, Kao accepts the interiority of principle in the mind. He also sees the process of investigation of things as one that incorporates internal as well as external sources. And he, like Hu Chü-jen, places tremendous importance upon the individual life as the ground for investigation as well as the extension of knowledge. With this model, the exhaustion of principle is seen in terms of the act of nourishing and preserving the mind.

Kao P'an-lung was also one of the most significant practitioners of quiet-sitting. He related such practices to basic positions of the Chu Hsi School, upholding the *Great Learning* strategy of learning through investigation and extension, though the model relied heavily upon a sense of investigation in tandem with preservation and nourishment. He continued to maintain, however, that even with the capacity for interior principle of the mind and thus a model of investigation as interiorly based preservation, there were still differences that separated the Ch'eng-Chu position from that of the School of Mind, even from its contemplative wing.[29]

The differences remain primarily issues of practice and revolve around the continued insistence of the Ch'eng-Chu School to recognize the validity of sequential steps of learning, rather than relinquishing all such learning strategies to a nondifferentiated experience of innate knowledge. As such, Kao criticized the radical wing of the School of Mind for its antinomianism and destruction of learning. He had a more difficult time criticizing the contemplative side of the School of Mind, and commentators have suggested that there was in fact little difference,[30] though he maintains a difference in terms of basic Ch'eng-Chu categories. This subtle line between the Chu Hsi and Wang Yang-ming schools maintains itself through the growth of Neo-Confucianism in Japan and is eventually a pressing question for Okada's lineage.

Tokugawa Neo-Confucianism, Ch'eng-Chu Teachings, and the Yamazaki Ansai School

With the initiation of the Tokugawa period, Japan underwent profound change from a medieval culture to a state poised with the seeds of modernity. The study of the intellectual foundations of this period began in earnest with *Studies in the Intellectual History of Tokugawa Japan*, by Maruyama Masao[31] a work that has posed a rigid interpretation of the role of Confucianism in Tokugawa ideology. To Maruyama, Neo-Confucianism is a monolithic system of thought little changed from its own foundation in Sung China. As a closed and rigid system, it could only contribute to what Maruyama sees as the inherent conservatism of Tokugawa ideology, the ideology that had to be destroyed to allow modernization to take place. This interpretation has now been challenged in serious ways by a number of scholars.[32] Neo-Confucianism is clearly not the rigid monolithic system of thought that Maruyama proposes. It has undergone growth throughout its history in China and Korea before its continued development in Tokugawa Japan. The sense of Neo-Confucian orthodoxy plays not only different roles in varying cultures, but in addition, as we have seen, means many different things. It can serve as the official state ideology and as a personal and individual religious worldview. Its capacity for individualism, humanism, and moral action on behalf of real problems of the world, *jitsugaku*, or "practical learning," renders an image of conservatism inappropriate. In fact, it appears that such "practical learning" of the Neo-Confucians aided rather than abated the seeds of modernity and played a role itself in the transformation of Tokugawa ideology to the modern Japanese state.

Tokugawa culture was pervaded with a Neo-Confucian worldview at both elite and popular levels. The concern during the Tokugawa for a stable and harmonious society lent a sympathetic ear to the Neo-Confucian regard for the fundamental equilibrium between human being and cosmos.[33] The founders of Neo-Confucianism in Tokugawa Japan, Fujiwara Seika (1561-1619) and Hayashi Razan (1583-1657), inherited a rich and complex form of Ch'eng-Chu teaching, the Sung teachings of the Ch'eng-Chu School filtered through the Ming period as well as further refinement in Korea, particularly under Yi T'oegae (1501-70). In many respects, the Japanese formulation of Neo-Confucianism shared close links with its Chinese roots. This can be seen in the manner in which orthodoxy was understood in terms of state ideology and individual religious learning. It can also be seen in the role of orthopraxy, the official state sponsorship of the Confucian temple as well as the individual forms of ritual and self-cultivation. It is, of course, far too simplistic to suggest that Japanese Neo-Confucianism is a mere copy of its Chinese roots. In the words of Peter Nosco, Japanese Neo-Confucianism is a "refashioning" of Confucianism to meet the specific characteristics of Japanese culture as well as the Japanese polity.[34] While the Chinese polity remained essentially bureaucratic, the Japanese polity was feudal and militaristic. This difference and its impact upon Neo-Confucianism has been suggested by W. T. deBary as the difference between "Mandarin orthodoxy" and "Bakufu orthodoxy."[35] There is also the potential role of Japanese nativistic thought in the formulation of Neo-Confucianism in Japan.[36]

We have seen in the late Ming period a figure such as Kao P'an-lung who turned away from the Chu Hsi model of externally directed learning to a far increased sense of internal learning. Rather than the broad-based learning scheme characterized by the investigation of things and the exhaustion of principle, there was a recognition of the internal dynamics of principle and the ability of the individual to preserve and nourish this internal source, particularly through contemplative means. Looking at the whole spectrum of Ch'eng-Chu learning, however, there remains an openness to both the rational and empirical method of learning as well as the internal mode. As we begin to see the adaptation of Neo-Confucianism to the Japanese setting, both of these strains assert themselves.

In the beginning phase of Ch'eng-Chu teachings in Japan, Fujiwara Seika played a major role in an attempt to synthesize a number of strands of the Neo-Confucian tradition.[37] He remained within the Ch'eng-Chu School, but he was also influenced by the School of Mind. He has a certain interest in the rational and empirical tendencies of the Ch'eng-Chu tradition, particularly as represented by the Ming figure Lo Ch'in-shun (1465–1547), but he also shared an intense interest in many of the prevalent Ming models of meditative self-cultivation and self-articulation of the religious life. He is represented as upholding of the Ch'eng-Chu School, but clearly must be seen through the expansion of the Ch'eng-Chu model during the Ming as well as the continued expansion in Korea under the influence of Yi T'oegae. His approach to Neo-Confucianism stressed the personal and experiential side of internal learning.

The second figure often associated with the founding phase of Neo-Confucianism in Tokugawa culture, Hayashi Razan, a prominent adviser to Tokugawa shoguns, was a student of Fujiwara Seika and embraced the Ch'eng-Chu teachings. His approach to the teachings differed, however, from Fujiwara Seika, for he came to reject the internal-directed model of learning, the late Ming model of personal experience, and embraced instead the rationalistic tendencies of Lo Ch'in-shun. This adaptation of Lo Ch'in-shun's interpretation of the Ch'eng-Chu teachings has important ramifications for the role of Neo-Confucianism as official state orthodoxy in Japan,[38] but it parts company with the teachings that maintain a strong focus upon the personal religious life.

Yamazaki Ansai (1612–82) and Ishida Baigan (1685–1744) both maintain the interest in the interior model of learning. Yamazaki Ansai represents these teachings at the official and elite level, Ishida Baigan at a more popular level.[39] Both extrapolate and appreciate the dynamics of the learning of the mind (*shingaku*). Ishida Baigan, however, was more directly a follower of Wang Yang-ming, and Okada does not include him in *Zazen to Seiza,* even though Yamazaki Ansai and Ishida Baigan support a religious life infused with contemplative practice. It is instead Yamazaki Ansai and the Kimon School that forms the foundation of the Japanese lineage to Okada.[40] Yamazaki Ansai was profoundly influenced by the late Ming focus upon the interior experience and practice of the religious life. He saw the Ch'eng-Chu teachings as providing a direct means to the religious life and to experiences that would confirm the Chang Tsai vision, as detailed in the *Western Inscription,* of the unity and wholeness of human being and cosmos. The focus was upon an internal model, one that defined the investigation of things as within the context of the self and its moral action, rather than a broad-ranging model of rational and intellectual knowledge.

Yamazaki Ansai placed particular emphasis upon meditative practice. It is in his school that we find the tradition of quiet-sitting in possibly its fullest form within Japanese Neo-Confucianism. One of Ansai's disciples, Satō Naokata (1650–1719), is known for his particular emphasis upon quiet-sitting in self-cultivation. Another major figure of the school, Yanagawa Gōgi, also emphasized quiet-sitting. In a work compiled by Yanagawa Gōgi, *Collection of the Sayings of Chu Hsi on Quiet-Sitting (Shushi seiza shusetsu),* the postscript states what he considers to be the significance of the practice of quiet-sitting and chastises recent Confucians for failing to undertake meditative practice.

> The absolute importance of a scholar's practicing quiet-sitting is like the necessity of a boat having a rudder. How can one be indifferent to this? Those who aim at the learning necessary to become a sage come to this point of view. How is it possible that generations of recent scholars have drowned in the midst of their own baseness and banalities, never knowing the original instructions of the sages and worthies? In every case they are simply washed away. In my heart I feel sorry for them. It is for this reason that I have copied passages from Chu Hsi on quiet-sitting and collected them together into a book. This fall I edited it, requested and obtained a preface from Satō Naokata, and have had it printed so that it might be shared by a community of friends.[41]

Quiet-sitting is viewed as the means of guiding the development of the inner life; it is equivalent to the rudder in the boat. In turn, it is only with this development of the inner life that the affairs of the world can be attended to. Without this centering activity, one's life is reduced to baseness and one is swept away by the ways of the world. To Yanagawa it is only when Confucians return to contemplative practice that the teachings and instruction of the sages and worthies will again be heeded and made concrete in a world crying for moral restoration.

Satō Naokata contributes the preface to the same work and also writes about the importance of the tradition of quiet-sitting.

> Activity and quietude are the key to the natural Way of Heaven and by concentrating upon quietude to regulate activities, the scholar will truly cultivate this state. The former sages and worthies followed the guidelines of the *Great Learning* and the *Elementary Learning (Hsiao-hsüeh)*

and they excelled in teaching about abiding in reverence and exhaustion of principle. The followers of Lao Tzu and Buddhism have rejected activity and sought only quietude. This is an incomplete picture of the Way of Heaven. Most Confucians, on the other hand, act, but they do not understand the importance of regarding quietude as fundamental and therefore their activity is of little use. How is this sufficient to warrant the title "scholar"?

What the Ch'eng-Chu School has called quiet-sitting is in fact the necessary foundation for the scholar to preserve his mind and accumulate virtue. Of those who wish to learn the way of the sages and worthies, if they do not put forth energy in this direction, what can they hope to obtain? There are those, however, who are anxious about quiet-sitting and some fall into the errors of Buddhist practice. But if one complies with Chu Hsi's clear admonitions and uses this practice in a practical way, then one can be called someone who is good at learning.[42]

The passage outlines the importance of a quietistic worldview, but cautions that there must be a balance between quietude and activity. If quietude prevails and if the admonitions of Chu Hsi are not followed, then the practice may lead into Buddhism. On the other hand, the major significance of quiet-sitting is also stressed. The Confucian is almost by definition committed to activity, to the performance of the moral act. Satō Naokata stresses that such activity needs to be grounded in a thorough-going contemplative model. Activity is not clearly directed or focused without the centering of the self, and the centering process can be established only by the practice of meditation. The call for moral action remains, but moral action itself must be firmly grounded through meditation in a thoroughly centered self. This model becomes the heritage of the Yamazaki Ansai School and one that attracts the teachers of Okada.

The Tradition of Kusumoto Tanzan

The major Ch'eng-Chu teachers of the nineteenth century included Kusumoto Tanzan (1828–83), Kusumoto Sekisui (1832–1916), and Ōhashi Totsuan (1816–62). To these figures, learning and self-cultivation were primarily grounded in interior learning, contemplative practice, and personal experience. There was a strong reaction against the traditional view of the Chu Hsi learning as mandating a broad form of learning, equating, for example, the methods of investigation and extension with extensive book learning. As Okada has suggested, these followers of the Ch'eng-Chu School argued against such learning when it was equated, as in the case of the Hayashi

Razan School, with close textual study, memorization, and exegesis.[43] To these Ch'eng-Chu followers, book learning was to be grounded in interior reflection and personal experience.

The Wang Yang-ming followers of the same period had a similar point of view stemming from their focus upon innate knowledge. To them, the Ch'eng-Chu followers were now saying the very same thing, and there was no reason why there should not be a reconciliation between the schools. It was the Ch'eng-Chu followers who continued to argue that even with the added sense of interiority of learning in their own school, that still did not bring the schools together. At the heart of this was the approach to learning and, as we have seen in Kao P'an-lung, the necessity of a sequential development of learning that could not be reconciled.[44]

The retention of a difference between the schools is a subtle question to pursue. This applies in the Chinese context and it certainly remains such in Japan as well. On the one hand, the Ch'eng-Chu teachings had adopted an interior-focused mode of learning as well as strategies of quietude for self-cultivation. In turn, the Wang Yang-ming School had developed in one of its branches a focus upon quietude as a mode of self-cultivation. This causes the borderline between them to be remarkably thin. A closer look at the lineage of teachers that leads to Okada bears out the complexity of this issue.

Okada's own teacher, Kusumoto Masatsugu (1896–1961), was the grandson of Kusumoto Tanzan. Kusumoto Tanzan, in turn, received instruction from both Satō Issai (1772–1859) and Tsukida Mōsai (1807–66).[45] Tanzan studied for a time at Satō Issai's school in Edo (now Tokyo). While there, he was able to hear discussions between several of Issai's senior disciples, Yoshimura Shūyō (1797–1866) and Ōhashi Totsuan. Ōhashi Totsuan, as we have already noted, was to emerge as one of the major Ch'eng-Chu teachers of the period, but that was to be later. Satō Issai himself was a follower of Wang Yang-ming though also interested in the late Ming Ch'eng-Chu model of learning. Totsuan and Shūyō represented a contrast in learning. To Totsuan, figures such as Kao P'an-lung and Liu Tsung-chou (1578–1645) represented the ideal of learning, figures representing late Ming Ch'eng-Chu teachings and a reconciliation of Chu Hsi and Wang Yang-ming learning respectively. For Shūyō, it was Wang Yang-ming who presented the best model. Shūyō, of course, went on to become one of the leading Wang Yang-ming followers of the period.

Kusumoto Tanzan's reaction to this encounter of contrasting models of learning was to side with Ōhashi Totsuan and his interests in the Ming figures Kao P'an-lung and Liu Tsung-chou. As Okada describes various details in the development of Tanzan's thought, it is interesting to see how Tanzan leaves Totsuan to return almost directly to these Ming roots. There is an initial inclination toward one, then toward the other, indicating something of the potential closeness of these two figures. Each is enriched by the School of Principle and the School of Mind, and it is merely a matter of degree as to the dominance of one school over the other. The borderline between the School of Principle and the School of Mind is perhaps more closely drawn with these figures than with many others. In addition, what makes Kao and Liu seem even more closely associated is the emphasis they both gave to the practice of quiet-sitting. Because of Tanzan's interest in both Kao and Liu and the emphasis they give to quiet-sitting, Tanzan is tied not only to the Ch'eng-Chu teachings of quietude, but to the quietist branch of the Wang Yang-ming School. Thus, through his interest in Liu Tsung-chou, he is led to the study of Nieh Pao and Lo Hung-hsien, the major representatives of the quietist branch of the Wang Yang-ming School. In the end, however, it was his correspondence with Tsukida Mōsai which lead him to his serious engagement with Yamazaki Ansai and his view of the correctness of Ansai's interpretation of the Ch'eng-Chu teachings.[46]

Often in these discussions Okada seems to deal more with personal anecdotes of the figures than their teachings, but much of the heart of their teachings is contained in this anecdotal form. Okada points to the continuity between Kusumoto Tanzan and Yamazaki Ansai and the role that Satō Issai and Tsukida Mōsai play in Tanzan's development. He discusses at length the character of the teachings represented by these figures. He describes the relation between Tanzan and his younger brother Sekisui and in turn their relation to and understanding of the various branches of the Wang Yang-ming School. It is a complex context and a story infrequently told in the standard treatments of Japanese Neo-Confucianism.[47] Out of it emerges Okada himself, a living representative of the complexity of this lineage and a living teacher whose roots share this lineage. He represents a school of Confucianism that has chosen to center its religious life around the practice of meditation and has sought to serve the world from the foundation of contemplation. He is today in many respects the major repository of knowledge about Confucian meditative practice and its relation to moral action.

2. CENTERING THE SELF IN QUIET-SITTING

Okada's centering of self-cultivation around the Confucian contemplative practice of quiet-sitting makes him the inheritor of a rich and long-standing tradition of Confucian practice. Those who advocated quiet-sitting discussed various details of the practice, and it is much of this information that Okada has included in *Zazen to Seiza*.[1] There are questions of the origin of the practice, though little is actually known of its origin, and in turn about the manner in which it was described as a meditative practice. For Okada himself, it is the discussions of quiet-sitting by Kao P'an-lung and Kusumoto Tanzan that play the central role in his own interpretation and practice, though it is also important to recognize that as a follower of the Chu Hsi School of Neo-Confucianism, Okada, like Kao and Kusumoto Tanzan, looks back to Chu Hsi himself. And, in the case of the practice of quiet-sitting, while Chu Hsi qualified its use, he continued to practice it and to write about it. His own understanding of the practice then is seminal to the interpretation by later followers of his school of Neo-Confucianism.

The discussions of quiet-sitting by Chu Hsi, Kao P'an-lung, and Kusumoto Tanzan and others revolve around the importance of the practice either as a complement to study or as something that will penetrate into the interior realms of the mind. In turn, there is the ever-present importance of addressing the relation of quietude to the responsibility to act in the world. Attention is also given to the difficulties of contemplative practice, particularly the problem of thinking about quietude rather than becoming quiet by not thinking about it. Occasionally a few comments will be made about the practice

Plate II. Okada in His Garden.

itself, but this is the least emphasized feature of the discussions. For some persons or particular situations, it demands strict rules and physical isolation, but for most it is a relaxed model of meditation. There are also references to the use of sayings by various Neo-Confucians as a vehicle for quieting the mind. This involves the recitation of sayings to put one in the right frame of mind to let the mind begin to quiet itself. Very little is said about breath control, and for most Neo-Confucians breath control apart from a slowed and regular breathing technique was not to be employed, for it all too easily resembled the techniques of Buddhists and Taoists.

Often these discussions of the practice concern the way this practice relates to larger issues of Neo-Confucian learning. We have already seen the importance played by the *Great Learning* and the amount of debate surrounding the interpretation of the steps of learning. What does it actually mean to engage in *ko-wu,* the investigation of things, or *chih-chih,* the extension of knowledge? For Chu Hsi, much of this learning process was described in terms of the exhaustion of principle, the thorough-going search for and study of principle, and the importance of the correct mental posture, called abiding in reverence, if the search was to be successful. There was also a role for "preservation and nourishment" of the nature of goodness, that is, the attempt to preserve the nature of goodness inherent within the human being. This, however, received a smaller role as a focus of the learning process than the exhausting of principle and the attitude of reverence. Such learning strategies are the very foundation of the practice itself. Is its role than to facilitate the exhaustion of principle, to assist in the thorough-going search for and study of the principle of things? Or can its role be seen more directly in aiding the development of the correct mental attitude, the state of abiding in reverence?

The issue becomes complex because there are many interpretations of these strategies of learning. Furthermore, we have the general change from Chu Hsi to the Ming followers of Chu Hsi, which witnesses a greater emphasis placed upon interior dimensions of the learning process with an investigation of things still discussed in terms of the exhaustion of principle, but one that has shifted from external to internal sources of principle. As such, the process of exhaustion becomes more clearly a process of preservation and nourishment. In turn, while Chu Hsi downplayed the role of preservation and nourishment, it emerges afresh as a key principle for the interpretation of the exhaustion of principle by the late Ming Chu Hsi followers as well as for the lineage of teachers culminating in Okada. This is also the point at which the teaching of Chou Tun-i, regarding quietude as fundamental, can begin to reemerge as a central teaching for the process of learning complementary with the interior directedness of the later interpretations of the Chu Hsi learning.

All of these elements play an active role in the discussion of quiet-sitting. This makes the discussions at times seem complex and perhaps even a little more abstract than the practice itself would require. But for those who practice quiet-sitting, it is clearly an important issue to be able to understand and articulate exactly where the practice fits in the largest model of the learning process. The reason behind this appears to be the caution Confucians feel to begin with when it comes to issues of meditation. There was always the fear that too much meditation or too structured a meditative practice would commit one to a form of quietism and thus an inability to respond by moral action to the problems of the world. This tendency, from the Confucian point of view, was clear in the quietistic excesses of Taoists and Buddhists alike, and it was critical that a distinction be maintained from their forms of quietism. One of the best ways to do this was to insist that meditation fit into a total framework of learning that retained the ideal of a sage cultivating quietude and committed to serving the world.

The Origins of Quiet-Sitting

The origins of the practice of quiet-sitting are discussed primarily in terms of the critical role played by the Ch'eng brothers, Ch'eng Hao and Ch'eng I. There is an important connection to Chou Tun-i as well, however, for both Ch'eng Hao and Ch'eng I are students of Chou and received his teaching on regarding quietude as fundamental. No references appear to be made to the actual practice of quiet-sitting with Chou Tun-i but, rather, the importance of establishing a perspective of quietude. It is the Ch'eng brothers who appear to turn this into an actual contemplative practice, though the details are not extensive.

Chu Hsi received the teaching of quiet-sitting from Li Yen-p'ing (1093–1163). Both Li Yen-p'ing and Lo Ts'ung-yen (1072–1135) were students of Ch'eng I. This would appear to indicate that the practice may originate with Ch'eng I, but the *Records of Learning of the Sung and Yüan Confucians (Sung-Yüan hsüeh-an)* states that Lo Ts'ung-yen, at least, received the teachings on quiet-sitting from Ch'eng Hao rather than Ch'eng I.[2]

Some sources have suggested there is a secret, or esoteric, transmission, implying influence from traditions other than the Confucian.[3] This seems frankly rather unnecessary. It is quite obvious that many Neo-Confucians studied both Taoism and Buddhism, and some frequently practiced meditation in Buddhist monasteries and retreats. If there is influence, it need not be in the form of a secret teaching tradition, but simply the impact upon the Confucians of the model of the religious life; or more specifically the contemplative life, lived by both Taoists and Buddhists. This does not mean, however, that Neo-Confucian quiet-sitting is to be understood and explained as a borrowed practice. The Confucian tradition can support its own meditative practice metaphysically as well as practically, though these other traditions could have served as a backdrop model that stimulated the Confucians to look more seriously at the self-reflective, introspective, and eventually contemplative potential of their own tradition.[4]

Both Ch'eng Hao and Ch'eng I practiced quiet-sitting. The discussions of quiet-sitting by the Ch'eng brothers are simple and straightforward, and the themes that emerge remain central to the practice by later practitioners. In the case of Ch'eng I, for example, we have the following description:

Someone asked how Ch'eng I taught people quiet-sitting. Chu Hsi replied: "He saw that people were filled with anxieties and desires and instructed them to collect the mind together by means of this [i.e., quiet-sitting], just this and nothing else. If it is a case of one who is just beginning his learning, it is exactly the same!"[5]

Quiet-sitting's task is the calming of the mind and the elimination of anxiety and desire that keep the mind from reaching a stage of quietude. The initiation of this process is referred to as collecting the mind together or unifying the mind. This simply means that the digressions of thought produced by anxiety and desire will be gradually eliminated, and with this elimination will come a unification as the mind becomes attentive to its roots of quietude and stillness. Okada includes several passages in *Zazen to Seiza* where Ch'eng I speaks of the need to see meditation as one form of learning among others. One is not to focus solely upon meditation. In addition, meditation is not to eliminate all thought, but simply to calm the mind.

Ch'eng Hao also gives a description of the nature and function of quiet-sitting as interpreted by Chu Hsi:

One day [Ch'eng] Hao said [to a group who traveled to pay their respects]: "All of you who are engaged in this [learning], it is nothing other than learning someone else's interpretation. Why don't you go out and make an effort to put it into practice yourselves?" Two of the gentlemen said: "We are those who lack the capability of practicing it." Ch'eng Hao replied: "When you lack the capability to practice it, then go and practice quiet-sitting." When you practice quiet-sitting then the original foundation will be nourished and gradually become settled. When the gathering together of your [mind] has been completed then you have a resting place although you do not avoid worldly affairs. It is similar to a person going on a journey: they travel but when they return they still have a dwelling wherein to rest. If there is not the nourishment of the original foundation and one freely follows things in the world, then when one wants a return of the unified mind, one will lack the dwelling place for the self to rest in![6]

The theme is again the establishment of a mind that is collected together or unified. But here Ch'eng Hao addresses the practical issues of learning and suggests that learning is to be an experience, not simply an accumulation of learning of what other people have thought. As an experience, learning is something that is acted upon. If one can't go out and actually practice the learning, then what kind of learning is it? There is thus the need to establish within the individual the foundation of a unified mind so that learning is, from Ch'eng Hao's point of view, true learning. The role of quiet-sitting is the establishment of this foundation, a point of stability or rest and of quietude from which to journey and to act, but in turn a point to return to. Quietude is the foundation. It does not rest in itself. It pursues the journey and the act, but it also remains at the center as the point of unification.

Chu Hsi and Quiet-Sitting

Chu Hsi practiced quiet-sitting and in turn interpreted its role for Neo-Confucian learning. In his early training under Li Yen-p'ing he was taught a form of quiet-sitting that sought to reach the inner depths of the mind.[7] Li Yen-p'ing did not see quiet-sitting as a mere complement to study, a kind of quiet reflection. He saw it instead as holding the capacity to penetrate the innermost recesses of the mind. In the model of mind used by the Ch'eng-Chu School, this meant that quiet-sitting could not only deal with issues of the *i-fa,* the manifest mind, but could as well penetrate to the depths of the *wei-fa,* the unmanifest mind.[8] This was a perspective with roots in an interpretation of the early Confucian classic the *Doctrine of the Mean (Chung yung),* originally a chapter from the ritual classic, the *Book of Rites,* and a passage that became the *locus classicus* of references to the unmanifest mind. "Before the feelings of pleasure, anger, sorrow, and joy are aroused it is called equilibrium (*chung,* centrality, mean). When these feelings are aroused and each and all attain due measure and degree, it is called harmony."[9]

This passage was the source for the distinction between the unmanifest and manifest capacities of the mind, but more important, was drawn directly into the discourse regarding meditation. We find Lo Ts'ung-yen saying, for example, "In quiet-sitting one is capable of seeing pleasure, anger, sorrow, and joy while they are yet unmanifest (*wei-fa*) and have not assumed material form."[10] Li Yen-p'ing's position is virtually identical as to the capabilities and object of the practice of quiet-sitting. In fact, Li Yen-p'ing instructed Chu Hsi that if he were to practice quiet-sitting, he would be able to perceive directly the Principle of Heaven, *T'ien-li,* within the unmanifest mind.[11]

Chu Hsi apparently followed this instruction for a short time, but was then influenced by Hu Hung (1106–61) of the Hunan School, and this became a decisive influence that turned Chu Hsi away from the practice of quiet-sitting as a means toward experiencing the unmanifest mind.[12] Hu Hung argued that attention toward the unmanifest mind alone might be the way to understand the substance of the mind, but it failed to take into account the importance of the function of the mind, the active component or the manifest mind. This is a standard and well-known metaphysical distinction in Chinese thought, *t'i* and *yung,* or substance and function, and was employed here to warn Chu Hsi that the critical balance between understanding and acting could not be preserved if self-cultivation was allowed to be dominated by a practice of this kind. As Okada argues in *Zazen to Seiza,* this represented a major change in Chu Hsi's learning and was a critical one for the future interpretation of the practice of quiet-sitting.[13] Chu Hsi followed Hu Hung's advice and thereafter severely qualified the use of quiet-sitting to the model captured by the phrase "a half-day quiet-sitting, a half-day study."

This may still seem to be an inordinate amount of time spent in meditation, but the real intent of the passage is to suggest that the function of quiet-sitting is as a quiet complement to study rather than a practice exercised unto itself for an exploration of the unmanifest mind. From this point of view, anyone who exercised quiet-sitting as an exploration of the unmanifest mind was ignoring function or activity and was running the risk of being incapable of distinguishing himself from Buddhism or simply falling into Buddhism entirely. For Chu Hsi, quiet-sitting was a part of the total model of self-cultivation. He thereby preserved at least a role for the practice.

Though Chu Hsi qualified the use of quiet-sitting and this in itself has extremely important ramifications for the history of the practice, yet the fact that he advocated the role of a half-day of quiet-sitting and a half-day of study suggested, as we have seen, that the practice had an important role to play, even if qualified. One of the themes that emerges as essential for Chu Hsi is the necessity of balancing study and quiet-sitting. It was study that would carry out the basic learning process called the exhaustion of principle, but quiet-sitting was still necessary in this total process. In certain respects, this role of quiet-sitting was to facilitate study itself. Chu Hsi tells the story of the scholar who had a bad memory until he read Mencius' teaching that the whole purpose of learning was nothing more than to regain the mind that had strayed.[14] With this in mind, he began the practice of quiet-sitting and found that his memory reached a point of high development. Clearly quiet-sitting was advantageous to study.[15] Chu Hsi reinforces this point even further.

> In reading, first collect together mind and body, and quiet the mind a little. Then open a book and it will be far more effective. If the mind is driven toward external things and is chaotic, then the mind is completely separated from the Way. In this kind of situation one cannot read. There is no need for any explanation, just simply shut the gate and for a period of ten days to two weeks sit correctly. After that when one looks at books one will understand that what I say is not nonsense.[16]

These passages make quiet-sitting sound as if its only purpose is as a complement to study in order to enhance the role and function of study itself. There is more to it than this, however, for study itself is aimed at the process of uncovering the true nature, ultimately in the state of sagehood itself. Learning is the learning of sagehood. For quiet-sitting to be a complement to this suggests that even for Chu Hsi its role was important in the process of self-understanding and self-realization. Chu Hsi's qualification was that it serve a model of learning and self-cultivation that saw study in the framework of the learning process that focused upon the exhaustion of principle and abiding in reverence as the primary means for the realization of the goal of sagehood rather than a model that emphasized quietistic and contemplative models of practice toward a quietistic end.

Quiet-sitting does have an important role to play for Chu Hsi, and this can be easily overlooked in the kind of qualifications he places upon the practice. As the following passage demonstrates, quiet-sitting in its capacity to establish a person's nature is central to the learning and self-cultivation of the individual.

> People today are not willing to focus upon the fundamentals. They take note of a word such as "reverence" as something for future concern and are concerned even less for things from the past. The foundation has not been established and therefore the rest is fragmented. The moral effect is without a collected and calm dwelling. Ch'eng Hao and Li Yen-p'ing

taught people quiet-sitting. From their perspective it was quiet-sitting that was essential.[17]

While Chu Hsi would qualify the position of Ch'eng Hao and Li Yen-p'ing, he seems here to be in fundamental agreement that there is a necessity to establish this quiet foundation.

The issue that haunts Chu Hsi's discussion of quiet-sitting is the relation of the practice to moral action in the world. Here too is the ground for his caution with the practice. Clearly a practice that focuses too heavily upon quietude runs the risk of either being disinterested in acting in the world or, at a more serious level, perhaps incapable of moving from quietism to activity. Instead, both spheres are essential, as is the ability to move from one to the other. "The terms 'activity' and 'quietude' are opposites of each other and yet they cannot be unrelated to each other, for if they are, then the spontaneity of the Principle of Heaven would not be accomplished by human effort."[18] In other words, activity and quietude are interconnected, and self-cultivation, particularly quiet-sitting, must display its capacity for its interconnectedness with activity. Chu Hsi argues that quiet-sitting, then, when it is practiced correctly, will by its nature show its relation to activity. It is, according to Chu Hsi, the sage who understands this best. "In his activity the principle of quietude is not yet done away with and in his quietude the source of activity is not yet stopped."[19] Quietude is at the foundation of the sage's activity, but in turn there is a commitment to activity even when in the midst of quietude.

It is the balance that remains critical in the relation of quietude and activity. For Chu Hsi, even a normal level of practice of quiet-sitting may be judged excessive in terms of specific duties that may require one's action.

Although we speak of "regarding quietude as fundamental" this is not the rejection of activities or things. Since to be a human being one must set forth service for superiors and parents, communicate with friends, comfort wife and children, and manage servants, one cannot cut oneself off completely, simply shutting the door and practicing quiet-sitting. When there are issues of concern one must not leave them and respond by saying, "Just wait until I have finished my quiet-sitting." Not to respond is simply unacceptable.[20]

This balance of quietude and activity keeps the practice for Chu Hsi different from Buddhist meditative practice. It can still lead to depths of understanding even though it has committed itself to a balance of quietude and activity. But it does not involve itself in the technicality and formality of

Buddhist meditative techniques.

> Quiet-sitting is not required to be like the sitting meditation practices [of the Buddhists], entering concentration and cutting off thought and cognition. It is just the gathering together of the mind. Without rambling activities and idle thought this mind naturally becomes focused and at one with unperturbed calm and no affairs. Even if it has affairs then it abides by those affairs, fulfills its duty and then returns to being unmoved and calm.[21]

The commitment remains to a practice that responds to the real problems of the world. And yet the practice brings the individual to a perception of what Chu Hsi calls being at one. This is the state at which the unity of internal and external, or the individual and the world, is seen; the point at which principle is seen as commonly underlying all things. This is the vision of the sage, a vision that results for Chu Hsi from the balance of quietude and activity. This is sometimes also referred to as "singleness of thought," *i-nien.*

> Someone asked: "When you practice quiet-sitting for a long time then singleness of thought cannot but become active. What does one do then?" He said, "You must see that singleness of thought in whatever you do. If it is a good matter and something that should be done, then it is essential to go out and complete it."[22]

For Chu Hsi, quiet-sitting has only accomplished its task as it permits the individual's nature to express itself in its capacity for activity—moral activity in the world. Self-cultivation is complete only at the point that the vision of unity is exercised on behalf of necessary activities and responsibilities. To Okada, this unity of quietude and activity is one of the most important characteristics distinguishing Confucianism from Buddhism. This is captured in the phrase, from Chu Hsi, "total substance and great functioning," a phrase Okada uses frequently to indicate the completeness of Chu Hsi teachings.[23] It suggests that in addition to the "total substance" of the mind, that is, its capacity to respond to the principles of all things, it also carries out a "great functioning," that is, it engages in the issues of the real world. For Okada, this is one of the unique and important features of the Chu Hsi learning and a feature that he sees as the product of a learning schema based upon a major role given to quiet-sitting.

Finally, Chu Hsi deals with the issue of intentionality in meditative practice.

> Someone said: "Each day I do a little quiet-sitting in my leisure time in order to nourish my mind, but I continue to be aware of ideas spontane-

ously and confusedly arising. The more I want to become quiet, the less quiet I become." Chu Hsi said" "When there is the presence of confused thought, then how much more thought will be added if you think about quietude? Moreover, one does not want to adhere oneself to something or to bind or oppress oneself. One needs to have a time for peace and rest." In addition he said: "To emphasize quietude it is first important to experience it. Then after that one can assist it to grow."[24]

Chu Hsi's response emphasizes the importance of not seeing quiet-sitting as a specific method that is to become the object of attention. In this sense, quiet-sitting is just quiet-sitting. In fact, he himself says: "Quiet-sitting is just to be considered quiet-sitting. Do not seek for some more leisurely form of activity and do not seek for some more leisurely form of thinking. It is without method."[25] This does not trivialize the practice. If anything, it makes it all the more subtle, for there is the recognition that quietude is a great deal more than the intellectual understanding of it and the conscious pursuit of it. To make it an object of attention or a focus of practice is to create an intellectual category of quietude that remains separate from the actual experience of quietude. The only directive for the practice is to aim at the experience of quietude itself. Chu Hsi says: "When quiet-sitting is without scattered and miscellaneous thought, then it is nourished and in a flourishing state."[26] And one cannot force the dispersion of such thoughts. One can only sit quietly and let the mind become calm on its own. This too is a point that will be central to Kao, to Kusumoto Tanzan, and to Okada in the practice of quiet-sitting. It is this lack of intention that permits the emergence of the naturalness of quietude. In turn, it is this naturalness of quietude that permits it to form a natural bond with activity in the world.

Chu Hsi's own discussion of quiet-sitting is thorough-going. The issues involved in the interpretation of the practice for Chu Hsi reemerge as salient issues for the later Ming dynasty Chu Hsi scholars and the lineage of scholars leading to Okada himself. The relation of quietude and activity, the actual practice of quiet-sitting and questions of method, the problem of intention—all are later articulated. But they are articulated in a changed environment, one that has seen the reassessment of quietude.

The Reassessment of Quietude

The revitalization of the practice of quiet-sitting by the Ch'eng-Chu School during the Ming centered around several crucial factors. There is the shift from external- to internal-directed learning. With this we see a heightened importance given to processes of self-examination and modes of expression of self-reflection, particularly quiet-sitting. There is also an attempt to restate the importance of the Sung philosopher Chou Tun-i, not for the metaphysics he was already well known for, but for his emphasis upon quietude and his principle of regarding quietude as fundamental. In turn, there is a willingness to see an expanded role for quiet-sitting, to place it in the model of the manifest and the unmanifest mind and recognize that the practice of meditation has the capacity to explore the depths of the unmanifest mind, though still with the qualifications of Chu Hsi that it was not to lose its connection to the activities and concerns of the world itself.

Chu Hsi played a key role in what W. T. Chan has called the "completion" of Neo-Confucianism.[27] He synthesized a number of different elements taken from various teachers to create what became known as the School of Principle. In this process, he was highly selective and had a certain image in mind of the perimeters of orthodoxy. The philosopher Chou Tun-i plays a key role in this synthesis in one sense, but in an equally important sense he is left out. He is included for his metaphysical speculations, the so-called Diagram of the Great Ultimate,[28] a Neo-Confucian cosmogony, and in this he plays a seminal role. What he is not included for, however, are his ideas about self-cultivation and the worldview that was the foundation of his practices. What he emphasized in this respect was regarding quietude as fundamental.[29]

To Chu Hsi this posed a model of self-cultivation that ran the risk of being too quietistic, and in the end Chu Hsi chose to emphasize Ch'eng I's principle of abiding in reverence rather than Chou Tun-i's regarding quietude as fundamental. Both remain central concerns, but the emphasis for Chu Hsi was clearly upon Ch'eng I's recommendation of self-cultivation rather than upon Chou Tun-i. The practice of quiet-sitting for Chu Hsi was to fit into the emphasis upon the abiding in reverence and the exhaustion of principle, while it was to shun its connection to a larger worldview of quietude that Chou Tun-i saw as central.

Okada, however, in *Zazen to Seiza* considers Chou Tun-i as the patriarch of Neo-Confucian learning not simply for his metaphysical contributions but, more importantly, for regarding quietude as fundamental. This is not to say that Ch'eng I's principle of abiding in reverence is taken less seriously but, rather, that it is reinterpreted and Chou Tun-i is appreciated for the world-view that he built around quietude. Even to Chu Hsi's charge that Chou Tun-i ran the risk of encouraging the error of quietism and its excesses in Taoist or Buddhist practices, Okada answers by suggesting that Chou Tun-i surpasses the learning of both Taoist and Buddhist alike. Okada interprets the Ch'eng brothers' focus upon reverence as in need of being clarified through Chou

Tun-i's concept of quietude. In this sense, the role of Chou Tun-i's regarding quietude as fundamental remains central to Okada himself.

This view forms the foundation of Okada's own interpretation of quiet-sitting, and in the first chapter of *Zazen to Seiza* he has attempted to demonstrate that quietude is the very root of East Asian thought. The argument begins by referring to both the *Doctrine of the Mean* and the *Great Learning* to demonstrate that, even in the ancient period, there was a common perspective that it was essential to cultivate a still and settled mind.[30] The Buddhist tradition has also focused upon the importance of the quiet mind, and in a work of some popularity in Japan, *Vegetable Root Discourses (Saikontan)*,[31] Okada demonstrates the degree to which East Asian thought has revolved around the importance assigned to the cultivation of a quiet mind. The question arises, for Okada, as to why the cultivation of the stillness or the quietude of the mind has remained such a salient feature of East Asian religious traditions. This may equally apply to other areas of Asia as well. Okada's focus remains East Asia. The answer that he gives in a sense links him directly to Chou Tun-i. He says that, for Chou Tun-i, regarding quietude as fundamental was an outgrowth of his cosmology of the Great Ultimate, *T'ai-chi.* The Great Ultimate begins in the *Wu-chi,* the Non-Ultimate. As the Great Ultimate was activity, so the Non-Ultimate was stillness and quietude.[32]

For Okada, therefore, nature itself is ultimately quiet. He uses the example of the *Book of Changes (I Ching)* and its hexagram "return," *fu.*[33] This hexagram, a common reference for Neo-Confucian self-cultivation, contains among its six lines one moving, or yang, line under five still, or yin, lines. It indicates the capacity for incipient activity within stillness or quietude. There is stillness, yet there is activity. As Okada argues, though there be both quietude and activity, the yin and the yang, it is the yin that is the foundation of the yang, the quietude that produces the activity. From this point of view, the *Book of Changes* begins with the foundation of quietude.

This is the answer to why it is necessary to cultivate a quiet mind. Mind and nature for Okada are ultimately one. If the state of quietude is the essence of nature to begin with, then it is the same for mind, and thus the way to penetrate to that same essence is to assume the state that is itself the essence—the state of quietude. Nature is quiet, mind is quiet, and through the practice of quiet-sitting one leaves behind the various false and selfish selves to arrive at the true nature of the self.

Okada carries the argument for the foundation of quietude in East Asian thought further by suggesting that the classical systems of Chinese thought all share in this essential nature and foundation of quietude. He refers to the systems as the realists, the transcendentalists, and the idealists. The realists are the school of philosophy known as the Legalists, the transcendentalists are the Taoists and later the Buddhists, and the idealists are the Confucians. His argument is an interesting one and certainly one of the very few attempts to put the entire foundation of Chinese thought into the context of the concept of quietude.

Metaphysically, quietude is the foundation, and its importance to Okada, as in the same way to Chou Tun-i, cannot be minimized. The perception of quietude as the Way of Heaven itself is for Okada probably the single most important perception arising from East Asian thought. And it is from this foundation that the practice of quiet-sitting grows. Only a reassessment of quietude and of Chou Tun-i can produce this perspective, a perspective that sees the centrality of quiet-sitting and the importance of those such as Kao P'an-lung who chose to focus upon it.

Kao P'an-lung and Quiet-Sitting

Kao P'an-lung, as we have already indicated, was a prominent Neo-Confucian at the end of the Ming period. He was associated with the Tung-lin Academy, a major private academy for learning and self-cultivation and represents the late Ming Ch'eng-Chu School.[34] With Kao, we have an extensive collection of writings that deal with the practice of quiet-sitting. He composed poems, journals, diaries, and a number of essays that touch upon the subject of contemplative practice. He seems to have had a deep sensitivity to the practice of quiet-sitting, its inner dynamics, and its potential for realization of the interior dimension of the self.

Kao wrote of his experiences in very personal terms, and this element relates the issues of contemplative practice in a very direct fashion to others attempting to follow similar practices of self-cultivation. Okada, like his teacher before him, finds Kao's autobiography to be a particularly poignant portrayal of the difficulties of practice and translates a portion of it in *Zazen to Seiza*. The section that Okada has included relates the struggles in the life of self-cultivation, the struggles that produce the title of the autobiography itself, *Recollections of the Toils of Learning (K'un-hsüeh chi)*.[35] In these sections, Kao indicates his growing awareness, during the course of a journey, of his lack of knowledge of his own nature and the need to involve himself in a practice that would bring him face to face with his nature and give him knowledge from experience, not just the accumulated learning from what is found in books. The crisis of realizing he had no understanding brought him to the point of engaging in serious contemplative practice.

The next day in the boat I arranged the mat and seriously set up rules and regulations as well as practicing what Chu Hsi called "half-day of *seiza,* half-day of study." When the mind would become unsettled during the practice of *seiza* I would consult the teachings of Master Ch'eng and Master Chu and practice one by one Ch'eng Hao's "sincerity and reverence," Master Chou's "regarding quietude as fundamental," Yang Shih's [1053–1135] "viewing of pleasure, anger, sorrow and joy when they are unmanifest," and Li Yen-p'ing's "sit in silence and purify the mind; realize for oneself the Principle of Heaven." In fact I kept these in front of me throughout the entire day. At night I did not undress and only when weary to the bone did I sleep. When I awoke from sleep I again practiced *seiza,* repeating and alternating these various rules.[36]

The journey lasted two months and later on the trip Kao describes an enlightenment experience that follows from extensive contemplative practice. The experience is psychologically shattering and thorough: it penetrates, as Kao says, to the very core of his nature. The description Kao gives of his enlightenment experience is remarkably detailed.[37] This experience is a kind of watershed for Kao, for it forms a foundation of experience that, regardless of the conditions of toil and turmoil of the later years of his life, is something to fall back upon. And for those such as Kusumoto Tanzan and Okada himself, such an account gave a firsthand description of what the practice could lead to in terms of direct experience.

Kao himself did not regard the enlightenment experience as the conclusion of the practice, but continued throughout his life the toils of learning and self-cultivation and continued to write of his practice. Okada refers to a short essay, *Agenda for Dwelling in the Mountains (Shan-chü k'o-ch'eng),* by Kao that describes the agenda for a single day to be spent in a retreat in the mountains.[38] It is a day filled with quietude, with study, and with the enjoyment of the beauty of the environs. Formal meditative practice is described and so too are the oppressive forces that perturb the mind's stillness and demand the return to meditative practice. In these writings, one can see Kao's thorough commitment to quiet-sitting and in a sense his joy in the return to practice.

Okada derives the name of his subsection of chapter 3, "Rules for Returning in Seven," from an essay by Kao of the same title, *Rules for Returning in Seven (Fu-ch'i kuei).* Here Kao advises a program of *seiza* practice based upon the *Book of Changes'* hexagram *fu,* "return," and the statement that on the seventh day comes return. The program that Kao advises is to restore one to calm and quietude and recommends a seven-day period be set aside for the full regimen. The first day is simply relaxation, but then one begins serious *seiza* practice, and by the third day one has begun to reach the subtleties of the practice. With the completion of the seventh day, calmness has been restored.[39]

From these essays and autobiographical writings, certain features of quiet-sitting begin to emerge. First, even in following Chu Hsi's rule of a half-day of quiet-sitting and a half-day of study, Kao can set himself to an extraordinarily arduous form of practice when it is felt necessary. In the particular conditions he describes in his autobiography, Kao has reached a spiritual crisis in his own life. He realizes for the first time that his learning has been without focus and without the establishment of an inner core or understanding. When confronted with this situation, he turns to contemplative practice, and his use of this practice is disciplined and arduous. He imposes the strictest of schedules and regulations upon himself and commits himself totally to quiet-sitting. On the other hand, the agenda for the mountains suggests a rather more relaxed mode of practice though there is still isolation from the events of normal life. The practice then can be both extremely rigorous and rather more relaxed, flexible to the particular conditions and needs of the time.

Second, Kao indicates the use of phrases from some of the major Neo-Confucians in the practice itself. He also refers at times to formal types of sitting, upon a mat for example, or in a cross-legged position. This tells us that there can be some importance to placing oneself in the correct position both psychologically and physically. The physical positioning is certainly not an end unto itself and has never been insisted upon, but at the same time there is also the recognition that it can be important to the initiation of the practice. So too are the calling to mind or recitation of expressions of various Neo-Confucians. Kao says that one repeats these phrases and that one thinks about them and that they become the basis for the initiation of a quieting process of the mind. This can facilitate the entry into the state of quietude.

Third, in addition to the rigorous nature of the practice, there is also an element of isolation suggested by these passages. Contemplative practice, at least in these particular selections, is not something carried out in a setting of moral activities. At the level Kao is discussing, it requires isolation, though clearly this isolation is not an end unto itself. It is to produce a level of self-reflection and experience, however, that is the product of the self dealing with itself and nothing else. This still tells us little of the actual questions of method in the practice, but we are fortunate that Kao addressed several essays more specifically to some of these questions.

The Idea of Method in Quiet-Sitting

Kao realized that there were difficulties in the interpretation of the practice of quiet-sitting and addressed two essays to answer some of the questions raised.[40] Okada translates both of these essays because of their importance in providing detail upon the nature of the practice itself.

The first of the essays, *A Discussion of Quiet-Sitting (Ching-tso shuo)*, discusses the subtlety of the cultivation of the state of quietude. *Seiza* is a method or technique, and as it is employed there is a conscious decision to pursue the state of quietude. The problem is that the intention toward quietude, however subtle, can, as Chu Hsi also noted, obstruct the experience of quietude, for the intention remains a conscious thought *about* quietude rather than simply the experience of quietude. In addition, in this intention toward quietude there is also the intention to rid the mind of its limiting and selfish dimensions so that the state of quietude alone remains. This can result in a concerted effort to drive out such limiting dimensions of the mind, and as such the mind is filled not with experiences of quietude but with the intention to drive from the mind all that is not quietude.

The issue of intention is critical and yet subtle in practice, but Kao cautions that the practice must simply initiate the emergence of the state of quietude. It must not try to force the creation of quietude. It should concern itself with something else. As Kao says, "It is a return to the quietude of human nature, not an adding of intention or knowledge. If even a single thought is added, the original substance is lost."[41] The key then is in what Kao calls the naturalness or the "ordinariness" of the practice, *p'ing-p'ing ch'ang-ch'ang* or *p'ing-ch'ang*. The degree to which it is natural or ordinary is the degree to which the practice is initiated without intention either toward the goal or away from the present perturbed state of the mind.

This state of "ordinariness" suggests as well the relation between activity and quietude. If the state of quietude is "ordinary" in the sense of lacking a specific intention toward its cultivation, then the movement from quietude back to activity should itself be ordinary. If these states are both "ordinary," then there is, according to Kao, no real transition between them. As Kao states, "When the transition from quietude to activity is an 'ordinary' one, then activity is itself quiet and the time of quietude and activity as well as activity and quietude are the same. It is simply 'ordinary.' Therefore it can be said that it is neither quietude nor activity!"[42] Kao admits that only the person who has experienced this state through quiet-sitting can understand the final conclusion.

In his second essay on quiet-sitting, *Later Discussion of Quiet-Sitting (Ching-tso shuo-huo),* Kao discusses further the difficulties inherent in the problem of intentionality.[43] The difficulties surround the practice of the beginner. The beginner is attached to the practice itself. It is a crutch necessary in the unsure world of contemplative practice and experience. When the beginner tries to emphasize the "ordinary," the mind only becomes scattered, rather than concentrated. Thus one must have a strategy; one must begin from the assumption of the unity of body and mind. This must be taken, as Kao says, as fundamental. The problem is, of course, that the moment it is recognized as fundamental, then there is an intention toward it. This in turn is an intention that should not be the object of attachment. But consciously not making it an object of attachment is itself an intention. Thus we have an intention to avoid an intention! How then to proceed? Kao's answer is just to carry on with the practice in an ordered and dignified manner; with time, the practice itself will mature and the state of the "ordinary" will be produced. If it is successful, quietude will be experienced and the transition between quietude and activity will be a natural one. This is the final standard for the practice. It must be in unity with the activity of life, and it must facilitate such activity. If it does, then the self is truly centered.

Kusumoto Tanzan, Seiza Realization, and Stored Wisdom

Okada can reflect back upon Kao P'an-lung and the importance of his practice and articulation of quiet-sitting, but a more immediate influence upon Okada in respect to quiet-sitting is Kusumoto Tanzan. Tanzan focused much of his self-cultivation upon quiet-sitting and also wrote of it extensively. Okada's work on Tanzan was an attempt to bring the importance of this figure and his practice to the attention of scholars of Confucianism, and in turn the attention paid to Tanzan in *Zazen to Seiza* centers this figure in the tradition of Confucian contemplative practice.[44]

For Tanzan, the naturalness or ordinariness of quietude as Kao discussed it was to become the principle for his own *seiza* practice, what he referred to as "*seiza* realization," *seiza tainin.* The pursuit of *seiza* realization for Tanzan was, according to Okada, of equal difficulty to the record preserved from Kao's autobiography. Kao's writing in turn played a major role in Tanzan's own practice. He specifically employed the techniques discussed in *Rules for Returning in Seven*. Initially, as we have seen, Tanzan followed the teachings of Liu Tsung-chou, a disciple of Wang Yang-ming. He was also interested in the quietist branch of the School of Mind, studying both Nieh Pao and Lo Hung-hsien. Here he found the focus upon Chou Tun-i's principle of regarding quietude as fundamental and, according to Okada, hoped to bring this back into the perspective of the Chu Hsi School. As his thought developed, he returned to the Chu Hsi teachings, attempting to relate Chu Hsi's teachings to his own theory and practice of *seiza*.

His theory of *seiza* rested upon a key phrase in his later thought, the wisdom that is stored, *chih-ts'ang* (Japanese: *chizō*).[45] According to Chu Hsi, goodness is stored in the Four Beginnings. Its capacity is in each of the Four Beginnings: humaneness, righteousness, propriety, and wisdom. In turn, wisdom is the endpoint of the Four Beginnings. It is the end, but it is also the beginning. It is a repository or storehouse for all things. Tanzan uses the metaphor of the seasons to describe it further, suggesting that wisdom corresponds to winter.

> Of the four seasons, spring, summer, fall and winter, wisdom belongs to winter, and of the four associated virtues, greatness, perseverance, cleverness and constancy, it belongs to constancy. Its substance is quiet and stores within it what is past. Its function is active and has wonderous effects of knowing the future. This is the beginning and end of all things.[46]

To Tanzan, wisdom becomes itself the substance of principle, and thus principle and wisdom are not different from each other. From Tanzan's point of view, this means that the very distinction that seemed so operative in Chu Hsi's teachings, dividing of internal and external, has no bearing. To posit the central role for stored wisdom is to transcend the distinction of internal and external. As Okada says in discussing Tanzan's theory:

> Stored wisdom is boundless and empty, but in it there is included all existence. It is the totality of principle with no distinguishing characteristic, but within it there is held a vigorous activity. Therefore it is the unity of existence and activity. In terms of the four seasons it is the moment of midnight of the winter solstice, and it corresponds to the point of time when quietude is completely exhausted and the subtle function is beginning to move.[47]

To Tanzan, since mind itself shared in this stored wisdom, the state of reverence could then reveal this hidden constancy of the mind itself. In his discussions of reverence, emphasis is placed upon the principle of regarding quietude as fundamental, and in order to facilitate this foundation of quietude, his idea of *seiza* realization assumes a central role. For Chu Hsi, this wisdom remains not the experience of the ineffable, but the quintessential role of goodness. For Tanzan, stored wisdom was in a sense the Absolute itself.

Tanzan's Method of *Seiza*

Kusumoto Tanzan has left us with an even more complete discussion of *seiza* than Kao P'an-lung, and Okada includes much of this in his discussion. One of the most important items is a lengthy letter Tanzan wrote in 1861 to Kōriki Sōseki (1829–61).[48] The letter, a summation of much of Tanzan's teaching, gives surprising detail on the practice of *seiza*. Tanzan quotes Atobe Ryōken (1659–1729), one of the major practitioners of *seiza*, who describes *seiza* in its physical characteristics, something that has been difficult to obtain any information about. In this description, it is contrasted with Buddhist *zazen*. *Zazen* is seen as a formal and technical practice. Legs must be folded, eyes focused upon the tip of the nose, mind focused below the navel. By contrast, *seiza* is discussed as a practice that can be undertaken at any time and in any context. Instead of the formal position, the legs can be crossed in whatever way one wants. One should make the body straight, but not stiff, simply folding the hands together and remaining relaxed.

Tanzan's instructions sound similar to those of Kao. He cautions that as the mind calms, numerous thoughts will begin to come out. This is natural and to be expected.

> When practicing quiet-sitting trifling and petty thoughts come out one after another. If you sweep them away still more continue to come out. They are the remains of actions already gone. It occurred to me that the reason these thoughts are produced is because the activities of our ordinary life tend not to accord with the Way.[49]

It is most important not to try to force these thoughts away. Tanzan quotes Ryōken as saying, "If one calms one's mind, wasteful thoughts will stop of their own. If one pushes them away and gets rid of them forcefully, without fail others will continue to come out one after another."[50] The key is relaxation and a practice that is not forced. His advice is to sit back and let quietude come about naturally, on its own.

Like Kao, Tanzan is also concerned with the issue of thinking about the experience of *seiza* realization. The experience can easily become itself an object of reflection. The moment that this happens the actual experience itself has been lost. In this respect Ryōken says, "The moment that one recognizes this as the point of the unmanifest, it is already the manifest."[51] The object is only to experience, not to think about the experience itself. Ryōken describes the experience of the unmanifest in greater detail: "The point of the unmanifest is before the voice of the bird or the sound of the wind echoes to the mind. If one recognizes that it is the sound of a bird or the wind, then it is the manifest."[52] It is not that the sound of the bird or the wind has been excluded from perception itself, but simply that the sound is sound as such and not identified as the sound of a particular object. There is sound, that is all, and it is accepted as sound. It is not questioned as sound to identify its source. Tanzan goes on to describe the same phenomenon with objects we observe through sight. Whether it be birds flying or the wind moving the leaves of a tree, there is a seeing, but not a questioning.

Tanzan also quotes Ryōken to describe the way in which the practice and experience of quietude begins to have an effect on the way one hears or sees. "When one encounters things after practicing *seiza,* one does not have this same questioning mind."[53] Thus there is just the hearing or just the seeing, and from Tanzan's point of view, this is a direct contact with the unmanifest itself. Tanzan describes this point in detail.

At the point that one calms the mind by quiet-sitting, the eyes see color as it actually is, the ears hear sound as it actually is, the nose smells odor as it actually is, the movement of the hands and feet is in accord with the process of creation of things as they actually are, and the self has no relation to the activities of the hands and feet; the substance of the mind becomes vigorous, it penetrates the forces of Heaven and is free of abstracts. In this is found the sincerity of the man of humanity. It is unfathomable and still like a deep abyss, it is broad and expansive like Heaven. Everything becomes whole and one and merges together. Man is Heaven, Heaven is man. To be enlightened to this is true enlightenment; to cultivate this is true cultivation.[54]

On the other hand, if there is questioning or for that matter agitation, then this foundation of quietude has not been established. Even if one practices *seiza* and yet approaches daily activity or things of the world considering them from the perspective of the daily mind of habit, then whatever quietude has been built up will itself be lost. It is essential then to ground oneself according to Tanzan in Chou Tun-i's principle of regarding quietude as fundamental and to view all activity from this perspective. If this can be done, then the result will be similar to what Kao discussed, an ability to move from quietude to activity with little or no transition and in the end to experience no difference whatsoever between quietude and activity. Ryōken says in this respect, "One must be careful to conduct daily activities more and more in quietude. If one does not lose the mind of *seiza* even for a little while, then the effort of regarding quietude as fundamental can be achieved."[55]

Okada's discussion of Tanzan's practice of *seiza* ends with the inclusion of a daily schedule of self-cultivation that Tanzan wrote for his students. It is very similar to two of the writings included from Kao P'an-lung, his *Agenda for Dwelling in the Mountains* and the *Rules for Returning in Seven*. Both of these writings laid out the activities that should make up a day of learning and self-cultivation, and Tanzan's text is doing the same thing. What is different about Tanzan's is that while Kao's were written with a specific sense of isolation in mind for the practitioner, Tanzan intended his rules to apply to the normal day of a student. In this schedule, *seiza* is balanced with other activities. There is study of the Classics and of the philosophers, there are long walks, there is composition, and there is *seiza*. This reflects Chu Hsi's own rule of a half-day of quiet-sitting and a half-day of study, but it also illustrates the degree to which Tanzan saw the practice as forming the foundation for all activities, permitting those activities to unfold within a self thoroughly centered in quietude.

From *Seiza* to *Kotsuza*

In his volume *Zazen to Seiza*, Okada attempts to show the importance of the practice of *seiza* in historical Confucianism and for the world today. Okada engages in the practice as it has been handed down to him, representing the traditions of Kao P'an-lung and Kusumoto Tanzan that have been the focal point of his own discussion. It is, from his point of view, one of the essential ingredients if the contemporary world is going to be able to return to its true humanistic roots. When I was with Okada on that first visit, in 1977, it was clear that *seiza* was viewed as the salient means to the centering of the self. When I returned in 1983 to interview him, I found that as I posed questions about *seiza*, he was patient with me and answered the questions, but it was as if we were discussing a historical practice rather than a pressing existential concern. I wondered why there seemed to be this distance from the practice. The answer lay, as I was soon to find out, in Okada's new thinking about meditation, and his feeling that there was a meditative practice that went beyond the limits of *seiza*. This seemed difficult to imagine, since both Kao as well as Tanzan had viewed *seiza* as the very basis of their enlightenment experience. Okada was not, it turned out, challenging the practice itself, but suggesting that some of the very problems that both Kao and Tanzan had seen in the practice could be met and overcome through a new orientation in the practice itself. This new practice he referred to as *kotsuza,* a term difficult to render into English, but having the sense of "just sitting." I sat enraptured with his enthusiasm for this new practice. Here was a man who from a young age had focused his learning and self-cultivation around the practice of *seiza,* and yet now at the age of seventy-four he was informing me that only very recently had he realized that there was another approach possible and that it better suited his own present thinking and practice.

The new practice, *kotsuza,* means "just sitting" and nothing more. But what is this "just sitting"? It is as its name suggests—just sitting. The point of focusing upon just sitting, however, is so that the mind will not be focused upon anything else. To Okada, this is the way to let the inner nature of the mind emerge. As he says, "With just sitting the experience of the inner nature becomes manifest and there is true inner subjectivity" (*naimen teki shūtaisei*).[56] But how is this different from the model of *seiza* he followed? It is not different in terms of the description of the process that the practice will lead one through but, rather, in terms of its capacity to realize this goal with a minimum of difficulties encountered.

Quietude is produced by assuming a position of quietude, and nothing should interfere with this quietude. Here, however, is where both Kao and Tanzan experienced difficulties. It seemed time and again that it was all too easy for things to interfere with that experience of quietude, particularly the thought processes concerned either to rid the mind of extraneous thought or the thought about the experience of quietude itself. Thus conscious attempts to make the mind quiet or to preserve the experience of quietude are themselves a clear hindrance to the actual quieting process. And for Okada, this hindrance seemed to be intimately connected to the formality of the practice of *seiza* itself. *Seiza* is far more relaxed and informal than many of the forms of Buddhist *zazen* and therefore from the Confucian point of view freer of this problem than *zazen,* but for Okada there was a problem in this area, and the solution lay in renouncing even further the formality of the practice.

This realization that methods tend to produce too much thinking about quietude and not enough of the actual experience suggested that the practice should itself not be a method with its own rules and regulations. It is, of course, a method to the degree that it is the doing of one thing rather than something else, but it is method-free to the degree that it remains free of thinking about itself in terms of specific rules and regulations or even thinking about itself as something that will produce particular results. Kao talked in a similar way and suggested that this point of practice had to be method-free even though it employed method, and ultimately only the person who was practicing and experiencing quietude could understand the nature of a method that could not be a method. For anyone else, it remains only an intellectual framework, and this in itself gives it the "thinking-about" quality that already gravitates against the retention of the experience. Better to stop talking about it or, in this case, better just to sit—and not to sit with a method.

The practice, according to Okada, still is rooted in the teachings of Neo-Confucianism, and there is still the general principle of a balance of quietude and activity, but as *kotsuza* strives to diminish elements of method, none of these elements can assume any conscious or articulated status. There is, after all, just sitting, and anything else is the creation of an intellectual understanding which by definition is the ruination of the experience itself. As Okada says, *kotsuza* is not different from the teachings of Confucianism; in fact, it is the ultimate form of these teachings, but it is nothing other than just practice.

What then of the practice of *kotsuza?* It reflects a new stage of Okada's understanding. Can it be described and discussed?

> It is not impossible to explain something of *kotsuza*, but frankly I prefer sitting with other people as an "explanation" of just sitting. . . . *Kotsuza* is a part of Chu Hsi and Wang Yang-ming. But I don't want to give an analysis of *kotsuza*, for the more that is explained, the less that is understood. I may sometime have to explain something about *kotsuza*, if I live long enough![57]

What followed Okada's discussion were a series of questions I asked Okada about *kotsuza*. The first question that interested me was the relation of *seiza* and *kotsuza*. Did one begin, for example, with *seiza* and move on to *kotsuza*? His answer was that one should begin with *kotsuza*. This seemed to me to present a real problem for the beginning student who might very well be in need of a method, or of something to hold onto. How would the directive, just go and sit, be effective in that case? But to Okada the practice is simple and so too its final state. Nothing complex is needed either at the beginning or at the end. He compared self-cultivation to the study of a tree. One can begin with leaves and branches, or the trunk, or one can go directly to the roots. *Kotsuza*, for Okada, is going directly to the roots. This has the same application to the beginner that it has to the person experienced in the ways of contemplative practice.

I was curious as well about the relation of the quietude of *kotsuza* to the world of activity, a point that has been stressed by Okada in his discussion of the practice of *seiza*. And we have seen the degree to which Chu Hsi, Kao, and Tanzan all are concerned that quietude and activity come to assimilate themselves thoroughly to each other, that the so-called transition between quietude and activity and between activity and quietude come to be no longer a transition at all. For Okada, *kotsuza* is to do the same. In fact, it might even be argued that *kotsuza* possesses the capability of making this transition less difficult precisely because it does not set itself the task of defining the characteristics of the method and state of quietude. By not engaging in the process of articulating a method of quietude, it has not defined the state that stands in distinction to activity. If quietude is not defined, then in turn activity remains less rigidly defined, and the transition from one to the other can proceed with only a minimum of hindrance. Such is the point of view of just sitting, not a state confined to sitting alone, but an attitude that attempts to remain free of inserting content into the attitude, that begins and ends with the experience of quietude.

Yet we have just said that there is no difference between quietude and activity. Were one to begin and end with quietude alone, a difference of quietude and activity would be created and maintained. Thus to begin and end with quietude means to begin and end with both quietude and activity and, from a Confucian point of view, without the activity the real task of rescuing the world has not been realized. We take then the contemplative model, the state of quietude, and we see that it acts in the world with thorough-going moral commitment. From a contemplative model, we move to moral action and to the conclusion of Okada's thought—a conclusion that grounds the world of quietude in the world of actual problems.

3. MORAL ACTION FROM A CONTEMPLATIVE MODE

The model of *seiza* upon which Okada built his own practice ends with the conclusion that ultimately there is no difference between the world of quietude and the world of action. As this practice becomes thoroughly integrated into one's own life, all actions come to reflect the depth of the reservoir of quietude that has been established. Throughout the discussion of quiet-sitting itself, we have seen the emphasis that has been placed upon achieving a state of quietude that has this capacity for action inherent within it. A quietude that is only quiet, from Okada's point of view, serves no purpose whatsoever. But more important, a quietude that is incapable of moving into the context of activity has little to claim for itself as a state of quietude.

This echoes back to an earlier issue of contemplative practice: the degree to which it is relatively easy to attain a state of quietude in a quiet setting. The problem arises when one attempts to take that state of quietude achieved in a quiet setting and move into a setting of activity. The quietude is thoroughly dissipated unless the training has been long and arduous and has stressed the need for quietude to provide an access to activity. This is really the key issue. Unless one is simply going to retire from the world into a hermitage of quietude, then the world needs to be brought into the framework of quietude itself. We have seen the way in which Okada has stressed those discussions of *seiza* that have been concerned to integrate and assimilate quietude and activity thoroughly. Kao P'an-lung stands out as a prominent figure in this respect. In his essays on quiet-sitting, the transition between quietude and activity must be a thoroughly natural one. In the end for Kao, as we have seen, there is no transition at all, because there is no difference between the states.

This integration of quietude and activity is represented even more clearly in Okada's discussion of his movement from *seiza* to *kotsuza*. As we have seen, *seiza* is interpreted as a practice and technique, and while its conclusion is to transcend its role as a specific technique by bringing about this union of the realms of quietude and activity, it remains for Okada the object of thought. As an object of thought, it creates an intellectual model for understanding the relation of internal and external realms, the spheres of quietude and activity. Thus for Okada it becomes necessary to break down this last intellectual barrier to allow quietude and activity to coalesce without an artificial technique. This is *kotsuza,* just sitting. Activity is in this sense no different from the wellspring of quietude within the depth of the individual. Activity and quietude, quietude and activity: from this perspective they are the same. They are not the subjects of abstract intellectualizing; they are simply the reality of living each day.

The position that Okada represents stresses the importance of carrying the contemplative vision to the world of action. This unity of quietude and activity is in itself an important indicator of the religious structure of Okada's point of view and the religious structure of the Confucian tradition itself. Much interpretation of the Confucian tradition has rested upon a model of moral and social action. The Confucian was identified primarily through his role of serving in government or serving his family and ancestors. The capacity for responsibility in moral service has remained one of the chief features highlighted in the tradition, and yet little attention has been paid to the interior developments of the self that result in such moral responsibility from learning and self-cultivation. This foundation for moral action in society is clearly rooted in the focus placed upon learning and self-cultivation. Service in society is the outgrowth of the interior dynamics of self-development.[1]

In religious terminology there is a further dynamic to this understanding of the relation between the internal and external spheres. Joachim Wach, in his characterization of features of religious experience, has drawn attention not only to the internal features of the religious experience, but to its external ramifications as well. He suggests as a fourth and final characteristic of religious experience that it must issue forth in action.[2] It is not enough, according to Wach, simply to stop with religious experience itself. This would be equivalent to someone claiming to have a transformative experience, but then saying that there was nothing to be done for the world or for one's fellow human beings.[3] As Wach's discussion suggests, such a person's actual experience would be doubted. One would demand to see the way in which the experience would bring about a commitment to action to help transform the condition of the world.

If we entertain this notion of issuing forth in action as an essential characteristic of the religious experience, then we bring a new dimension of understanding to the age-old description of the Confucian tradition, the description that sees Confucianism as a system of social ethics rather than as a religious tradition. If we bring Wach's point of view to the Confucian materials, we can say that this commitment to social ethics is not an end unto itself. Such social ethics, if that be the correct term, are the very product of the interior religious dynamics of the tradition itself. Specifically, the Confucian commitment to activity is that element that Wach has described as the issuing forth into action from the genuine religious experience. What then has for so long been identified as one of the salient features, if not the salient feature, of the Confucian tradition and an element that seemed to preclude seeing the tradition as a religious tradition becomes an outgrowth of the interior religious dynamics of the tradition itself.

There remains, of course, the argument that the tradition is unable to engage in internal religious dynamics, because it is only a form of humanistic reflection or of moral action. It would seem, however, that we are beyond this argument in the general study of Confucianism and that the religious nature of the tradition has been substantiated, particularly the religiously transformative nature of its goal, sagehood. If this is accepted, then its commitment to activity is a religious commitment, and the context of Wach's category an appropriate one for interpreting the religious dynamics of the tradition.[4]

As we bring this model back to Okada, we can see that Okada's commitment to activity does not stand in contradiction to a contemplative mode or a religious dimension. In fact, quite the contrary. His commitment to activity, to serving in the world and trying to rectify its problems, is a natural outgrowth of his particular focus upon the internal dynamics of a contemplative mode. If he were not to conclude that such action were necessary and essential, then he would have said nothing different from those who perfect quietude in a quiet place and seize hold of the opportunity to retain their quietude by abiding in quietude alone. But this is not by Confucian standards genuine quietude; it has not assimilated quietude with action itself.

For Okada, genuine quietude demands placing oneself in the context of activity. This is the point of departure for his criticism of Buddhism. Okada condemns those who cultivate a model of quietude and then remain within the sphere of quietude, serving no role nor carrying out any responsibility within the framework of activity in the world, at least as Okada himself understands it. While the Zen model of contemplative practice is a significant one for Okada, he is also critical of Buddhism and in particular of Zen. The lines of this criticism are focused upon the frequent failure of Zen practice to issue forth in action, that is, to make a commitment to serving and transforming the world.

In *Zazen to Seiza,* Okada summarizes his criticism of Zen under six headings: first, Zen does not know ethics; second, Zen does not focus upon the governing of the world; third, the nature of mind in Zen has no integration of interior and exterior; fourth, in Zen the mind is divided; fifth, Zen actually does not obtain absolute nothingness; and sixth, Zen does not obtain absolute freedom.[5] From Okada's perspective, these criticisms are decisive in pinpointing the weaknesses of Buddhism. In turn, for our analysis such criticisms clearly define the degree to which Confucianism must remain in a posture addressing real problems of the real world. This is even more important when one is dealing, as we are with Okada, with a part of the tradition that has sought a contemplative model of learning and self-cultivation. On the surface of it, it would appear that a contemplative model would be the least interested in active participation in the world. Yet as our study of Okada's *seiza* and *kotsuza* has indicated, such contemplative practices are judged genuine only if they issue forth in the call to activity within the world. Buddhism in this respect is insufficient for Okada. The answer is to be found only in the Confucian model of a contemplative realization activating itself to the problems of the world, a model of moral action as an outgrowth of the contemplative mode.[6]

A Contemporary Imperative to Act

In all that Okada says in *Zazen to Seiza,* the directive is to develop the contemplative mode in order to realize the state of quietude thoroughly, and then to carry this internal quietude into the world and make it the basis for moral action in the world. This was the foundation of Okada's remarks to me when I first met him. The world is in moral decline, what can we do about it? How do we set ourselves about the task of rectifying the ills of the world? Now one can see the foundation of thought and practice that produced this very simple yet thoroughly penetrating question. One can see the degree to which it is an outgrowth of Okada's entire life of learning and self-cultivation. It is a religious response to the world, coming as it does from his own profound religious insight into his life and the world.

In *Zazen to Seiza,* the foundation is laid for moral action from a contemplative mode, yet the work remains primarily historical in its focus. Thus the foundation is laid, but there is no formulation of action to be carried out. In this sense, the imperative is there, but there is no specific response to specific temporal and spatial conditions, that is, to the world as we know it today. I could not help but wonder if it would not be appropriate to invite Okada to respond to the particular conditions of the world today. It was this thinking that produced my trip to Japan in 1983, the trip upon which I interviewed Okada at length about his response to the conditions of the world today. Much of this focused on Japan as a highly technological society and the relation he saw between traditional Confucian values and the issues of modern society. A number of issues, however, had global significance as Okada talked of the very survival of the world itself.

In the history of Confucianism, there are many texts that illustrate the way in which a particular thinker, Chu Hsi for example, might respond to issues of his day, but for us today they are historical texts. What the literature has not produced is a contemporary Confucian talking about issues of our own day from nuclear war to biomedical research, abortion, technological society, and the future of world religions. This is the serious reflection of a contemporary Confucian on the issues of our day. Because it is not a historical text, there are those who will regard it as of less significance, and yet such a perspective fails to recognize the degree to which Confucianism in its innermost core has always seen its role defined in terms of individuals bringing their own inner understanding to bear upon the pressing issues of their day. Okada is no different in this respect. He is a Confucian, and his long years of contemplative practice have brought him to a certain understanding of the inner core of Confucian teaching. From this context of quietude, he can address the actions of the world. This dialogue with Okada becomes a text in itself, the latest of a long tradition of texts in which a Confucian is responding to the conditions of the real world and attempting to show the degree to which the Confucian contemplative experience can shed light upon the nature of the problems of the world and the way in which they can be rectified.

Okada's Response to the World

Okada begins with the affirmation of the goodness of human nature, the theory of the goodness of human nature first proposed by the classical Confucian thinker Mencius. It was Mencius who argued that all humans have a nature of goodness or a capacity for goodness, which can be fully developed through learning and self-cultivation.[7] It was Mencius who said that every person has a heart that cannot bear to see the suffering of another (*pu jen jen chih hsin*).[8] These arguments are not motivated by utilitarian standards,[9] nor are they seen as the basis for being rewarded in this life or in the next. In fact, Okada's discussion of death should eliminate any suggestion of an afterlife. The Confucian has always remained silent on the question of an afterlife,[10] and Okada is no exception. Here the focus is upon the issues at hand, and thus the importance of the concept that human nature is an embodiment of goodness. Yet the ideal of goodness and the apparent reality of conditions of the world are far apart. Instead of goodness, there appears to be a dominance of evil, evil from a Confucian point of view in terms of the selfishness that dominates much of the activity of the human mind, both at the individual level and at the level of societal, national, and even global spheres.

To Okada, one still starts, however, with the assumption of goodness, like Mencius' describing the simple incident of the child about to fall into the well.[11] For Mencius, human beings respond to this incident. They rescue the child and for no other reason, no ulterior utilitarian motive, than the simple fact that their moral natures cannot bear to see the suffering of another. For Okada, this is a too often unspoken assumption and therefore unrecognized statement about the nature of human beings. As he says:

> If we didn't believe in this ideal, how would it be possible to live to-
> gether as human beings? The very concept of the survival of humanity
> and the world is directly tied to it. Without Mencius' idea you would not
> be able to trust even the person standing in front of you. This is truly the
> basic point that all humans are by nature good.[12]

Our view of the world often, however, focuses upon the evil and the perpetuation of suffering that seems an almost ubiquitous characteristic of existence itself. Such evil seems only to have been exacerbated in the capacity held by modern society for its own total annihilation. As Okada says, there are many things about the world "that might lead us to a belief in the evilness of humans,"[13] and yet we must dissuade ourselves from this conclusion. The difficulty is that we look to Mencius' theory or other Confucian theories about human nature, according to Okada, as grounds for a rational proof. This is not, however, an issue of rational proof for Okada any more than Mencius intended his "arguments" with the philosopher Kao Tzu concerning human nature to be a proof, as we understand that term, for the goodness of human nature.[14] They are more in the nature of poetic insights into an experience of human nature. Thus Okada says:

The real understanding of this goodness must itself be the product of a deep inner experience. The idea doesn't come from a rationalistic observation of human conduct. It must in fact be considered in terms of religion itself. Thus, though there are many things that might lead us to a belief in the evilness of humans, we must accept the belief in the goodness of human nature.[15]

Okada's perspective on the issue of the goodness of human nature is not one that would be shared by all Confucians, nor certainly all scholars of Confucianism. It is, however, very clearly an interpretation that is an outgrowth of his own contemplative model of Confucian teachings. I raised this issue with Okada, and his response emphasized the role of experience over philosophical explanation. "As you say, there are many scholars who try to understand the goodness of human nature through rationalism. On the other hand, some try to consider the concept through their own inner experience. I try to understand the goodness of human nature through inner experience."[16]

If it is something that cannot be rationally proved, then prior to the inner experience of its truth, there will be a necessity of holding to the belief even if it has yet to be fully believed. In this sense, there is a risk to this belief and there is risk-taking involved in the attempt to live out the capacity for exercising faith in the potential of human nature. Facing the potential goodness of human nature thus takes on the character of a leap of faith. This is an issue of relevance to the individual in interpersonal relations, but it is equally relevant to the mass display of individuals in the facing of one nation-state by another. This does not produce for Okada the position of always trusting the "other" to fall back upon its goodness, and thus he is not suggesting the requiting of evil with goodness. There is a time and a place for punishment of evil and the exercise of good for Confucius,[17] and Okada does not differ from him in this respect. But there is also a necessity to see the capacity for goodness and to exercise a faith that in the end this capacity for goodness will emerge.

From Okada's point of view, one of the chief problems of contemporary society is the inability to understand this assumption of the goodness of human nature. This has disastrous effects on the individual and, of course, could have cataclysmic results for the future of the human race. Not only has education redirected itself away from value orientation and toward a technological knowledge, but it has also depreciated any form of learning other than intellectual and rational models. This means that the idea of the goodness of human nature is diminished in comparison to strategies of technological knowledge. In addition, the path of learning that necessitates an inner contemplative experience has lost all credibility as a pedagogical tool. What suffers is the individual and one's self-understanding, and in turn the world at large. To Okada, unless there is a radical reorientation that permits the faith in human goodness to move to an inner experience of that goodness, only the severest of consequences will follow for the future of humankind itself. One of the key issues in this problem is the arising of science, a science that has intellectually freed itself from questions of ethics and religion.

Science and Human Values

Okada expresses his concern about the way in which science has developed. Instead of developing hand in hand with humanity, according to Okada, it has become a threat to the very humanity it had set out to serve. Obviously one cannot stop the development of science, and this is not Okada's desire, but rather, to introduce into science a respect for human life, which he presently sees lacking. For Okada, the Confucian tradition and teaching could serve this end, for it begins with the assumption of the importance and inherent value of life, one's own as well as others, and sees the need for mutual respect for the value of life as a prerequisite for survival. We cannot but live with others, and the basis of living with others is the core of Confucian ethics—the exercise of consideration for others, the recognition of the feelings of the heart of the other person.

Does this mean that science and Confucianism are fundamentally incompatible? Okada thinks not and discusses the range of Chu Hsi's learning to illustrate the degree to which Chu Hsi himself would have found a compatibility with science.[18] The key for Okada, however, is to be found in Chu Hsi's concept of "total substance and great functioning." The phrase, as we have seen, has several meanings. It first means that the human heart or mind contains an essential ethical nature. Second, it means that the principles or laws of the external world or natural world are to be found as well in the human mind. Thus there is a direct correlation between the inner structure of the human mind and the natural world. If in this respect we call the natural world the macrocosm, then the human mind is a microcosm of it. As Okada remarks almost humorously, we in fact assume this correlation as the basis of our knowledge about the universe, for if the mind and the natural world did not share a common nature, knowledge of one by the other would be impossible![19]

On this most would agree; however, if the second point is allowed, that there is a common nature, then the first point, the ethical nature of the heart or mind, has an interesting ramification. If the human being and the natural world share a common nature and the human being in turn is ethical by nature, then clearly in this frame of thought the natural world or the universe is also ethical by nature. This is an argument that has long been at the center of Confucian thought, but here it is being applied to the issues of contemporary science and the modern scientific view of the universe. The application to the contemporary context suggests that science must allow for the fact that we may be dealing with a natural world and universe that is ethical by design, rather than the product of random chance.

The issue that Okada raises is a basic and essential one. He is arguing that a science that bases itself upon a view of the universe that lacks ethical structure has itself no basis for sustaining value consideration of the human beings it is attempting to serve. To describe a universe as possessing ethical structure is to say at the most fundamental level that the universe has meaning and purpose, and that it is directed toward some goal. In turn, this is also to say that the individual life also has meaning and purpose. For Okada, if science assumes no such purpose or meaning in the universe, then there is nothing upon which to build a science save utilitarianism and selfish concerns.

Rather than allowing science to perpetuate a process of development ultimately predicated upon the meaninglessness of the universe, Okada would recommend that science be incorporated into a system of thought that assumes there is meaning and purpose. Within this framework, science can do its work, and rather than bringing about the destruction of humanity, it will be seen as truly serving the deepest needs of humanity.

This bears upon the whole question of religion and its difference from an empirical or scientific worldview. Empiricism assumes a factor of mere chance or randomness in the foundation of the universe. There is no teleology, there is no purpose or meaning. A religious point of view, on the other hand, whether it be Buddhist or Christian, Hindu or Jewish, is defined precisely in terms of the component of meaning and purpose in the world. A religious point of view cannot sustain itself in a world of chance and purposelessness. The philosopher W. T. Stace has stated this clearly.

> Religion could survive the discoveries that the sun, not the earth, is the center; that men are descended from Simian ancestors; that the earth is hundreds of millions of years old. These discoveries may render out of date some of the details of older theological dogmas, may force their restatement in new intellectual frameworks. But they do not touch the

essence of the religious vision itself, which is the faith that there is a plan and purpose in the world, that the world is a moral order, that in the end all things are for the best.[20]

For Stace, religion can cope with changing scientific views of the universe—the new astronomy, the new geology, the new biology—but it cannot cope with a view of a universe without purpose or meaning or ethical structure. Confucianism is saying nothing different, and Okada would find himself, I suspect, in complete agreement with Stace on this point. In this way Confucianism is functioning like any other religious tradition by arguing that one cannot sustain a religious view of the world out of a view of the world as lacking all purpose.

Even with the perceived ambiguities of the world, the view, as Okada has expressed it, that evil is very obvious and goodness often hard to detect, there is still the clinging to meaning and purpose by a religious tradition. As Clifford Geertz has argued, this is basic to the very structure of religion itself.

The strange opacity of certain empirical events, the dumb senselessness of intense and inexorable pain, and the enigmatic unaccountability of gross iniquity all raise the uncomfortable suspicion that perhaps the world, and hence man's life in the world, has no genuine order at all—no empirical regularity, no emotional form, no moral coherence. And the religious response to this suspicion is in each case the same: the formulation . . . of an image of such a genuine order of the world which will account for, and even celebrate, the perceived ambiguities, puzzles and paradoxes in human experience.[21]

For a religious tradition, these seeming ambiguities, puzzles, and paradoxes cannot indicate the ultimate purposelessness of things, but only an inability to detect the underlying meaning and purpose. Confucianism is no different in this respect, and Okada's basic argument against science as a form of empiricism simply reconfirms his own fundamentally established religious orientation.

Until science adopts a point of view of moral order and purpose in the universe, its development will continue to run contrary to the interest of humanity itself. At a practical level, the only way this task will be accomplished, according to Okada, is to begin to change the educational system to include contemplative practice and self-cultivation. This will lead to the kind of inner experience Okada has emphasized, the true inner subjectivity, and as such will influence the way in which a scientific worldview will be entertained. Instead of an end in itself, it will be seen to reflect the meaning found in the inner experience of the self, a self that experiences its own meaning in the larger moral order and purpose of the universe itself.

Ethics and Animals

One of the topics that grew out of our conversations was the issue of ethical responsibility not only toward human beings, but toward other forms of life as well. This became the occasion for me to pose a series of questions to Okada on the Confucian response to animals and, in contemporary context of the issue, the case for animal rights and its relation to biomedical research.[22]

The issue of a Confucian response and attitude toward animals is not a new one. In fact, the tradition contains a number of statements pertaining to animals. Confucius is depicted as showing kindness toward animals,[23] and Mencius uses the example of a king who cannot bear the thought of an animal suffering as an example of the true feeling of humaneness.[24] Neo-Confucians in turn suggest that, as the unity of humankind with the cosmos is recognized, as they form one body with the universe, there would in turn be a display of humaneness toward animals.

An equally consistent theme in Confucianism, however, is a hierarchy in the feelings toward others. For the Confucian, the greatest level of humaneness is to be shown to the individuals who stand in a special moral relation. In turn, this level of concern is to be extended to larger and larger spheres, eventually extending to all living things. The Confucian is insistent, however, that the priority remain with those who are in closest moral relationship. If someone can express compassion toward animals but not toward his fellow humans or close relatives, then this is a skewing of the moral principles from the Confucian perspective and not a sign of virtue.

In this spirit, I posed questions to Okada. I asked initially whether the Confucian had ethical responsibilities to *all* forms of life, not just human life. Okada answered by saying: "Yes, I think we do. This idea of respect should be extended to all forms of life, animals and plants alike. The Confucian concept of being in community with other human beings can be extended to the community of life itself."[25] Okada agreed as well that we have a moral responsibility for other forms of life, and this is based primarily upon the argument of Mencius that we cannot bear to see the suffering of another. "That all humankind has a heart of commiseration that cannot bear to see the suffering of others, such an idea should be applied to animals as well."[26]

We then turned to the question of the use of animals in biomedical research. I acquainted him with the various ways in which this issue is approached in the West and the prominence that such discussion has now achieved in terms of animal-rights issues as well as serious discussion in the field of ethics. This was, he said, an issue that no one in Japan had asked him about and yet it was also an appropriate area for a Confucian response. The problem, as he saw it, was the conflict between the need to continue the development of science and the obvious suffering that is incurred by the animals in their sacrifice to the needs of science. His solution to the problem is again in terms of the phrase from Mencius, the heart of commiseration. This does not simply stop the suffering or the killing of the animals, but it places a value upon the lives of the animals and a moral responsibility upon the researcher. His example of eating of fish in Japan is to the point. "Let me put it this way: here in Japan we eat a lot of fish, and from time to time we have a memorial service for the fish that have been killed. If you think about the problem in this way, it might well be solved."[27]

The conclusion may seem ambiguous, and perhaps it is in terms of the response by animal-rights activists who would want to see a direct cessation of the researcher's work; but from the setting of the Confucian tradition a great deal is being said. There are times when the unity of humankind and animals should be emphasized, and there are times when the differentiation between them should be emphasized. This is something that will be clarified through one's own moral sensitivities to the issues involved, as well as an understanding of the heart of commiseration. Okada, by using the example of the eating of fish, is drawing our attention to the issue of human needs and yet also showing that such needs still must operate in a setting of moral responsibility and obligation. Here too there is even a sense of gratitude. The fish or the research animal is giving up its life so that others may live or scientific progress may be made. This is a sacrifice, and it needs to be understood in terms of the moral responsibility incurred by the individual who is responsible for this sacrifice. If the ethical dimensions of the issue can be seen, then the relationship between the researcher and the animal sacrificed changes, and with the change would come improvements such as a more conscious attempt to sacrifice less animals or to substitute cell cultures for animals themselves. The critical issue remains, bringing researchers to see the ethical dimensions of their work in terms of the sacrifice of life itself and making researchers aware of their own heart of commiseration and the appropriateness of a response, even their own, that cannot bear to see the suffering of another.

Biomedical Ethics and Abortion

Two topics that at present have engendered a tremendous amount of ethical discussion as well as simply political and topical opinion in Western societies are the issues of right to life and, in turn, right to death, and the controversies surrounding abortion and euthanasia.[28] These issues are not discussed in Asia to anywhere near the degree that their profile has assumed in the West. Still, I wanted to pose these issues with Okada, focusing first upon questions concerning the right to die, euthanasia, prolongation of life by artificial means, and the suffering that is caused both to the patient and to those in immediate relation, whether family or even medical staff. Second, I wanted his response to the controversy surrounding abortion. I approached these questions with Okada to find a strictly Confucian response to the issues.

His answers suggested a recognition of the extreme difficulty of the decision-making process and an understanding of the range of issues that become involved—social and economic, as well as ethical. First, in terms of right-to-die questions, he has little difficulty with euthanasia as a solution. To Okada there is no stigma in terms of the act of euthanasia itself, but clearly the issue is one that must be a product of moral reflection, allowing flexibility where it seems necessary. There is a fundamental moral responsibility to further the value of human life itself. This remains essential, but so too does the wisdom to see the point at which one is not so much prolonging the value of life as prolonging the suffering of the dying process.

On the question of abortion, Okada's response demonstrated both a very specific Confucian issue and a more general non-Western cultural point of view. The non-Western cultural point of view simply recognizes that many issues enter into the decision for or against abortion and that it is difficult to raise the issue to the level of absolute right to life for the fetus or, in turn, the absolute right of the mother to determine the decision. The role of the individual and its rights, whether fetus or mother, is simply not the same part of the issue as it is in Western technological societies. That in itself makes the issue of abortion a less significant one ethically within the setting of East Asian cultures.

There is, however, one response that is distinctly Confucian and in general would militate against abortion. This is the issue of ethical responsibility and its connection to special moral relations. If pregnancy occurs, then a set of Confucian ethical values is relevant, values that isolate the importance of specific moral relations and that argue that a parent's responsibility lies with the nourishing and caring of the child. As Okada says, "If the woman becomes pregnant, then the parents should accept the responsibility of the baby born to them and should carefully raise it. This is our fundamental purpose as human beings."[29] What stands out as fundamentally Confucian in this response is the assertion of ethical responsibility and the recognition of a special moral relation between the parents and the infant. This, as Okada says, is fundamental to our very purpose as human beings. In this way a response that denies this fundamental purpose runs counter to our role as human beings and, in turn, to the development of the cosmos as well. The ramifications of this position still need, however, to be put in the context of potentially different roles of individual rights as well as the extenuating circumstances that are appropriate justification for abortion.

Here again, one should not expect definitive positions or answers in terms of the controversies that surround both right-to-die issues as well as abortion issues in Western societies. Perhaps it is important to realize to begin with the degree to which these issues have not achieved the controversial nature they possess within Western culture. That in itself may be highly significant in terms of recognizing that these issues only emerge out of the development of certain technologies or certain philosophical and religious perspectives.

Okada, however, is still providing a basis for how a Confucian would address these questions, and in this respect he is saying a good deal about a Confucian response. Uppermost in that response remains the issue of ethical responsibility, whether one is dealing with a terminal illness or a decision on abortion. The emphasis upon ethical responsibility suggests that the way we relate to these questions should be a reflection of our own inner nature of goodness and our capacity for reflecting this goodness in natural moral relations. Thus we have moral obligations associated with the terminally ill just as we have responsibility in parenting. This does not mean that decisions for euthanasia or for abortion cannot be made and that at times these are the best decisions that can be made. But it does draw our attention to the seriousness of the decisions themselves and the degree to which the decision must mirror our own inner feelings of moral reflection.

Technological Society

Much of the world's population must recognize that it either presently lives in or is striving toward a highly technological society. How, within this framework, can we be fully human, that is, how is it possible to exercise our capacity for humaneness, to let emerge our heart of commiseration?

Okada responds to this challenge by suggesting that no matter how far science develops or how technological the society, we are still fundamentally dealing with the relation of one person to another. The Confucian never loses sight of the primary goal of establishing a true humanity. Okada admits that this search for the true humanity becomes far more difficult in a technological society.

The answer to this dilemma is to emphasize the internal dimensions of self-cultivation rather than simply an acquired knowledge of things.

The important issue is to establish one's own inner subjectivity within the mind. It has seemed to me that with the increase in scientific knowledge, there has been a loss in the inner subjective capacity of the mind. Scientific knowledge stimulates the mind, but it also causes the loss of inner subjectivity within our minds. In order to retain our inner subjectivity and yet still accept scientific development, it is essential that we have some means to maintain our inner subjectivity.[30]

Okada speaks of this inner dimension as the inner subjectivity of the mind and stresses that, while scientific knowledge is not to be neglected, it needs to assume its proper position, a position secondary to an increase in the subjective capacity of the mind. For Okada, this increase in the inner dimension of self-understanding, the "inner subjectivity" of the mind, is to be accomplished first and foremost by contemplative practice. He proposes that contemplative practice be initiated in standard educational programs, beginning even in primary grades, to begin to provide a means for students to establish the inner dynamics of their subjectivity much as they learn the skills of acquiring knowledge of the world. I asked Okada if anything else other than quiet-sitting was needed in order to live in the context of technological society. He replied, "The other major element is to teach children respect for human life, the life of others as well as their own."[31] Without the establishment of subjectivity and without the respect for others, technology has no means to control itself. This poses the grave danger of the destruction of humanity itself.

The Threat of Nuclear War

A technology gone wild, a science that feels no connection to ethical consideration of human life, nuclear war, nuclear winter, and the ending of life as we know it—an altogether too frequently encountered image of the future of planet Earth, but one demanding response and, in this case, the response of a Confucian. First is the question of our future. Will there be a future or are we fated to live out the nightmarish doomsday scenario? For Okada, "We are obligated to think that we shall triumph, even if we do not!"[32] His answer is in the context of the way in which Confucius answered the question pertaining to death itself. As Okada says:

It is obvious that everyone is born and everyone must die, but it seems ridiculous to think about death while we are still living. Humankind came to exist on this earth and it might disappear one day. That is a fact, and yet I am still opposed to thinking about the end of the world.[33]

What underlies this statement is a profound belief in the meaning and purpose of human life. We are not dealing with a heroic fatalism, an attempt to push on, surrounded by a meaningless universe. We begin with the assumption of meaning. If humankind disappears, then that too is part of the meaning of the universe.

There is, however, a real threat to human life posed by nuclear war, and Okada is very sensitive to the dimensions of the threat. This is a threat we need to react to, and it is here that we need to stress the respect for human life. This is not an issue, for Okada, of Confucianism per se; it is an issue of all humanity, it stretches across the border of East and West, it embraces all human beings. He does feel that at this largest level East and West have made different contributions, the Western analytic model and the Eastern model of wholeness, but that only through working together and assimilating these models will the continued existence of humanity have a chance.

On the very practical political level, Okada represents a traditional Confucian characteristic, a point of view informed by pragmatism and political realities. Unilateral disarmament does not face the realities of political power, he argues. We must begin by assessing human nature in a political mode, we must recognize the self-serving and utilitarian motives that dominate in the relation of nation-states. The response to this condition, for Okada, is to recognize the need for a balance of power between nation-states and then a gradual process of disarmament. The nation-state represents in a magnified sphere the problems of human nature itself. Human nature is good at its deepest layer, but it is also conditioned by circumstances, and this produces evil. This evil must be recognized and dealt with, not idealistically ignored.

Ultimately, for Okada, as the *Great Learning* itself says, world peace is an issue of self-cultivation, and the ultimate solution still lies in the inner dynamics of self-learning. Our plight rests with the degree to which the self has been turned away from, and the ways in which science and technology, when unrooted in moral values, have been allowed to project a future. The only solution for Okada is to take seriously the directive of the *Great Learning,* to cultivate the self before attempting to govern the world.

World Religions

I asked Okada to comment upon the role of religion in general in the world and the future role of religion. His response touches upon several points. First, he admits that in general religions have played a positive role. This has come about chiefly through their role of restraining human desires. There have, however, been negative features as well, chiefly the level of fanaticism and prejudice that religions have perpetuated. Okada expresses his own criticism of the Abrahamic traditions, feeling that through their insistence upon exclusive claims to truth they have perpetuated strife and conflict. He feels that Eastern traditions have demonstrated a much greater degree of tolerance and that they have tended to emphasize inclusiveness rather than exclusiveness. On the other hand, however, Western traditions have shown a capacity to face the real problems of society, rather than turning away from such issues. To Okada, it is only Confucianism among the Eastern traditions that shares this capacity for dealing with real problems.

The issue that remains central for Okada is the ultimate importance of respect for human life. From Okada's point of view, the degree to which a religious tradition supports this respect for human life is the degree to which it is valuable and can make a contribution. In a sense, the particular tradition is of little consequence.

And what of Confucianism itself? What does Okada as a Confucian think of the future of Confucianism? "We don't really need to have Confucianism as Confucianism in the future. All we need is the respect for human life and human dignity."[34] The issue is more fundamental than the particular name of the tradition, and the issue is the very core of Confucian teaching for Okada, human dignity and respect for human life. If this remains, then the teachings of Confucius will not have disappeared.

On Death

It is appropriate to draw our discussion to an end with an understanding of Okada's view of death. As he discussed death, he echoed the sentiments of the Confucian tradition, that what follows life is simply a mystery and it is pointless to try to speculate upon it. This point of view goes back to a statement by Confucius himself when he was asked about death. He responded by saying that he had yet to understand life and therefore could not be expected to know anything of death.[35]

The passage on death gives a very intimate view of Okada. He expresses the hope that there may be some form of afterlife, but there is the qualification that ultimately this remains unknown.

I want to think that when I myself die and go to an afterlife, I shall see my teacher again and I shall read books with him and study under him once again. Whether there actually is an afterlife or not, my teacher lives on in my heart. In a similar way my parents, my brothers and sisters, they all live on in my heart.[36]

Or further:

> From my own point of view, the relation of life and death is that of cause
> and effect. Because something is born, it will die. This is simply the law
> of the universe. Now if I know that I am going to die, then I would
> simply say I am following that principle. In my heart I would worry, of
> course, about my family, about society and the state. I guess too that I
> would be saying to the dead, "I'm coming to see you!" I would be
> thinking this way until my actual death.[37]

The hope is for an afterlife, and yet there is the final confession that death is
an unknown. This in turn suggests the importance of holding the memory of
loved ones closely in one's heart.

And what of Okada's own role as a teacher? The hope is that something of
good has been accomplished, and that some other person has received some
help, that the heart of commiseration has shown its humaneness in the respect of other people. If this much has been accomplished, then life has been
worthwhile and its meaning has been fulfilled. Such are the reflections of a
Confucian upon his life, a life of quietude and action, a life whose perimeters
define the religious within the Confucian tradition.

PART II
SELECTED TRANSLATIONS
FROM OKADA TAKEHIKO'S
ZAZEN TO SEIZA

4. *SEIZA:* A Prefatory Discussion

There is a proverb that says: To the lover's fond eye a pock mark will appear as a dimple. That the pock mark is seen not as a pock mark but instead a dimple is because of the slanted perception of our mind. If the mind is instead like a clear mirror or still water, then the dimple will be seen as a dimple. In these times, there is a worldly spirit in Japan. People look to go this way or that in a world that has been rapidly transformed. They seem to have many different viewpoints and do not know what is correct. They dispute with one another and act without consideration of others. I feel that little by little there will be a loss of the humanistic spirit and an unsteadiness in the subjective spirit. If the humanistic spirit is lost and the subjective spirit unsteady, then neither individual nor society can make a correct judgment or act in the correct way. What then does one do to restore human nature and reestablish subjectivity? In this respect it is important to learn and master various forms of knowledge, and it is also essential to gain wide experience. The most direct and rapid method is religious belief together with *zazen* and *seiza,* which the ancient sages of East Asia transmitted to us.

The beginning point of *zazen* and *seiza* is the art of settling the mind, that is, the art of concentrating and uniting the spirit. If *zazen* and *seiza* aim only at this, however, they are less than fully understood. In order for them to have their full meaning, they must also illustrate a metaphysical concern. This means that the practice must include a worldview of human life and society. The concern of this book is *zazen* and *seiza* in this latter sense.

Zazen and *seiza* both aim at the quietude and emptiness of the mind. The search for the quietude and emptiness of the mind is not, however, limited only to *zazen* and *seiza*. In East Asia this kind of thought has had a widespread influence. This book tries to clarify the nature of quietude and emptiness in Asian thought in general. Up until now there have been explanations of many specialists concerning *zazen*, but few have touched upon the broader Asian context and almost none upon *seiza*.

When *seiza* is mentioned, many people are reminded of a method for body and mind hygiene. Few ever notice that *seiza*, unified together with metaphysics, is itself something deep and profound. It may also be said that there are few who understand that it holds a different purpose and meaning from *zazen*. *Seiza* is something that focuses upon quietude and emptiness, but it also contains a means to solve real problems in the world in positive ways. Accordingly this book spends many more pages on the discussion of *seiza*.

Seiza and the Contemplative Mind

Seiza is sitting with the body still. However, it is not limited to the body, for the aim of *seiza* is the stilling of the mind. That is to say, *seiza* is practiced with the purpose of stilling the mind. However, since strictly speaking the mind is never still for even as much as a moment, is it possible to still the mind simply through the practice of *seiza*? With deeper examination of the topic many questions begin to arise. Might not the attempt to think about the stilling of the mind, for example, already have become a disturbance to the mind? In examining the topic in this way the questions themselves become more and more complex.

We know, however, through our own experiences as well as common sense how important it is to still our minds in daily life. How many are the persons who experience the onslaught of failure and misfortune brought upon themselves through anger and violent emotions. *Seiza* is focused upon the stilling of the mind; however, that is by no means its only purpose. There is in *seiza*, as I shall explain at a later point, a profound meaning and purpose for human life. Nevertheless, simply on the issue of stilling of the mind, *seiza* is both a good and a simple method. In Japan from our childhood onward we know, from often hearing or reading in books, how to calm the mind. For example, it is common knowledge that when the mind is unsettled, it is good to do such things as count from one to ten silently, concentrate one's strength in the abdominal area, or simply breathe very deeply.

Seiza is an excellent method for stilling the mind, but it should not be interpreted as something that must be practiced in compulsory fashion. From this point of view, to still the mind is to fail to realize true stillness; it is, on the contrary, to create harm. On the other hand, there have been many different ways of thinking about true stillness of mind. For example, if one speaks of resentment, that is, of righteous indignation rather than selfish resentment, then although the resentment exists, the mind can still dwell in the equilibrium of a quiet environment in the manner of "a clear mirror and still water." Although resentment exists, there is also something that transcends it. People of ancient times expressed this kind of neutral state in phrases such as "quietude in the midst of activity."

The ancients taught that when the true way is followed, then whatever circumstances are encountered, the mind will remain settled and still. The work called the *Doctrine of the Mean* expresses this in the following way:

> The gentleman acts according to his position, he has no desire to go beyond it. In a position of wealth and honor he acts in accordance with wealth and honor. In a condition of poverty and extremity he acts with a proper sense of poverty and extremity. Amongst barbarousness he acts according to what is proper amongst barbarousness. The gentleman is in possession of himself regardless of his situation.

This passage means that the person regarded as a gentleman has settled himself within his own circumstances and follows the true way in accordance with the particular context, seeking nothing in excess of this. For example, in wealth and honor, one acts in a way that is in accordance with the situation rather than contrary through arrogance or indulgence. In poverty and extremity, one acts in accordance with those conditions and is thus free from servility or sycophancy. When forced to live among barbarians, one acts in accordance with those conditions, and even under extreme conditions one continues to accord with them. Thus those who are gentlemen have a mind at peace whatever the circumstances might be. The work called the *Great Learning* says: "When the point of rest is known, then there is settlement; with settlement one can become still." Whatever the circumstances, it is essential to realize that it is best to follow them quietly. If the circumstances are first examined, then one will not be at a loss and the direction of one's intentions will be settled. When the mind is like this, it can be said to be calmed and still.

Discussions of *seiza* suggest that the mind loses its stillness through the entanglements with external things and that it is thus essential to preserve the mind free from such enticements. For the famous Neo-Confucian of the Sung period, Chang Tsai, who aimed at what he called a settled nature, that is, a calming and a settling of human nature, the mind was entangled by external things and could not avoid agitation. He sought a solution to this problem. Ch'eng Hao wrote an essay in reply, *On Calming the Nature (Ting-hsing shu),* and pointed out the errors of his method as well as discussing the correct way of settling the nature, though it is best to understand nature as mind. This is what Ch'eng Hao said of calming the nature:

A calm and settled nature is a mind that is calmed and settled whether in a state of quietude or in a state of activity. In such a state external things, like a reflection in a mirror, neither advance nor retreat and the mind is not internal, nor are things external. If one regards what is differentiated from oneself as an external thing and in turn tries to conform to it and follow it, then the nature becomes divided between the interior and the exterior. If the nature complies with external things, what happens to the interior aspect? This is to cut off the external entanglements but without knowing that there is in fact no interior or exterior in the nature. If you think in terms of internal and external as two separate parts, then the calm and settled nature is something that can't be obtained.

Mind extends throughout all things of heaven and earth; however, the Way of Heaven, and of earth, is not to be equated with the selfish human mind. The emotions of pleasure, anger, sorrow, and joy move in accordance with all things; however, the constant way of the sage lacks emotions that are self-generated. The sage is the gentleman's source of learning; his mind is refreshingly impartial and unselfish, and when he encounters affairs he adapts himself to them. Often, however, one labors strenuously to remove external enticements and although a single enticement can be eliminated, there is no limit to other enticements appearing immediately and constantly. In addition, human emotions build upon one another, and they become contrary to the Way. In most circumstances it is only the selfish human mind and selfish discriminating knowledge that are used. When the selfish human mind is acted upon, it is not behavior in compliance with the Way, and in turn when selfish discriminating knowledge becomes the basis of judgments, the judgments are no longer judgments that are appropriate and natural.

To try to find what is real with a mind that despises external things is comparable to looking at things in the back of a mirror! Rather than judging external things false and internal things true, it is better to forget entirely the duality of internal and external. When duality is forgotten, then the mind is clear and does not busy itself with things. If there is no busying with things, this is the beginning of the calming and settling of the nature. If the nature is calm and settled, then the truth contained in external things will be understood. When the truth of phenomenality is understood, the point has been reached in which there are no entanglements.

Even someone who is a sage, however, is not insensitive or lacking in feelings. It is proper to be happy when the time calls for happiness, angry when the time calls for anger. Since happiness or anger at such times is directly connected with the object that is the source of the feelings rather than the mind itself, then when the external object disappears the happiness and anger disappear as well. Thus the sage is not troubled in dealing with externalities, and so it is not essential that following external matters be viewed as wrong while seeking the internal be considered right. To think of the true happiness and anger of the sage in terms of happiness and anger based upon the selfish human mind and selfish discriminating knowledge is simply an erroneous point of view. Anger is the emotion common to every person, easy to vent and difficult to restrain. When such anger is vented, if it could suddenly be forgotten and viewed instead within the context of the true right and wrong found in stillness, then it would be understood that it is not worthwhile to hate external enticements, and the Way would be fully comprehended.

Ch'eng Hao describes the calm and settled mind in phrases such as these: "the feelings possess no emotions in responding to the myriad things," and "expansive and impartial, it adapts to things as they arise." Therefore we need not be intent upon first expurgating those externalities regarded as enticements upon the mind to preserve what is within the mind. Instead, make the effort to observe the principle of right and wrong in things without either self-discriminating knowledge or selfish emotions. The expressions of Ch'eng Hao, of course, become frequently quoted sayings for later Confucians, though care needs to be exercised that Ch'eng Hao's expressions are not interpreted as indicating a transcendental point of view.

From what has been said it seems that it is not essential that a calm and still mind be based upon the practice of *seiza*; however, *seiza* has a purpose and meaning befitting it. There is a work entitled *Vegetable Root Discourses* with which the Japanese have long been familiar. The work, whose title is taken from words by the Sung dynasty Neo-Confucian Wang Hsin-min, "If men regularly gnaw at vegetable roots, then all things will be accomplished," discusses in simple terms the cultivation and nourishment of the mind as well as the essential conduct of life. In it, it is said, "If when man is quiet and sitting alone deep in the night, he contemplates the mind, then delusions will disappear, he will feel the truth revealing itself and gain the understanding of the macrocosm." That is to say, at the time deep in the night when not a single sound is to be heard and the person is at rest, only then alone in the practice of *seiza* and the contemplation of the mind do false and deluded thoughts disappear and the true mind, that is, the original mind, appear. Thus the self-existent mind free of obstacles arises in the manner of the expression, "The bright moon shines in the empty sky everywhere clear and penetrating." There appears to be no difference between this and the realm of the mind expressed in Zen enlightenment.

If one speaks of the true mind in Zen Buddhism, it is said that true and false are not two and that there is no distinction between the true mind and the false mind. That is to say, the true mind does not exist apart from the mind of delusions, and the mind of delusions is not separate from the true mind. It is the same as the relation of ice and water or water and wave. The work *Meditation Hymn (Zazen wasan)* by Hakuin (1686–1769) states, "All sentient beings are originally the Buddha. In the likeness of water and ice, ice does not exist apart from water and there is no Buddha separate from sentient beings." This simply states in a different manner that truth and falsity are not two separate paths. The third patriarch of the Ch'an School, Seng Ts'an, suggests a similar point in his *Mind of Faith Inscription (Hsin-hsin ming)*: "Two views do not exist; be on guard not to pursue them." In other words, the point of view distinguishing truth and falsity is the perception of two aspects of the Great Way, which is in actuality one.

Truth and falsity are not two. Thus to eliminate falsity and seek the true mind gives rise to the distinction between truth and falsity as well as that between right and wrong, and, of course, one's own original mind is lost. What we are suggesting in discussing the contemplation of the mind in *seiza* is that the original mind is perceived by a clear mind in *seiza* and the life of humankind should be guided by such activity. In other words, *seiza* is a method for realizing the fundamental meaning of the universe and articulating the correct Way.

In *Vegetable Root Discourses*, the contemplation of the mind and the experiencing of the Way within the state of quietude is considered profound, and its subtle effects are said to be immeasurable. "If thought is clear in the midst of quietude, then the true substance of the mind is perceived; if the physical form is composed in the midst of activity, then the true essence of the mind is recognized; and if the tensions are calmed in the sphere of transitoriness, then the true meaning of the mind is grasped." To speak of contemplating the mind and experiencing the Way is never a simple matter, much less speaking of enlightenment within the center of stillness. The ancients suggested that even when one thinks one has obtained enlightenment within the setting of a quiet environment, when affairs are encountered often times the enlightenment is of no use whatsoever. Thus some say it is far better to seek enlightenment in the midst of activity. For them enlightenment in the midst of activity is many times more difficult than enlightenment in quietude, and if enlightenment is realized within activity, then there is virtually no significance to enlightenment in quietude. If a peaceful and quiet mind is obtained in this fashion, then gaining a quiet mind while in a quiet environment is simple. At this point, however, even to speak of seeking a quiet and peaceful mind raises many inherent complexities.

Quietude and Nature

As has already been indicated, *seiza* is a simple and rapid way to obtain a quiet and still mind. That the practice of *seiza* presupposes the unity of the body and the mind should be quite obvious. Why is it, however, that the mind must be quiet; in other words, what is the purpose behind this? If this is not fully understood, the purpose of *seiza* itself is increasingly ambiguous. It is critical, then, on this basis to understand in general terms the thought surrounding the search for a quiet and still mind; otherwise misconceptions of the practice of *seiza* will arise.

The philosophy of quietude attained a remarkable degree of development in East Asia, and it is no exaggeration to say that the significance, value, and authority of Eastern thought have been preserved through it. What then is the reason for the value placed upon quietude in East Asia? There are various reasons, but primarily it is because the world of nature was regarded as ultimate. People oriented themselves to it, and they sought to establish their belief in and around it. In China from time immemorial there has been a focus upon Heaven. Heaven was regarded as the absolute authority, and even the emperor dared not turn his back on the directives from Heaven. Heaven was considered to have a mind in the same fashion as people, that is, an individual character and existence, and for this reason was called Heavenly Ruler. Heaven or Heavenly Ruler was regarded as the ultimate source of government, morality, and religion. Thus, if the emperor turned his back on Heaven, perpetuating evil government and violence, the emperor would incur the anger of Heaven. How would the emperor know of Heaven's anger? That anger is known, so it is said, by the sound of the people's resentment as well as through various natural calamities. However, after the time of Confucius, Heaven came to be understood as rational and could be expressed by the word "nature." It was thus sought after as something to follow and comply with. Of course, the word "nature" has been used in a vast number of ways, but in East Asia it is an expression that reveals the idea of Absolute Truth. It developed to a point that it possessed authority equivalent to the idea of God in Western Christian teachings.

Nature, with the presupposition of absolute authority, is seen as the foundation of art, literature, and thought. Rather than seeing them as abstract objects of speculation, however, there has been a tendency to focus upon the relation of life and life's activities with nature. This meaning of nature was often expressed by phrases such as the "mind of nature," the "Way of nature," and the "mind of Heaven and earth" and was frequently sought after through conformance with the natural world. A haiku by Bashō (1644–94) suggests that one must look carefully to see the bloom of the Nazuna flower in the fence and thus points to one feature of this view of nature. Bashō observed in the tiny bloom of the Nazuna flower by the side of the fence both the mind of spring and the mind of the life-producing Heaven and earth. That is to say, he observed the mind of nature.

One often hears it said that those referred to as sages and worthies of antiquity would pursue discipline and self-cultivation deep in secluded wilderness areas in order to investigate the secrets of the Way thoroughly. It was during the Taisho era (1912–25) that a French *littérateur* by the name of Paul Claudel stayed in Japan for several years while serving as ambassador. At one point he lectured in Nikko, giving his impressions of Japan. He makes an interesting point in the context of his lecture: "In Japan it is the custom that elementary school teachers accompany the children on their excursions, excursions that are often to shrines located in the midst of thick forests. Why are such places chosen? It is to be awakened to the essential union of man, gods and nature while the child is yet unknowing and unconscious of it." Quite apart from whether Claudel's view is correct or incorrect, humankind in East Asia has selected lonely places deep in the wilderness to seek after the Way, thinking that in such places Heaven, earth, and human will become whole and form a union, and in such a way the mind of nature will be realized.

Whether nature is prior to the human being, more than the human, or within the human, in East Asia nature has been thought of as something still and quiet. Saying it is still and quiet does not mean it is lifeless or moribund. Quite the contrary, it contains the vital force and subtlety of the spark of a flintstone, of a bow drawn to the full or a cat facing a mouse. When it is presented in this light it appears difficult to say that nature is still and quiet. The work called the *Book of Changes,* which is composed of eight trigrams and sixty-four hexagrams, contains one hexagram that is called "return." It is written ☷☳ and contains the activity of one yang line under five yin lines. This is what is called the return of the one yang line. The *Book of Changes* interprets this rhetorically: "To return, is this to perceive the mind of Heaven and earth?" The mind of Heaven and earth is the mind of nature, that is to say, it is nothing other than this very idea of nature itself. Yin is quiet and still, yang is activity, and the hexagram "return" illustrates the adumbration of activity within stillness. For the *Book of Changes* this is understood as the mind of nature. Under such circumstances there are those who interpret the mind of Heaven and earth as quiet and those who say it is active. Yet though it is said to be quiet, there is incipient activity within it; and though it is called active, there is dormant quietude within it. Even in terms of quietude or activity, it is not easy to understand. In general terms, the East Asian perspective is to seek the way of quietude, regarding quietude as the basic foundation of activity. It goes without saying that such a quietude embraces both quietude and activity; it is not simply quietude in opposition to activity. Thus one is dealing with something that is fundamentally metaphysical in character.

Though the way of the *Book of Changes* is spoken of as quietude, when it is compared with Taoism, Buddhism, or other traditions it is more appropriate to say it has an active standpoint. This is because the *Book of Changes* is different from the Taoist and the Buddhist with their belief in the quietude of nature from an other worldly point of view. Instead the *Book of Changes* seeks conformance with what we might call natural law, holding there to be purpose within nature as well as a teleological view in conformance with the natural world, which emphasizes the ethical dimensions of good and bad as well as fortune and misfortune.

For this reason the *Book of Changes* regards the active mind of nature as the Way and establishes an active orientation toward the world. In fact, the title *Book of Changes* means precisely this. Change means constant transformation. It actually has been treated as having three separate meanings: continual transformation, constancy, simplicity. Continual transformation means that things are not fixed or still. This is a far-reaching point of view; however, it is essential to know that this is also an unchanging law. Thus to be able to perceive an unchanging law in the midst of ceaseless transformations eases the difficulty of a human life constantly subject to change. Change, in addition to its meaning of continual transformation, also means what is simple and what is constant, though the root meaning retains the sense of continual change. Thus change is based upon a view of the world from the standpoint of activity. Knowing that the *Book of Changes* speaks of the appearance of the world in terms of the two primary forces yin and yang, this is even clearer.

The *Book of Changes* has explained the appearance of the world through a movement of opposites. There is the rise and fall, the comings and goings, as well as the blending and transformation of the two opposing aspects of the single vital force, namely, the positive force yang and the negative force yin. The saying that yin and yang constitute the Way suggests a law of activity. It is within this context that there exists structure and order for people to base themselves upon. Though the *Book of Changes* is a work on divination, it does not begin with fatalism, nor does it end with mechanism. There is meaning and direction to this law, and it suggests that life itself has a purpose. This is the reason for the inclusion of ethics within the *Book of Changes*. We cannot overlook the traditional ethical standpoint of the unity of self and others. Thus, while the *Book of Changes* discusses a dialectical relation, it still takes the position of purpose, harmony, and cyclic change. From this perspective, change can be considered to hold to the thought of quietude.

Of course, it should be obvious that this kind of quietude is different from that of Buddhism and Taoism. It is clearer if this particular characteristic of change is compared with Mao Tse-tung's view of the world from the perspective of the dialectical materialism of communism as well as his explanation of the phenomenon of the world by the same dialectical process. In the *Book of Changes* contradiction is something that can be settled by harmonizing the originally conflicting elements, but for Mao it is only settled by conflict. Thus the two positions are fundamentally different from each other. This applies to the view of nature as well. In the *Book of Changes* nature is the eventuality and goal of human life, but for Mao it is something to be changed and reconstructed along with society itself, to provide for the progress of humankind and the development of history. If the two are in opposition, the thought of Mao seems active while that of the *Book of Changes* seems quiet. The position of Mao is to sweep away the traditional thought of quietude and transform history.

Quietude and Stratagem

For what purpose and under what circumstances did someone seek a quiet mind in East Asia? Take, for example, three individuals who have each sought the same quietude. One extricates the self from any concern with honor or wealth, seeking instead a mind empty and carefree. Another tries to restrain the mind, focusing upon a mind of reverence and thus attempting to avoid violating the ways of a human being. Yet a third controls the mind through quietude solely to seek a scheme to control others. Each of these three persons places importance upon a quiet mind, though in each case the purpose is entirely different. It follows that the inner content of the mind must differ as well. The condition of quietude itself is the same; why then do such differences themselves develop? It is because there is a different purpose involved; that is to .say, there are different views of humankind and nature.

The Chinese from time immemorial have possessed three district ways of philosophy. One of these ways controls humankind and society by one's own whims, basing itself upon the utilitarian nature of people. Another rids humankind entirely of suffering and repression in order to reach the world of absolute freedom and eternal light. The third relies upon the virtuous nature of humankind in order to realize the ideal society, the way of "one mind and a single body." These can be designated the realist, the transcendentalist, and the idealist respectively. Each of these three ways regarded nature as the endpoint and for this reason spoke of the quiet mind.

Realism sees humankind entirely within a utilitarian context. Based upon this kind of utilitarian view of the person and society, the philosophers called the Legalists—Shang Yang (d. 338 B.C.E.), Shen Pu-hai (d. 337 B.C.E.), Han Fei-tzu (d. 233 B.C.E.)—as well as others, emphasized law and governmental strategy through the principles of centralized authority and autocratic rulership as well as trickery and scheming. The diplomacy of Kuei-ku Tzu and others emphasized tactics of persuasion in which there was no visible display of skill. The military strategists Sun Tzu and Wu Tzu emphasized a strategy of victory based on relying upon the enemy itself.

When humankind, society, and nation are viewed from a utilitarian viewpoint, there is a relation of opposition, conflict, and strife, and one cannot but seek after some secret way of completely controlling others. In other words, "The way to handle people is not to be handled by people." Shang Yang saw Legalism primarily as a form of law with excessive punishments, while Shen Pu-hai saw in it the tactics to control others completely without revealing one's own position. Han Fei-tzu, speaking of the combined use of the two, said they are like the two wheels of a cart or the two wings of a bird and that it was essential not to lack one or be biased to the other. Instead true law must include tactics, and true tactics must include law. These kinds of law and tactics demonstrate the subtle essence of absolute control.

In Sun Tzu's strategy, law is the normal and standard method, while tactics are used for surprise. The regular way is to set out flags fairly, deploy troops, and launch a frontal attack. The surprise element is gaining a victory through catching the enemy off guard. Sun Tzu especially favored the surprise element. Of course, if surprise is employed on too frequent a basis, the effect will be lost. Thus if there is not constant switching between the regular method and the surprise tactic, then their true worth will remain undemonstrated. It is in this that the secret of strategy is found. In a book dealing with strategy called *The Classic of Control (Wo-ch'i Ching)*, it is said that victory is won by surprise attacks and that the surprise attack is the general's prerogative. Surprise implies deception, that is, it violates honesty.

Sun Tzu said that the military follows the way of deceit and stands on falsification. Although deceit involves cheating, it does not include evil in ethical terms. In Han Fei-tzu's tactics, what is called the employment of deceit is used as a technique to control the subjects of the state. The Confucian Ōta Zensai (1759–1829) interprets deceit as duplicity. If it means duplicity, then in Sun Tzu's strategy it is like pretending to be far away while actually being close or pretending to be close while actually being far away. Or in the same way pretending to have an advantage when one is actually at a disadvantage and pretending to have a disadvantage when one is actually at an advantage. Enticing others with what appears advantageous to them is like catching fish with bait; it is winning victory by holding the very power of life and death itself. Sun Tzu's strategy exemplifies this deceitful approach: "If one appears in the beginning like a tender maiden, then the enemy opens the door. Afterward he runs like a rabbit and the enemy has no defense."

We have already said that the way of surprise contains the secret of certain victory in its strategy, but it was in the hands of persons of knowledge that it was conducted successfully. For this reason, Sun Tzu valued knowledge. He cited five virtues with which the general is endowed: "The general is wise, sincere, humane, courageous, and serious." Wisdom was the most important. In Japan the work on strategy, *Classic of Combat (Tosen kyo)*, is different in its point of regarding courage as the most important of the general's virtues. How is such knowledge obtained? Kuei-ku Tzu spoke of avoiding "harmful openings." This means the same thing as when Lao Tzu says to "shut the openings"; in short, to make the mind quiet and empty one must eliminate thought, intention, deliberation, and knowledge.

In the area of strategy or diplomacy a resourceful mind is crucial, and a quiet mind is the essence of such resourcefulness. Thus Kuei-ku Tzu has said:

The mind must be peaceful and quiet; thought and deliberation must be deep and profound. When the mind is peaceful and quiet, profound intelligence will prosper; when thought and deliberation are deep and profound, commendable plans will be established. When profound intelligence flourishes the wise cannot deceive us, and when commendable plans are established the man of ability is not able to defeat us.

Sun Tzu has said, "For a general, subtlety is through quietude, and governance is with fairness." What does this mean? The Japanese Neo-Confucian Ogyū Sorai (1666–1728) has explained it in the following way: "This is a statement concerning a general's way of thinking to control his subordinates. Quietude has neither sound nor smell and is immeasurable. Subtlety means there is not so much as a clue to be seen. Governing fairly means to prepare strategy with a determined attitude."

According to this, what Sun Tzu refers to as quietude involves within it knowledge to command subordinates without displaying one's tactics to the enemy. This is no different from the skillful scheming involved in the statement, "The fish must not be allowed to leave water. The sharp knife that governs the country should not be displayed to others." This statement is found in the writings of Lao Tzu, though in the case of Lao Tzu it is really quiet unsuitable to interpret it as a discussion of scheming and plotting. After all, it was the later followers of the Legalist School of philosophy who interpreted it in such a manner.

Summing up then, realism, basing itself upon a view of the person and society as utilitarian, regards the relation between self and others as that of opposition, conflict, and strife. Quietude is considered the best weapon in the control of others. In the mind that is quiet, such skillful knowledge is hidden and it is considered essential to control the mind through quietude. In China the philosophy of quietude had a significant import even in realism where the focus remained upon the art of scheming.

Quietude and the Transcendental

The traditional philosophy of quietude is a form of transcendentalism, a transcendentalism that includes Taoism and Buddhism. Both hoped to reach the unchanging Absolute through the transcendence of and deliverance from this world with its limitations and suffering where human life and society are filled with contradictions and difficulties. Although they deal with transcendence and emancipation, there is for the Taoists and Mahayana Buddhists a concern about the phenomenal world, and transcendence and emancipation were thought of as essentially aiming at a salvation in this world. The phenomenal world in which salvation is sought, however, is not precisely the same as what Confucian idealism calls the phenomenal world. To idealism the phenomenal world is humankind in society. Buddhism and Taoism focus primarily upon human suffering in the world rather than the harmony of human and society. The Neo-Confucians, or idealists, criticize the Buddhists and the Taoists on precisely these grounds. That is, they tend to forget that humankind had from the beginning existed in society and, instead, concentrate themselves solely on the salvation of the individual. Because of this they know nothing of the way to govern the family or the nation, and what they really sought was simply the way of self-aggrandizement.

Lao Tzu shares the identical transcendental point of view, but it is from a rather different perspective, for Lao Tzu has a very strong interest in government. Chuang Tzu (369–286? B.C.E.) differs from Lao Tzu in this very respect, scorning government as so much refuse. There are some scholars who say that Lao Tzu discussed the way of serving the world in the same way as the Confucians. However, Lao Tzu also possesses the transcendent perspective, and he is thus thoroughly committed to the way of quietude. Lao Tzu's philosophy of quietude suggests a denial of humankind and a return to the naturalness of Heaven's ways. It is said that only through these means will human beings be able to live out their years and the world be free of strife. The Confucians, from a Taoist perspective, speak of humaneness and propriety to rescue humankind and society, and this itself disturbs the true nature of the human being, which is quiet. Of course, the result for the Confucians is then the direct opposite of what they desire. In addition, for the Confucian learning is esteemed, the knowledge of the sage and the talent of the worthy are valued, yet these only encourage the covetous ambitions of humankind, and Lao Tzu rejects them. In short, Lao Tzu said that the simplicity of humankind's original nature of quietude must not be distorted through morals or learning. Humankind's ambitions and schemes must not be encouraged, and the peace of the world must not be disturbed. His reason for saying this is that he felt he had seen how an idealist who talks of learning, humaneness, and righteousness actually behaves in the world.

Thus Lao Tzu's philosophy suggests that human behavior cannot avoid opposition and contradiction. This is the reason he so highly recommends naturalness and nonaction, speaking not only of the support for the human spirit, but of concrete modes of behavior as well. In a word, he trod the path of lowliness and withdrawal, and the myriad things were entrusted to the course of action of the great way of nature. Lao Tzu spoke of softness rather than hardness, quietude rather than activity, withdrawal rather than advancement, lowliness rather than height, dullness rather than sharpness, and simplicity rather than wisdom, suggesting the extraordinary strength that was exhibited in lowly qualities. No one demonstrated better than Lao Tzu the power of noncontention and withdrawal from real society.

What is Lao Tzu's view of the ideal government and society? He has this to say:

> It is ideally a small kingdom with few people. Even though the people have great talents, such abilities are not to be implemented. The people think of life as something important and death as a serious matter. Their lives are simple, yet rich. There is no inclination to move to distant places; even though there are means of transportation, there is no desire to travel. Though they have helmets and weapons, there is no strife in which to employ them. The people return to a state like the simplicity of ancient times where contracts were concluded with the knotting of a rope. In a government of this kind, people are pleased with their food, find pleasure in their garments, are peaceful in their domestic life and happy in their ways. Though neighboring states are close enough to be seen and the crowing of cocks and barking of dogs can be heard, they are satisfied with their own land and do not travel, though they grow old and die. A kingdom of this kind is a utopia.

Though the same position is maintained in terms of the philosophy of quietude as well as the transcendental, Chuang Tzu differs significantly from Lao Tzu. The philosophy of Chuang Tzu is religious and thus different from the realism of Lao Tzu. Because of influences from the Sophist School as well, the development of his philosophy is a very complex process. Such influence resulted in the sharpness and profundity of Chuang Tzu's critical spirit. Thus the absolute, or ideal, world that was sought came to be entrusted with a deeply religious nature. Beyond a brief summation, the philosophy of Chuang Tzu is outside the scope of the present work.

It is a common experience to find that in arguing with others it is exceedingly difficult to understand the position of the opposite party. During the period in which Chuang Tzu lived, there were many schools of philosophy, one vying with another. The two greatest rivals were the Mohists and the Confucians, and it seemed as if all the scholars in China could be divided into these two schools. Both spoke of love, but for Mo Tzu there was a utilitarian focus, while for Confucius the emphasis was upon propriety. What one thought to be right, the other considered wrong and so they argued on and on. Chuang Tzu criticized them sharply, arguing the relativity of right and wrong for each. For Chuang Tzu, value judgments by humans are subjective, thus they cannot be but relative. There are, for example, the cases of

Mao-ch'iang and Li-i, both considered women of unequal beauty in the eyes of men, yet how were they considered among other living things? As soon as a fish sees them it hides itself in the water. When a bird sees them it is frightened and flies up into the sky; a deer sees them and immediately runs away. Value judgments differ from person to person, and the circumstances for the very same person can change as well. Chuang Tzu suggests this by telling a story.

> Long ago in a certain state there was a very beautiful girl. This girl was loved and cared for by her parents, but there came a time when a king from a neighboring state attacked and she was taken away. At first there was not a day the girl did not cry over the harshness of her misfortune as she recalled her parents and her native place now far distant. As she came repeatedly to share the king's bed, however, she wondered why she had previously been so sad.

Since human value judgments are relative or subjective in this way, although someone thinks that what they said is correct, others regard it as wrong, and while someone thinks that what others say is wrong, for those people it is correct. Accordingly in a dispute when an adamant position is taken, there is no way to decide which position is actually correct. If yet a third party adds a point as to right and wrong, since this is also a relative and subjective point of view, it is no more an assertion of truth than the others. If this can be understood, then, according to Chuang Tzu, one will know it is a mistake to explicate and adhere to one's own point of view.

How then can one reach a correct judgment? It is by abandoning subjective and relative judgments in favor of the naturalness of the Great Harmony. Chuang Tzu has called this "adapting to circumstances." Through "adapting" it is possible to bring an argument to an end, leaving each point of view as it was. In addition, it is possible to bring the positions together while maintaining individual differences. For Chuang Tzu this is explained with terms such as "Heaven the equalizer," "Heaven the unifier," "following both alternatives," and "pursuing two possibilities." "Heaven the equalizer" refers to the natural harmony; "following both alternatives" means that one can walk on different paths at the same time; "pursuing two possibilities" means different alternatives are acceptable. In other words, these are explanations of the basic truth of the mutual relation between opposites. Chuang Tzu's form of critical philosophy also raises the specter of doubt on those who would regard strife and opposition as the essential truth.

From what we have seen, Chuang Tzu points to the relative nature of human values and judgments, that is, their subjective nature, and seeks a critical point of view from a higher perspective. Chuang Tzu definitely, however, does not end in skepticism. In a work called the *Lieh Tzu,* which in general follows the same point of view as that of Chuang Tzu, there is an interesting story along this line:

At the time Confucius traveled to an eastern state he unexpectedly encountered two children who were engaged in an argument. One child said, "The sun is closest at sunrise and furthest at noon. This is because it is as big as an umbrella at sunrise, while at noon it is as small as a dish. When you look at something far away it is small, while when you see something close at hand it is large." The other child said, however, just the opposite: "The sun is furthest away at sunrise and at noon it is closest. This is because it is coolest at sunrise and warmest at noon. Something far away feels cool while something close feels warm." The two children each insisted that they alone were correct and they would not give way. Confucius thought he could put a stop to the argument by handing down a decision on right and wrong; however, he was at a complete loss as to how to figure out which of the children was correct. The children, seeing Confucius' perplexity, ridiculed him, saying, "Throughout the world you are honored for your wisdom, what an absurdity!"

Such a statement gives the impression of skepticism, but in fact this is not the case. Instead, right and wrong are truly rectified by a form of wisdom that transcends ordinary relative knowledge. Chuang Tzu also sought this form of wisdom. In this way it was thought possible to reach the Great Goodness, that is, what is truly good.

Certainly the most fascinating topic in what we are calling transcendentalism is Zen Buddhism. Zen has become a matter of very serious study among the present generation of scholars, and because of its greater preservation in Japan than in China, European as well as American scholars who are interested in Zen come to Japan. The entire topic of Zen I want to postpone, however, until the next chapter.

5. A CRITIQUE OF ZEN

Up to this point I have discussed realism and transcendentalism, suggesting that quietude played a major role in both systems. Now I want to discuss the question of quietude in idealism. I have already distinguished between *seiza* and *zazen*. *Seiza* is a method that searches for the quiet mind in what I have called idealism; *zazen* is a method that searches for the quiet mind in what I have called transcendentalism. As a result of this distinction, the content of the two in terms of the quiet mind is very different. Even in idealism, the ultimate Way is attributed to nature, but it is very different in its content. Realism, as we have seen, skillfully utilized its law of nature and sought the way to govern and control others. Idealism, however, regards human beings as possessing an affectionate heart with which they mutually understand each other. It regards the human being as having a virtuous nature and anticipates a virtuous society based upon the already virtuous nature of the individual. It is this that is taken as the Way. The two systems of thought both speak of the Way, but the content is different.

This can be explained by a simple illustration. The Legalists take a position of realism and, like the idealism of the Confucians, discuss justice, righteousness, and the universal Way. However, individual freedom for the Legalist is completely excluded. It is only justice and righteousness for the way of the nation and the public. If the individual is completely obedient, the nation will become strong of its own and in the end such benefits will be received by the individual. This was thought of as justice and righteousness. However, for the Confucian justice and righteousness that support the common life of

Plate III. Okada in His Study.
The wall hanging behind him and to his right reads
kotsuza, "just sitting," the term Okada uses to
describe his contemplative practice.

human society are considered originally endowed in the human being. Humankind and society as well as humankind and nature will come together and be one naturally. In this way, the ideal society and the ideal world will become a reality. In this fashion, the Confucian way is filled with purity and warm love, while the Legalist way is strict and harsh. There are two proverbs that exemplify this: "If you see a man, you think him a robber," and "In traveling, good company; in the world, goodwill." The way of thinking of the Legalist is based upon a view of society and the person as illustrated in the first proverb. The Confucian's view of society and the person is illustrated by the second.

Idealism, unlike transcendentalism, which is established upon the denial of the person, is built upon the affirmation of the person. Therefore, for example, the way of Lao Tzu and Chuang Tzu follows the Way of Heaven and eliminates the way of humankind. Confucius and Mencius, on the other hand, regard the way of humankind as following the Way of Heaven. Long ago Chuang Tzu said that attaching a rein on a horse's head or putting a rope through the nose of a cow was contrary to the original nature of the horse or cow and that we must follow the Way of Heaven, not the way of humankind. The Sung period Confucian Yang Shih said, however, that Chuang Tzu's discussion was incorrect. Instead he suggested that if you attached a rein to the cow's head or put a rope through the horse's nose, that would be contrary to the original nature of cows and horses! Doing what Chuang Tzu condemns is in fact following the original nature of the cows and horses, and it is proper that the human way follow the Way of Heaven.

Transcendentalism, as we have already seen, is a denial of human life. This point of view is taken more seriously in Buddhism than it is for Lao Tzu and Chuang Tzu. It is common knowledge that Buddhism views humankind as possessing karma and as suffering in the flames of passion. Lao Tzu and Chuang Tzu do not share this harsh interpretation. They also have a deeper concern for human society than Buddhism. Idealism, on the other hand, establishes itself on the affirmation of humankind. Even if there are contradictions in the human being and human society, the original nature of the human being is thought to have within it the Way that sustains all life.

In the *Analects*, there is a story that illustrates this point. Once when Confucius traveled to another state he passed a place where two hermits were living. They had retired from the world and made their living by plowing the fields. This was because they felt it unsuitable to live in a world where the Way of righteousness had degenerated and government was in chaos. However, Confucius traveled from state to state attempting to rescue the world.

He preached the Way to each of the feudal rulers of the various states, but he was not well received. Nevertheless he did not stop his travels from state to state. The hermits regarded it as foolish to undertake this kind of activity willingly in a world where one's contribution is of no consequence. In a world that is thoroughly chaotic it is simply impossible. In such times, they said, rather than wandering about, it is better to retire to live a peaceful life in the manner they had done. So saying, they ridiculed Confucius. Confucius answered them that such retirement was too simple. With defiance Confucius said, "I am a man among men." The mind of the "man among men" is exactly what is called goodness. This is the warm spirit of respect for the person, and in this lies the true meaning of idealism.

In idealism, as we have already seen, nature was regarded as the ultimate Way. This vast and quiet Way is that which continues the motion of the four seasons and is responsible for developing into the life of all things. This is also what is behind government, and it was considered that the ideal government operated even with the hands of the ruler folded. That is to say, the ideal world is realized by doing nothing. In this kind of world, each person is settled. Each person preserves virtue as a member of a family and pursues public morality as a member of society. The person who rules others preserves the Way; the person who is ruled in turn preserves the Way. People and oneself are of one mind and one virtue. Each person works in an occupation suitable to his or her respective talents and supports the great Way of Heaven and earth, developing each and every thing and participating and developing in the reality of the ideal society. The ancients in speaking of this kind of world expressed it well by phrases such as "Heaven and earth are positioned and all things are reared," or "The hawk flies up to Heaven and fish swim deep."

Since idealism establishes the spirit of respect for humankind, it respects traditional culture. Confucius spoke of a creative Way, yet he said of himself, "I am a transmitter, not a creator." His Way follows the tradition, and he himself saw in it nothing more than that. However, idealism is not something that holds rigidly to tradition. The famous expression of Confucius, "I search into the old and thereby know the new," is an example of this. The aim is to create the world anew and stamp out the traditional. Otherwise, although it is called idealism, it doesn't deserve its name! However, from the perspective of transcendentalism one cannot but criticize culture. This is because of their perspective of the denial of humankind. "Leave humankind, seek Heaven," "Abandon entering the world, seek leaving the world." Even though there is a transcendentalism in East Asia, there is also a tendency to remember humankind even from the viewpoint of the transcendent way. The result of this has been to create a unique culture. This is Zen culture, and the spirit of East Asian culture cannot be discussed without Zen culture. How much more is this true in terms of idealism?

Quietude and Abiding in Reverence

The *Doctrine of the Mean* considers Centrality and Harmony to be the way of idealism: "If you reach Centrality and Harmony, Heaven and earth are established and the ten-thousand things reared." Centrality and Harmony are the way of peaceful accord. For the *Doctrine of the Mean* this way acts by means of the Mandate of Heaven, and it is something that is also immanent in humankind. Therefore it says, "Before the arising of pleasure, anger, sorrow, and joy, this is called Centrality. When they arise and develop, this is called Harmony." The author of the *Doctrine of the Mean* hopes that people would seek this by focusing upon their own minds. In later times Centrality became known as the Centrality of the unmanifest, and Harmony was called the Harmony of the manifest. What was the reason for these designations?

In the *Book of Rites* one finds the following statement:

For man at birth to be quiet is the nature of Heaven. To be moved by things is the desire of nature. As things appear, the intellect comes to know them; after this, likes and dislikes are formed. If likes and dislikes have no due degree internally and if one cannot reflect upon oneself without his knowledge tempted by external things, then the Principle of Heaven is brought to destruction.

This means that the human being's heavenly nature is originally peaceful and quiet, but when it comes into contact with affairs of the outside world, perception grows and the feelings of likes and dislikes become active. Thereupon these feelings lose their standard and perception becomes seduced by external things. If at that point there is no close introspection, then the Principle of Heaven, that is, nature's principle of the correct Way, will be lost. Human nature is peaceful because it is the Principle of Heaven and has quietude as its substance. In the *Doctrine of the Mean* it is called Centrality. Centrality is the way of accord without excess or deficiency and without bias. This is the way in which the use of the unmanifest Centrality and the manifest Harmony can be understood in the *Doctrine of the Mean*.

What is the relation of Centrality and Harmony? Centrality is substance and Harmony is function. Substance and function are whole and of one root, though they appear as two: substance seeking to reach function, and function searching for substance. If substance and function are spoken of in terms of activity and quietude, then substance is quietude, and function is activity. It is a very difficult question, however, as to whether this is something that is affiliated with time or transcends time.

If we speak of substance and function as a tree, substance is the root and function is the leaves and branches. In this context the root is nourished, and the leaves and branches flourish. This is more direct and complete than the nourishment of the root from the leaves and the branches. Thus in the case of Centrality and Harmony, if the substance of Centrality is sought, the function of Harmony will naturally be practiced. Accordingly, rather than seeking Harmony where the feelings of pleasure, anger, sorrow, and joy are already roused and then reaching to Centrality afterward, it is more important to reach the substance of Centrality first in a quiet place where the feelings are unmanifest. This is the reason that the effort of the unmanifest and quietude are required.

In idealism during the Sung period, partially because of the influence of Zen Buddhism, more and more serious consideration was given to the understanding of the mind. For this reason Neo-Confucianism has been called a school of mind in ways similar to Zen Buddhism. Mind, from the Confucian learning, is the ruler that controls the nature of humankind as an internal principle. This is the true being that is the foundation of the universe, and human life is its manifest activity. Therefore nature does not exist separate from mind. However, the substance of the true nature is quietude, and it is for this reason that it was thought that there must be a quiet mind in order to seek the true nature.

This is the reason that Chou Tun-i, who is regarded as the patriarch of the Neo-Confucian learning, considered the special and distinctive feature of learning to be regarding quietude as fundamental and thought it possible that the very foundation of the Great Ultimate, the cause of all life and the root of human life and the universe, could be expressed by means of regarding quietude as fundamental. He originally had pursued the learning of Lao Tzu and Chuang Tzu and said that he also practiced cultivation with an interest in Zen Buddhism, but in his teaching of regarding quietude as fundamental he surpassed the thought of Lao Tzu, Chuang Tzu, and Zen Buddhism and established the way of the Neo-Confucian learning. Therefore it must be considered to have a different content from Zen Buddhism, Lao Tzu, and Chuang Tzu. Master Chou said that regarding quietude as fundamental is a condition without desires. His understanding of no desires is different from that of Lao Tzu, Chuang Tzu, and Zen Buddhism. Its meaning is to remove those desires that create evil in human relations. It does not mean to remove all desires, good and bad, but only to remove those that are selfish. If all selfish desires could be eliminated, then regarding quietude as fundamental would be obtained. Master Chou spoke of regarding quietude as fundamental, but for the sake of indicating that it was something different from the quietude of Zen Buddhism he went on to provide an explanation, saying, "no desires, consequently quiet." However, if quietude is by no desires, then it should not be necessary to have to describe it in terms of regarding quietude as fundamental.

Since Master Chou used the phrase regarding quietude as fundamental, however, he seems to have recognized the significance of the effort to quiet the mind directly. That is to say, he thought that when the mind had been quieted it reached the point of naturally having no selfish desires and returned to its original nature. If you look at the entirety of Master Chou's thought, what he calls quietude is doubtless something different from entering concentration through *zazen* as in Zen Buddhism. However, he did not state the distinction of the two very clearly. Therefore it is important to understand the meaning of the phrase "no desires, consequently quiet"; otherwise there may be some concern that his discussion of regarding quietude as fundamental will slide off into Zen Buddhism. Accordingly the elder and younger Ch'eng brothers, who were his disciples, did not speak of quietude, but used the term "reverence" instead, though they did not intend to deny quietude entirely.

Master Chou had the appearance of being free of human cares. The famous poet Huang Shan-ku (1045–1105) commented on his personality: "Clear and lucid, like a bright moon after a storm." Ch'eng Hao together with his younger brother Ch'eng I received the teachings of Master Chou. After they returned from meeting him they spoke of Master Chou's mind: "He can sing to the wind and return playing with the moon." In ways such as these the bounds of Master Chou's personality were remembered. It might be his own nature or it might be the result of his learning, regarding quietude as fundamental.

When Master Chou said, "no desires, consequently quiet," he taught Ch'eng Hao that this did not mean simply to be without desires. When Ch'eng Hao was sixteen or seventeen years old he loved to go hunting. He decided, however, on the basis of self-reflection that this was something that was bad and worked to eliminate the desire, thinking he would be able to in the end. He went and told Master Chou his principle. Master Chou replied that it was easy to make this kind of statement. One might think that the desire is eliminated, but it is not; it is only concealed, and as it begins to stir it will return again. One day twelve years later Ch'eng Hao was watching people hunt, and he realized that what Master Chou had said was true.

Ch'eng Hao also knew well the importance of a quiet mind. In a phrase from one of his poems he says, "When all things are viewed through quietude, all things realize peacefulness: the beauty of the four seasons is identical with humankind." Here through engagement in quiet contemplation we come to understand that all things under Heaven have their own place and are peaceful. This suggests that we ourselves are no different from the beauty of the four seasons, and that human society itself is the same in this respect. Ch'eng Hao considered what he called "quiet contemplation" especially important. Quiet contemplation means to seek enlightenment in quietude. For Ch'eng Hao this meant that all things are filled with harmonious vital force and life production. The mind is clear with no attachments and obtains the way of highest equality. When this state is realized all things come to exist in rapport with each other and there is true freedom. This can be seen in the words, "After quietude all things possess the spirit of spring," or "Vast and clear, whatever comes the mind can comply with it." Based upon what has been handed down to us, it is said that Ch'eng Hao practiced *seiza* the entire day as if he were a statue, and in his case, the harmonious vital force overflowed.

Ch'eng Hao's younger brother, Ch'eng I, also practiced *seiza*, and when he would see someone practicing it would say, "excellent learning." However, Ch'eng I's *seiza* was different from his brother's, for there is a spirit of strictness and solemnity in Ch'eng I. The relationship of the two brothers has survived in an interesting anecdote. One day the two brothers accompanied each other to the town's gay quarters. Ch'eng I saw the town prostitutes and thought them odious, but Ch'eng Hao went and took his pleasure with them. When the two brothers returned home, Ch'eng I was still opposed to these women. Thereupon Ch'eng Hao reproached him, saying, "A prostitute was with me, but not with my mind!"

In another story, Ch'eng I was practicing quiet-sitting one day facing a cliff. A disciple came to visit him, and Ch'eng I noticed him but pretended to be unaware of his presence, continuing as usual his *seiza*. Consequently the disciple waited a long time and eventually, it is said, several feet of snow had accumulated outside the hall. From this kind of tradition it appears that Ch'eng I was strict in dealing with his disciples' questions and learning. He spoke clearly to the distinction of right and wrong, and good and bad, and he forgave nothing.

The method of instruction of the older brother, Ch'eng Hao, was just the reverse of this. Tradition says that he did not make as clear a distinction of right and wrong or good and bad as Ch'eng I. From disciples' remarks it appears that, when sitting opposite Ch'eng Hao, they came to have a feeling of a peaceful atmosphere as if they were sitting in the middle of a spring breeze. In Ch'eng Hao's bearing, it can also be seen that there is something transcendent. This can almost be felt when reading the phrases of a poem by him. Actually, however, Ch'eng Hao's relation to the real world was conscientious and thorough. This can be seen clearly in these words from one of his poems: "The Way penetrates outside of the forms of Heaven and Earth: Thought enters in the midst of the transformation of wind and cloud." The first sentence speaks of the transcendent sphere; the second relates thought for the world with its many transformations. Ch'eng Hao was himself at the point where the two joined, and he spread his knowledge and gentle personality to the real world.

Ch'eng Hao's essay *Discussion of Understanding Goodness (Shih-jen p'ien)* represents this viewpoint. There is a section that stresses the importance of studying.

The student should first of all understand goodness. The person of goodness forms a unity with all things. Righteousness, propriety, wisdom, and faith—all of these are goodness. If the principle of this is understood, then goodness can be preserved with sincerity and reverence. There is no need to avoid things, nor is there any need for an exhaustive search. If you are not negligent, then what would there be to avoid? If principle has not been obtained, then there should be an exhaustive search, but if goodness is preserved for long, it will naturally become clear. Why is it necessary to have an exhaustive search? There is nothing equal to this Way. All understanding is insufficient to understand its greatness. The activities of Heaven and earth are entirely my own activities. Mencius says, "All things are complete within me," and that "if you are sincere and reflect upon yourself, it is the greatest pleasure." If in reflecting upon yourself you do not act with sincerity, then there will be nothing but opposition. Although one tries to unify self and other, there will be nothing in the end. How does one obtain happiness? The intention of Chang Tsai's *Settling Obstinacy (Ting-wan)* refers directly to this. If it is preserved by means of this intention, then nothing else needs be done. "There must be an attempt made; however, it must not be helped by the mind, which is expecting a result. Don't forget it, but do not assist in nourishing it." Do not exert the strength of even so much as a single hair. This is the way to preserve it. If it is preserved, then you can reach the end, for the innate knowing and innate ability cannot be lost. Since, however, the conventional mind is not removed, one must learn to preserve this mind. If it is preserved for a long period of time, then the old ways will disperse. The principle is extremely simple, though I fear that it is extremely difficult to preserve it. But if you embody it yourself and take pleasure in it, then there will be no fear of being unable to preserve it.

What is called *Settling Obstinacy* is from the writings of Chang Tsai and is usually called the *Western Inscription*. Chang Tsai once wrote the inscription on the wall of his study. The *Western Inscription* is the origin of brotherly love, that is, the original of what Ch'eng Hao calls goodness. It is presented with a religious feeling toward Heaven and a sincere feeling toward the family. Together with Ch'eng Hao's discussion of "all things form one body," it presents the viewpoint that Heaven and humankind are one, based upon the humanism of Confucianism and the true spirit of oneself and others as "one body."

My own teacher, Dr. Kusumoto Masatsugu, tried to give a general interpretation to the *Western Inscription*. He said that Chang Tsai attributes the universe to the meeting and parting of material force and the transformation of the two elements yin and yang. The law that controls yin and yang, as is discussed in the Chinese classics of philosophy, is the law of natural necessity of Lao Tzu and Chuang Tzu, and the law of intention of the *Book of Changes*. The later notion of intentionality is in agreement with natural necessity. It should be obvious that the former, though it is called natural, has an intention to it and is attributed to what can be said to be the life of the universe. In turn, Chang Tsai's philosophy of vital force in its ethical thought has a tendency to conform to nature. Thus when we discuss conduct on the basis of what is "natural," we find that it was by no means strange to the ancient Chinese philosophers such as Sun Tzu, Han Fei-tzu, and Kuei-ku Tzu to fall into a cold-minded utilitarian tendency to reduce it to a necessary scheming relation. The human being is regarded as an animal seeking material profit and wealth. It is not rare that human beings are at the mercy of necessity and simply fall into quietude with no feelings whatever.

Kusumoto also said that Chang Tsai, regardless of his not believing in spiritual forces outside of the transformation of yin and yang, discussed the morality of goodness and love based upon respect and awe with a religious feeling, a feeling in no way inferior to other major religious traditions. For Chang Tsai, Heaven and earth are regarded as father and mother and the human being is placed between them. The human body is not distinguished from the vital force of Heaven and earth; the body spread out overflowingly throughout Heaven and earth. Moreover, human nature is no less than that of the ruler of Heaven and earth, and there is mutual penetration with Heaven and earth. All people are one's brothers, and all things ones companions. The ruler is the son of one's parents, and the minister is the family minister to the son. Thus, respect the aged based upon the parents regarding elders as their own elders, love the lonely and the weak based upon the parents regarding the young ones as their own young. The sage is the one who unites the virtue of the mother and the father, the worthy is the one who exemplifies the excellence of the mother and the father. The sick, the orphaned, the widow, and others—all are one's brothers who have stumbled and fallen and have nowhere to turn. Thus under Heaven and earth the life of the society is regarded in the same way as the life of the family and the feelings of goodness. Love and virtue as the basis of the family are turned toward all in Heaven and earth.

Kusumoto went on to say that in facing Heaven and earth, however, humankind has the attitude of respectful awe and absolute belief. Serving Heaven and earth is to serve one's parents. In facing Heaven and earth there is a universal feeling urging the individual all the more firmly. There is a feeling of absolute dependence that is unavoidable. The second half of the *Western Inscription* was considered to relate this feeling. Whatever it might be, the feeling of absolute dependence brings peace of mind. The *Western Inscription* concludes with the statement, "I shall follow and accord with things." That is to say, if the self is in accord as far as possible, the attitude in facing Heaven and earth, and mother and father will be no different. "When I die I shall be peaceful." That is to say, I leave this world with a peaceful mind. Thus the virtue of family, society, and the nation is full of the practice of parental love and natural reverential thought. From my point of view, when the love from the family is directed toward Heaven, then the natural world together with society and nation all become the object of warm affection. In turn, when the thought of awe and reverential faith is transferred to the family, then the relation of love comes to be filled with devotion and belief. This is the way in which the circumstances of Heaven and humankind as one are revealed.

From my point of view, Ch'eng Hao and Ch'eng I both spoke of the original foundation of human life and the universe as Principle. Principle had been defined by Han Fei-Tzu as "the pattern for completion of a thing," that is, the reason that something is completed. If we speak of it in terms of human society, it is principle that composes the human being's common life, and it is also the true reality of the universe. Since this is endowed by Heaven it is also called the Principle of Heaven. This Principle of Heaven is in everything, and it is the law that acts as the foundation of each thing. Of course, originally it was thought of as something external to humankind. However, the principle of external affairs of the world and the principle of the foundation of our mind are said to be one; consequently there was neither interior nor exterior in the nature or in principle. Accordingly, to exhaust the principle of the external world results in the exhaustion of the principle of the mind and vice versa. Thus when principle is exhausted, the principle of the mind is exhausted. In fact, the principle of the external world comes to be exhausted. If one thinks of it like this, when only the principle in the middle of the mind was sought, it was thought that there was fear of falling into Zen Buddhism. If, however, the mind is excluded, then the true root of the union of the external and the internal cannot possibly be exhausted. Thus, together with exhausting the principle of the external world, there must be a mastering of the self internally, and it is essential to preserve and nourish the mind that responds to things.

Ch'eng I called the way of exhausting the principle of the external world "extending knowledge," and the way to nourish and preserve the mind "abiding in reverence." The former is the effort of knowing, the latter is the effort of practice. To cultivate learning it is necessary to extend knowledge; to cultivate the nature it is essential to abide in reverence for the nourishment and preservation of the mind. This becomes a mutuality that is indispensable, the same as the two wheels of a cart or the two wings of a bird.

Master Chou's teaching of regarding quietude as fundamental is an effort to seek a return to the pure original nature through a quiet mind, and can also be called preservation and nourishment. Why did Ch'eng I call it reverence and not quietude? Since human nature is something that exists regardless of the activity or quietude of the mind, to search the nature by the nourishment and preservation of the mind was not thought to be limited to quietude alone. What Master Chou called quietude was the original substance, and what he meant by quietude was not necessarily distinguished from activity. However, it is true that he mainly aimed at the quieting of the mind. For Ch'eng I, this was a biased position in favor of quietude. Instead, the preservation and nourishment of the mind should be practiced through both quietude and activity rather than being biased in favor of quietude. When it is biased toward quietude, then there is a fear of sinking into Zen Buddhism. Ch'eng I in this fashion suggested that effort be on reverence to penetrate both activity and quietude.

As far as the term "reverence" is concerned—and later there will be an opportunity to discuss it more fully—reverence is the effort to exhibit the original essence of the mind free of any and all evil intent. There is an expression in the *Doctrine of the Mean* that says, "Be fearful, be cautious," and another that says, "Be cautious when alone." There is also the expression in the *Book of Poetry (Shih Ching)* that says, "Fearful and cautious, like walking on ice." In short, the kind of thing indicated by passages like these is that reverence is an effort at a modest level of introspection. Among some it is said that reverence is the mind becoming devoted, such as toward Heaven. Although it may be spoken of as introspection, this is not necessarily its full meaning. There is also an element of activity to work with the nature and the original mind. If this is forgotten, then the main point of the discussion of abiding in reverence by the Neo-Confucians will have been lost.

Both Ch'eng I and Ch'eng Hao spoke of reverence. However, the method of Ch'eng I was strict, while that of Ch'eng Hao was flexible and more broad-minded. At any rate, this was what Master Chou called regarding quietude as fundamental and the Ch'eng brothers referred to as abiding in reverence. Later generations of Confucians emphasized either the principle of regarding quietude as fundamental or the teaching of abiding in reverence; however, they were also sometimes opposed and sometimes combined. The discussion in Neo-Confucianism became more and more complex in this area. The ones who emphasized regarding quietude as fundamental made much of the practice of *seiza* and continued to say that it was different from concentration through *zazen*. Not only those who emphasized abiding in reverence, but also those who emphasized regarding quietude as fundamental opposed Zen Buddhism and were very critical of its practices. From what position do they criticize Zen Buddhism? When this point is not clearly understood, regarding quietude as fundamental and abiding in reverence may appear closely compatible with the Zen theory of the mind.

A Critique of Zen

In the work *Vegetable Root Discourses*, there is a saying:

The true Buddha is within the family, the true Way is with daily activity. If one is sincere and at peace, of good countenance and amiable words, then among the father, mother, elder brother, and younger brother, all members of the family unite into one and all minds achieve understanding. This is ten thousand times superior to breath control and concentration of the mind.

What is the meaning of this passage? For some the Buddha is an external figure, but in fact it is nothing external. There is indeed the Buddha within the family who dwells together with father, mother, elder brother, and younger brother. In addition, in the world the Way is often considered something distant, but in fact it is within our own daily lives. Thus if we hold our sincere and honest mind, calm our feelings, relax our countenance, temper our expressions, and if at the same time there is mutual understanding of minds among father, mother, elder and younger brother as if they were together as a single body, this should be called the true Buddha and the true Way. It is also said that this is far superior to the breath control and contemplation of the practice of *zazen*. In short, rather than deeply seeking the Way in the midst of one's mind by means of *zazen* in physical isolation, it is far better to seek the true Way through creating unity and harmony within the family. This is very different from discussing contemplation in an isolated setting in the middle of the night.

In ancient China in the state of Ch'i, there was a king by the name of Hsüan. One day the king was looking out from his window and saw a sacrificial cow being pulled along to be offered in sacrifice. Accordingly the king made an inquiry, asking where the cow was being taken. The reply was that a bell had been completed and that a blood sacrifice was to be carried out for the spirits and therefore the cow would be killed for the sacrifice. The cow appeared, however, to sense that it was to be killed, and it was apprehensive and trembling with fear. When King Hsüan saw this he could not bear to see the cow killed with no crime and he ordered a halt to the killing. Mencius heard this story and went to see King Hsüan, saying, "This is the art of goodness." He explained to the king that if this mind of goodness were to be applied to the people and in turn were to become the way of governing, then the Way of the ancient kings could be realized. For Mencius this was the virtue of goodness: the mind of man that cannot bear to see the suffering of others, that is, the mind of commiseration. This, according to Mencius, is endowed in the original nature of humankind. There is a mind of shame and disgrace, a mind of deference, a mind of right and wrong—these are endowed in the original nature of every person. The mind of commiseration is the beginning of goodness, the mind of shame and disgrace is the beginning of righteousness, the mind of deference is the beginning of propriety, and the mind of right and wrong is the beginning of wisdom.

The basic requirement of being a human being is to possess these Four Beginnings. It is said that if these Four Beginnings are not there, then a human is not different from an animal. When these four virtues, goodness, righteousness, propriety, and wisdom, were combined with faith, they became known as the Five Constants, or Five Virtues, and were considered to be the root and trunk of basic human relations. Among them goodness penetrated the other four and was regarded as the central virtue. These virtues were thought originally to be endowed in human nature, and in the sense that they are the root and the essential reason for the life of human beings in society, they may be referred to as principle. Principle is simply something that exists in any discrete phenomenon, irrespective of issues of the internality or externality of body and mind. As the expression has it, "If there is a phenomenon, there is a law." This principle exists within things, and the Five Constants are its general guideline.

According to idealism the nature and mind of humankind possess this original principle. Therefore mind and nature are real, not vacuous. That is to say, since there is principle that exists and regulates internally, within things, therefore it cannot be said to be empty. It is real and thus different from Zen Buddhism. Although idealism is similar to Zen Buddhism in seeing the foundation of learning as the study of human nature, idealism on the contrary engaged in a search for real principles. Even if principle of this kind was not denied in Buddhism and its existence even acknowledged, in the end it was less than positive and given no more than a secondary role. For this reason Neo-Confucians were very critical of the Buddhists. It was because these Confucians followed the spirit of Confucius himself and felt that the Confucians have a mission to be with people of the world and be engaged in the construction of the ideal society.

I would like to give a general outline of the Neo-Confucian criticism of Zen Buddhism. Through this process we can hope to gain a clue of understanding of the relationship between *zazen* and *seiza*.

Zen Is without Ethics

When Wang Yang-ming was young, probably because of his poor health, he practiced what the Taoists called nourishing life and was interested in Zen Buddhism. At the age of thirty-one he suffered from an illness and retired from the world to a place far from people, practicing meditation in order to rid himself of discursive thought. However, whatever the means he used he simply could not eliminate it. This was because he could not separate from his mind his concern for his father and his grandmother. It was at that point that he became aware of his own heart. To think of these relatives—this is something that is within our nature. Taoism and Zen Buddhism try to eradicate this kind of thought, but you cannot reach the point of eradicating completely the very foundation of the life of humankind. Thus we can see the error of Taoism and Zen Buddhism, and this was changed in Confucianism so that human relations were regarded as of the utmost importance.

Wang Yang-ming became ill with his practice of the nourishment of life. He went to West Lake in Ch'ien-t'ang and visited a famous old temple in the area. When he went to the temple he saw a Zen monk who had for three years cultivated "nonspeaking, nonseeing." Yang-ming cried out to him, "Abbot, the whole day you are chattering, why do you chatter? The whole day you look about, why do you look about?" The monk stood up astonished. Accordingly Yang-ming gently inquired as to whether he didn't have a mother in his old home, and the monk replied that he did have a mother. Yang-ming asked if he didn't think of her, and the monk replied that he did think of her. Consequently Yang-ming instructed the monk that such thought of the parents was in the nature of human beings and then he left. On the very next day he came again to the temple, but the monk was no longer there.

For Yang-ming to suggest to the monk that he chattered and looked about all the time even though he was practicing "nonspeaking, nonseeing" naturally astonished the monk. In this way Yang-ming was able to point out the error of Zen by using the technique of Zen itself. Long ago this was called "gripping the sword and entering the house," that is, snatching away the sword of the opponent and defeating him by his own sword. The Sung period Neo-Confucian Yang Shih said that you must use this kind of method if you are going to criticize Zen Buddhism.

From this story, the Confucian criticism of Zen Buddhism is that it has abandoned human relations. This was the Confucian opinion toward not only Zen Buddhism, but the totality of Buddhist teachings as well as those of Lao Tzu and Chuang Tzu. However, among the Confucians some said that Lao Tzu and Chuang Tzu were a little better than Buddhism because for Lao Tzu and Chuang Tzu only the mind was empty and there was still principle to support the way of the common life of human beings, that is, the family, society, and the nation. But in Buddhism in addition to the mind, even principle was said to be empty and still. In addition, in Lao Tzu and Chuang Tzu, though principle is not regarded as the root of the Way and the substance is seen as empty, still they did not reach the point of regarding basic human needs as unnecessary. However, Buddhism was criticized for what it calls true emptiness, which was seen as a way to make even these things unnecessary.

A Confucian at the beginning of the Sung period, Shih Chieh (1005–45), spoke of the significance of human relations, saying that there must be righteousness between ruler and subject, love between father and son, discretion of husband and wife, the trust of friends, and the priority of elder and younger brothers in the life of people. If these do not exist, then all under

Heaven will lack order. That Buddhism and Taoism do not concern themselves with these is something that goes against the characteristic Chinese
way of ordering the world.

Zen Declines the Governing of the World

A Confucian in the middle of the Sung period, Chang Chiu-ch'eng, was
said by many Confucians to be influenced by Zen. Chu Hsi reproached him,
saying that his learning was more harmful than the injury of a wild animal or
a flood. Even though he received this kind of criticism, he in turn also
criticized Buddhism. In this respect he said that the government of goodness
can be carried out only through the mind of goodness, that is, the mind that
cannot bear to see the suffering of others. However, if it is only a mind that
cannot bear to see suffering and it cannot be enlarged to a government of the
kind that cannot bear to see the suffering of the people, then it is too narrow
and the knowledge too petty. To carry into place the government that cannot
bear to see the suffering of others through the mind that cannot bear to see
the suffering of others—this is the nature of the Principle of Heaven. However, since Buddhism considers the world to be illusory, it does not recognize
the function of the Principle of Heaven. In Buddhist teaching you are given
mind and stomach, but deprived of hands and feet. Thus you cannot act!

Lu Hsiang-shan was also criticized as having Zen ethics by Chu Hsi and
the later members of the Chu Hsi School. The distinction, however, between
Confucianism and Buddhism lies in the disparity of serving the world or
leaving the world. As a result, to distinguish between these two Lu sought to
make the distinction one of following the public way or following the private
way. Chu Hsi's eldest disciple, Ch'en Pei-hsi (1159–1223), says that Confucianism took the position of emphasizing the management, order, and institutions of the common life of humankind, while Buddhism took the position
beyond the world, searching in the dark and the boundless for the Way. The
Way, however, for Ch'en, was within human affairs. Since Buddhism regarded Heaven, earth, and all things as illusory transformations, discussing
them as "empty" or "nothing," he rejected Buddhism by saying that it disregarded human affairs. The scholar Ou-yang Hsiu (1007–70) said this was the
basis of the true character of Confucianism: the Confucians recognize the
actuality of the human being, and this is placed in relation to social institutions. He too opposed Buddhism.

Among the Neo-Confucians there were some who when they criticized
Buddhism did not criticize it from a philosophical point of view but instead in
terms, for example, of the strangeness of the monks wearing the habit; or by

saying that although it is natural that people cannot disregard the relation of ruler and subject or parent and child in order to live in the world, the Buddhists dislike it and try to evade it. That is, there are some who criticized it solely for its attitude of living and did not point out its errors from the point of view of the subtlety of the nature or the mind. To some this type of criticism was shallow, but Chu Hsi said that it hit the mark and was not superficial. The reason is that the subtlety of the nature or the mind is united with a tangible phenomenon. A criticism in a tangible area actually hits the mark. For this reason Chu Hsi admired this type of criticism.

From the Confucian point of view, Buddhism disregards basic human relations that should not be disregarded. In addition, the Buddhists say that the doctrine of emptiness has no role to play in serving the world. Any such attempt becomes a hindrance to enlightenment and thus is to be rejected, seeking only the way that is within the nature or the mind. The Confucians criticize this, saying that it is cutting off human relations and discarding things, and they are particularly critical of what the Buddhists call the hindrance of worldly affairs. For example, the Buddhists focus primarily upon the gate of the mind and regard the world as illusory. According to Chu Hsi and others, this expression "the gate of the mind" was something that occurred at the beginning of Buddhism rather than in the later period of Buddhism. In late Buddhism there is a focusing upon nature and mind, but it does not lose the actual world. For example, in Zen Buddhism there is the expression, "Activity itself is the real nature." When one says that activity is the real nature, it means that actual phenomena are the Buddha nature. Consequently when Buddhism in general and Zen Buddhism in particular are reproached, the discussions of the emptiness of nature and mind and the loss of the actual world are not adequate. The question may be asked as to whether or not human relations and the principle of things were regarded as of the first importance. Ch'en Pei-hsi commented on the Zen expression "Activity itself is the nature," and said that it regarded Heaven, earth, and all things as the eternal body of the Buddha (dharmakāya). Based on this, to go to the gay quarters and amuse ourselves as we might wish, this becomes the way of the Buddha and in such a case there was a genuine fear of the confusion of the Principle of Heaven with selfish desire.

In Buddhism there is an expression, "Sarvadharma (*chu-fa*) is dharmakāya (*shih-hsiang*)" (All things are the Absolute). This would indicate that Buddhism does not regard the actual world as immediately illusory and thus does not see alone the other world of the far shore. But what does this expression mean, "All things are the Absolute?" It is something that understood the actual world from the position of absolute emptiness. The Buddhist absolute denial is something that changes into absolute affirmation. This is indicated by the expression "All things are the Absolute", as well as the expression "Absolute and relative have no barrier." The same is also true of the Zen Buddhist expression "I am the Buddha." To them the self in the sea of passions is denied, but in the end the passions themselves become Buddhahood. The expression, "I am the Buddha," is of a very different nature and substance from the Confucian teaching.

Confucianism from its very beginning has taken the position of human affirmation and expects the perfection of humankind. What is this perfection? It is not outside the establishment of human moral principles. In Confucianism this kind of person is the original human. Accordingly, in Confucianism the public way, that is, the way of humankind, is respected, and the selfish desires are denied. They are very strict in wanting to distinguish these two. In the case of Buddhism, the public way is regarded as of second or third importance, and there is neither a positive stance nor a passion for it. Although Buddhism extends itself to serving the world in conformance with human relations, it is always something provisional and has only a tertiary role.

From the Confucian perspective there is an apprehension that the Buddhist discussion of "All things are the Absolute" will produce harmful effects by drifting with the currents of the age, whether good or bad, and being unable to hold critical knowledge. For these reasons the affairs of the world cannot be trusted to the Buddhists. In criticizing the Buddhist, the Confucian is simply saying that the Buddhists do not study the methods for the ordering of the nation or issues of peace in the world. If indeed we can transform the common life of humankind, then we have to search into human relations and we have to investigate things one by one, searching for the principles that are governing them. This is the reason that Confucianism places so much emphasis upon the importance of learning and knowledge. This method of study in Confucianism is what is called the investigation of things and the exhaustion of principle or the investigation of things and the extension of knowledge. Essentially this means that the principle of something is investigated in conformance with the thing itself, and through this process the knowledge of the mind is brought to a point of fulfillment. The existence or nonexistence of this investigation of things and exhaustion of principle is the basic distinction between Buddhism and Confucianism.

From the Confucian perspective, the way of Buddhism has no practical use. Specifically, for the common life of human beings and for the life of society it has no use whatsoever. Confucianism regards life as people together and a kind heart of mutual understanding. By employing the things of the world, it aims at serving the life of the human being in relation to others. Though it employs things of the world, each thing is to obtain its place in accordance with its original principle. If this is not the case, then it will be impossible to avoid sinking into a biased perspective. Therefore the use of things is nothing more than returning things to their origins. And in the learning of nature and mind there is no giving way to biased selfish intentions. Since Buddhist learning is not something that follows this kind of objective principle, inevitably it does not have a positive profile toward governmental policy and institutions that are responsible for guiding society.

In other words, Confucianism and Buddhism both aim at the learning of nature and mind, but the function is very different. That is to say, one method is seeking to serve the world, and the other method is seeking to leave the world. When it is thought of in this way, the two are the same in substance, but different in function. This is also called the same in root, different in branch. However, it is actually impossible that the root can be the same and the branches different because the substance and the function are of one body. When it is thought of in this way the discussion of the same root and different branches is simply an error. Confucianism and Buddhism are simply different in terms of roots and branches.

Since Zen Buddhism speaks of pointing directly to the human mind, its learning is the learning of the mind. The Neo-Confucian thinks of the mind as endowed with all principles and complying with all things, and they still advocate mind-learning. However, among Confucians there are some who say that in Confucianism when mind is discussed what is meant is principle, while in Zen what is sought after is the subtlety of the vital force. Others say that both discuss the mind's emptiness, but the Confucian follows human nature, while the mind is said to be empty. That is, human nature is real and not different from the laws that govern things themselves. The mind is empty and simply follows the laws of things in a state of no self and no mind though there is a regulation and direction within it. However, in Zen Buddhism the emptiness of the mind is spoken of, but there is no regulation and direction offered. There are some who have said that this is because in Buddhism human nature itself is regarded as empty. When based upon this, the distinction of Confucianism and Buddhism can be seen through the reality or emptiness of human nature. The expression "regulation and direction" is used frequently by the Neo-Confucians. Originally it was from the *Book of Changes*. The Confucians publicized this phrase and tried to confront Zen

Buddhism in this manner. "Regulation and direction" is to act in such a way as to be well controlled, having no excesses and no deficiencies. In other words, it is to guide society by the way of centrality and moderation. For the Confucian this was the way to realize the great way of the universe. In short, to the Confucian the serving or the nonserving of the world became the basis for the distinction between Buddhism and Confucianism.

Mind in Zen Fails to Unify Interior/Exterior

Ch'eng Hao said that for the Confucian, "one straightens the interior with reverence and settles the exterior with righteousness." In Zen Buddhism, it is only "straightening the interior with reverence"; there is no "settling the exterior with righteousness." That is to say, the mind-learning of Zen Buddhism stops with the interior. It is not something that penetrates both interior and exterior. In this way the existence or nonexistence of righteousness gives rise to the distinction between Buddhism and Confucianism. Ch'eng Hao's discussion of reverence and righteousness is based upon the *Book of Changes*. In the *Book of Changes* it is said, "The gentleman straightens the interior with reverence and settles the exterior with righteousness. When reverence and righteousness are established virtue is not alone." Essentially this means that if one straightens the mind without the loss of the right mind internally and acts with rectitude (acting in compliance with principle) externally, then virtue will increase, people will naturally help each other and not have to stand alone.

Later Confucians frequently discussed the interior and exterior aspect of reverence and righteousness based upon this passage from the *Book of Changes*. Confucians who placed importance upon the communal life of society naturally emphasized righteousness. This became the Confucian weapon against Lao Tzu, Chuang Tzu, and Buddhism. Ch'eng Hao held to righteousness and criticized Buddhism. In Confucianism goodness was regarded as the highest virtue, but in speaking of goodness most also speak of righteousness. True, goodness is something that includes righteousness, but when one speaks only of goodness alone without speaking of righteousness, then one slips into an undifferentiated love of others such as in the case of Mo Tzu or into an emptiness of the kind found in Buddhism. I am not saying that goodness does not have aspects of correspondence with what is called mercy in Lao Tzu and compassion in Buddhism, but righteousness and propriety are distinctive features of Confucianism.

At any rate Confucianism speaks of the internality and externality of reverence and righteousness. Therefore the Way is regarded as teaching both the internal and the external. The way of Buddhism, on the other hand, never goes beyond simply the interior. Why, however, did Ch'eng Hao criticize Buddhism in terms of righteousness only and not in terms of reverence? The reason is probably that if reverence alone were to be discussed, then all effort would be directed to the interior mind and there would be a real fear of falling into Zen Buddhism. When more deliberate consideration is given, then reverence may be seen as a mind of propriety. Accordingly, among the Confucians there are some who said that it is principle. Reverence does not simply limit itself to the interior; it penetrates as well into the external. Therefore it is fundamentally different from the Zen learning of the mind, which is solely concerned with the interior. Of course, reverence of this kind has in a sense transcended reverence! In other words, it is ultimately something without substance. Otherwise, for some it would be impossible to avoid attachment or even stagnation.

When we think of it in this way, we can understand that Confucianism and Buddhism are different, although they speak of the same effort of mind. In a question and answer between Wang Yang-ming and one of his disciples, this question was raised. "Buddhism practices the cultivation of the mind. In spite of this why can't they order the world?" Wang Yang-ming replied, "The cultivation of the mind by the Confucians does not separate itself from things. If you simply follow the law of the nature of things, you are naturally able to cultivate it. However, since the Buddhists cut things off entirely and instead view the mind as illusory, naturally they fall into emptiness, and eventually they have no relation to the world at all. Thus they are not able to govern the world."

In Zen the Mind Is Divided into Two

The Sung period Neo-Confucians Lo Ts'ung-yen and Li Yen-p'ing considered their learning to focus upon viewing of the vital force at the time that the feelings of pleasure, anger, sorrow, and joy were not yet manifest. In relation to this, Chu Hsi commented that the term "viewing" means "viewing it without viewing." What does Chu Hsi mean by this kind of statement? If one becomes attached to viewing, then one will slip into the complication of dividing the mind into two, the mind with which one views and the mind to be viewed. Chu Hsi discussed abiding in reverence in terms of the preserving of the mind, and in this case too he warned against the attitude of preserving the mind with reverence. According to Chu Hsi, reverence does not preserve and nourish the mind, but if there is reverence, then the mind is naturally preserved and nourished. Otherwise, one mind will be grasped by another mind, and already the mind is divided even though it is not in touch with the external world. For this reason Ch'eng Hao did not say to "preserve the mind by means of sincerity and reverence," but said instead, "preserve the mind by practicing sincerity and reverence." Kusumoto Tanzan also said, "Do not straighten the interior by means of reverence, but straighten the interior through the practice of reverence." In this same way, Chu Hsi pointed out that the Buddhist "contemplation of the mind" resulted in dividing the mind. "If you say that you constantly see the brilliance of this mind, then you acknowledge two masters. We don't know whether the true mind is the brilliance or whether the viewing of it is the true mind." In short, Buddhism sinks into the discussion of two minds. The question is whether the Buddhist is resigned to this criticism. Expressions such as "truth and falsity are not two" would seem to indicate such.

Zen Does Not Attain Absolute Nothingness
Wang Yang-ming says:

> Only one sage obtains true emptiness, that is, absolute emptiness, and though the followers of Lao Tzu and Chuang Tzu as well as the Buddhists speak of emptiness, they do not obtain its truth. That is to say, although the Taoists speak of emptiness, their real motive is to obtain the nourishment of life. In turn, the Buddhists discuss emptiness, but their aim is to separate themselves from the sea of suffering of life and death. Though the two each respectively search for emptiness and nonbeing, there is still the activity of a single thought and they are therefore not able to reach to the absolute emptiness and nonbeing.

To the Neo-Confucian, it was only in Confucianism that absolute emptiness and nonbeing could be obtained. In the same fashion, it was felt that only in Confucianism was there the obtaining of absolute understanding of substance and function as well as the physical and metaphysical realms.

Zen Does Not Obtain Absolute Freedom
Zen Buddhism explains the condition of absolute freedom by means of a gourd floating on top of the water. "It resembles a gourd floating on top of the water, having not the slightest obstruction. When it is pushed, it moves as it is pushed. When it is pressed, it tumbles. It is entirely on its own." However, a Confucian at the end of the Ming period, Liu Tsung-chou, explained enlightenment in the Confucian School as different from this. "It is something like the movement of a boat on top of the water. Since there is a rudder in our hand, although there are dangerous places everywhere, they are over-

come. And wherever one wants to go on shore, he can freely go." This expresses a special fact of the mind-learning of Zen Buddhism and Confucianism. Essentially the freedom of Zen Buddhism is a kind of blindness, the freedom of Confucianism has a purpose. Thus the mind that Confucians aim at ultimately is different from that of Zen Buddhism. Zen speaks of absolute nothingness and bases itself upon a transcendent condition that denies the independent nature of the human mind. From the Confucian point of view, the independent nature of the mind is itself the mind of the universe, thus "Heaven and earth are settled and all things are nourished." In other words, it is not merely a mind of freedom to move from one to another, but the mind that points in one direction. In other words, and this is Liu Tsung-chou's point, it has its own subjectivity.

We have related in a very rough way the Confucian criticism of Buddhism. In specific areas there would be much more that could be said, but my purpose has been to present a summary of the general problem. Obviously Buddhism has a rebuttal to these various points, but I have not included that here.

A Critique of *Seiza*

Among the Confucians of the Sung and Ming periods, there were many who leaned toward *seiza*, but there were also some who commented critically upon the practice. I want to speak to this critique in a general way. However, this introduction of the critique of *seiza* is not for the purpose of rejecting the practice of *seiza*, but out of my desire not to mistake the true intent of *seiza* or to harm it.

Those Confucians who explained the importance of *seiza*, like those previously mentioned, emphasized the difference between *seiza* and concentration through *zazen*, but there were others who said that *zazen* and *seiza* were the same in this respect. Since Wang Yang-ming used *seiza* to gain enlightenment, he spoke of enlightenment by *seiza* to his disciples. Shortly, however, he realized that it produced harmful effects, and afterward he spoke no more of it. The disciples did not understand the meaning of *seiza*, and they therefore came to look upon any activity with disgust. It also reaches the point where they were trying to reach enlightenment by seeking trancelike states. Wang Yang-ming discussed *seiza* with his disciples:

[*Disciple*]: At the time of quietude my intentions are in a favorable state, but whenever I try to do something, it can change entirely. What is the reason for this?

[*Yang-ming*]: This is because you know only to cultivate the mind in quietude and make no effort to overcome the selfish desires. When this is the case, then when you approach various worldly affairs they produce a trembling and shaking in the mind. It is better when you approach various matters to act with a mind that is forged and sharpened, and then you will be able to obtain a settled and peaceful mind. In doing this you can reach what Ch'eng Hao called, "Settled in quietude, settled in activity."

[*Disciple*]: When practicing *seiza* it seems that this mind is completely concentrated, but the minute you encounter some matter, the concentration does not continue and soon it reaches the point that there are many thoughts about it.

[*Yang-ming*]: It is only when the mind has been forged that there can be any effect to encountering various matters. If you dwell only in quietude, when it comes to affairs your mind will be agitated and in the end it will reach the point of not seeing any progress in your learning. And as for the effort at the time of quietude, although it seems as if the mind is quiet, in fact it is merely distracted.

Accordingly Yang-ming spoke solely of making an effort to preserve the Principle of Heaven by eliminating human desires and emphasized instead the importance of the removal of desires. Around the age of forty-six Yang-ming was sent by imperial command to pacify a rebel force. In the midst of this he sent a letter to his disciples, which spoke strongly of the importance of the elimination of desires. "Once I sent a letter to Yang Chi in which I said, 'Defeating the rebels in the mountains is easy; defeating the rebels in the mind is difficult.' When I pacified the escaping rebels, it was really nothing at all." Yang-ming pointed out the weakness of seeking quietude.

The foundation of the mind lies in quietude, but if you seek its foundation by quietude then the substance will be twisted. Activity is the mind's function, but if you fear the easy agitation of the mind, then the function will come to cease. The mind that seeks after quietude is active, and the mind that disdains activity is not quiet. In this way activity becomes active and quietude as well becomes active.

Thus seeking after the quietude of mind by *seiza* actually causes agitation in the mind. For Yang-ming it was most important to preserve the Principle of Heaven through the elimination of human desires regardless of whether there was quietude or activity. Otherwise, if one seeks a quiet mind, not only will it give rise to the harmful effects of preferring quietude to activity; in addition human desires, rather than being eliminated, will become hidden in the interior aspects of the mind and emerge when they wish. If one acts in such a way as to follow the Principle of Heaven, then the mind will certainly reach the point of obtaining peace and quiet. On the contrary, if one seeks only the peace and the quiet of the mind, one is not necessarily following the Principle of Heaven. In this way Yang-ming rejected the effort of regarding quietude as fundamental by pointing out the contradictory attitude of seeking only quietude.

The Ch'ing period Confucian Lu Fu-t'ing also said:

More than seeking quietude in quietude, a good method is to seek quietude in activity. Quietude is something that is settled in principle. At the time of the unmanifest one is settled in this Principle of Heaven and at the time of the manifest one is also settled in this Principle of Heaven. At the time of no-affairs one is settled in the Principle of Heaven and at the time of affairs one is also settled in this Principle of Heaven. In this way the effort gradually matures and the Principle of Heaven reaches the point of full maturity. When this happens, no matter how many changes or transformations, everything becomes quiet.

However, it cannot be concluded that Lu Fu-t'ing said that the study of quietude was wrong. Thus Lu Fu-t'ing did not criticize Lo Ts'ung-yen's teaching, "Observe the vital force of the unmanifest in quietude," or Li Yen-p'ing's teaching, "Clarify the mind in silent sitting and realize the Principle of Heaven."

For the beginner, however, Lu Fu-t'ing said, "*Seiza* is harmful. After the effort has had a chance to mature then this is not a hindrance, but the beginner who practices this type of thing will fall into Zen Buddhism." In this way he rejected *seiza*, saying instead that if one follows the Principle of Heaven at all times whatever one is doing, the time of quietude and the time of activity are both ultimately quiet. In the *Response to a Discussion of Learning (Lun-hsüeh ch'ou-ta)*, it is said:

Can you seek quietude of mind by the quieting of the body? Can you seek quietude of mind by the quieting of the mind? If you seek quietude of the mind by the quieting of the body, then if the body is active the mind will be disquieted. If you seek quietude of mind by the quieting of the mind, how can quietude be sought?

Lu also said, "If you seek, it is not quiet." Lu Fu-t'ing opposed the use of *seiza* by beginners in this way, but there are some who discussed the learning of quietude who felt that *seiza* was important for the beginner.

Zen Buddhism obviously regarded quietude as essential. Within Zen Buddhism, however, the Rinzai School stressed activities, while the Mokushō

School emphasized the position of quietude. Ta Hui (1089–1163) of the Sung period and Hakuin in Japan belong to the former kind of Zen Buddhism. Hung Chih (1091–1157) of the Sung period and Dogen (1200–1252) in Japan belong to the latter type of Zen. For Ta Hui and Hakuin, active effort is said to be a hundredfold more effective than quiet effort.

If the substance of the nature and the mind is said to be either active or quiet, I prefer to describe it as quiet. There is, however, the issue of the necessity of effort for quietude. An effort for quietude belongs in a temporal context and yet substance transcends temporality. This creates a difference in meaning of the two. Since, however, the substance whether in quietude or activity loses its real nature if separated from temporality, it is necessary to establish substance first by preservation and nourishment during periods of quietude. This is the main point of regarding quietude as fundamental.

Others thought that it was pointless to keep the mind in a vague state with seemingly no purpose. Since the substance was originally a metaphysical existence beyond feeling, it was thought that it could not be understood without developing its activity. Thus before making the effort to preserve and nourish quietude, it was first necessary to investigate the moral categories by which the substance acts. Without doing this, it was thought that one would fall into the emptiness of Zen Buddhism. This is the reason that for some what is called "understanding the manifest," or "understanding the beginning and the end" is regarded as the main point of learning. Those who take this position say that the learning of quietude has only substance, no function; that is, it is something that has lost the practical function and thereby sinks into emptiness.

Wang Yang-ming in a similar way opposed regarding quietude as fundamental and in his later years advocated the "extension of innate knowing," making it clear that it was found in life itself. Innate knowledge as it is in itself simply reflects moral law, and it was felt unnecessary to speak of quietude or activity. In this way it is simply being full of life. Innate knowing is the absolute quality of life, which advances and progresses by itself. For Yang-ming innate knowing is the substance that transforms itself and is itself the effort. Thus the substance is the effort as it is, and the effort is the substance as it is. That is to say, the substance is the effort and effort is the substance.

This kind of thinking is compatible with Hui Neng's (638–713) looking into the nature and sudden enlightenment. Hui Neng sought enlightenment in a direct fashion, seeing the original face with no consideration of good or bad. Hui Neng based this upon an existential point of view that sees the conformity of the mind and the Buddha nature. For example, when you are conscious of innate knowledge, all distracting thought is lessened and disappears. Innate knowing is of extraordinary power, like the alchemical transformation of iron into gold. Wang Yang-ming's saying, "Neither good, nor evil," means that there is simply no room to use the term "good", to say nothing of the word "evil." Therefore, for Yang-ming innate knowing is also existential. "In the human mind there dwells in each person a sage," or "Confucius is in the mind of each person respectively." This was something that he told his disciples to believe. Yang-ming called innate knowing "existential", but he also did not forget the importance of effort at the same time.

Wang Yang-ming did not speak of "innate knowledge"; he spoke instead of the "extension of innate knowing." The real meaning of this phrase is found in the term "extension." The effort of extension was considered to be the output of the very substance itself. If this is not the case and if the effort was considered to be in the seeking of the substance, then substance and effort would be divided and that which originally was one and whole becomes divided and inconsistent. Wang Yang-ming felt that Chu Hsi's idea of effort through toiling fell into this type of difficulty.

If the Chu Hsi learning and the learning of Wang Yang-ming are compared and if the Chu Hsi learning is spoken of in terms of Zen Buddhism, it should be called a cultivated experience and gradual cultivation. For Wang Yang-ming it should be called seeing into the nature and sudden enlightenment. In general those who are in a position of defending Buddhism have a tendency to criticize the Chu Hsi learning and the Yang-ming learning as a remolded and renovated Zen Buddhism, particularly the Yang-ming learning. Chu Hsi and Yang-ming were critical of Zen Buddhism and of Buddhism in general, but when you speak of it from the position of Buddhism, their arguments are said to be taken from Zen Buddhism itself. It goes without saying that although their Confucianism had a tendency to be realized through meditation like Taoism and Zen Buddhism, they adhere to a Confucian position and therefore they must be distinguished from either Taoism or Buddhism.

Wang Yang-ming's quest for the active expression of innate knowledge, what is referred to as his "existentialism," was promoted even more in his disciples Wang Ken (1483–1541) and Wang Chi (1498–1583), and in this was the establishment of the "existential" branch of innate knowing. This branch in turn criticized increasingly the discussion of innate knowledge as a process of cultivation. Among them they most keenly criticized the discussion of the quietist innate knowledge that regarded quietude as the basic principle of learning, seeing the substance of innate knowledge as quietude, dividing innate knowledge between substance and function, and seeing that only after the establishment of the substance could the function become operative. This is said to be a discussion of annihilation. According to the "existential" branch, innate knowledge is already perfect and complete. It does not permit a cultivation process; it must be a sudden enlightenment. When it is not this way, then one cannot avoid being attached and restrained and cannot obtain the true substance without obstacles.

The discussion of the "existentialism" of the two Wangs became increasingly popular. It also reached a point of being suitable to the ordinary person who had not a single letter of learning. A Confucian of the "existential" school, Chou Ju-teng (1547–1629), in a dialogue with his disciple Liu-ko, demonstrates one of the basic teachings of the school. Chou said, "When it is said that at present you are good, can this be believed?" Ko replied, "I can believe it." Chou said, "Then are you a sage?" Ko replied, "I am also a sage." Thereupon Chou cried out, "If you are a sage, you are a sage. It is not necessary to say 'also.' "

During this period in the late Ming, the Zen schools also had a similar tendency and together with the Confucians of this persuasion, they overran the generation. Then in the end there were those who preached that "the passions are the Buddha," and that "temptation for wine, women, and wealth does not hinder the way of the Buddha," and it became selfishness. This in general gave rise to a trend to rebel against the laws of the world. In any case, the Confucian discussion of regarding quietude as fundamental was knocked down entirely by this branch of Confucian learning.

6. A DISCUSSION OF *SEIZA*

It was after the Sung period, during the time that Confucianism was transformed by its contact with Taoism and Buddhism, that the Confucians came to practice *seiza* and find a deep and profound meaning in it. Chou Tun-i, who has been called the patriarch of the Sung learning, considered regarding quietude as fundamental as the basis of his learning. Master Ch'eng, who was his disciple and anxious that Master Chou might be biased toward quietude, spoke of the effort of reverence as including both quietude and activity, but did not abandon *seiza*. Among the disciples of Master Ch'eng, Yang Shih, Lo Ts'ung-yen and Li Yen-p'ing took quietude seriously. Chu Hsi, who was a disciple of Li Yen-p'ing, primarily followed Master Ch'eng's abiding in reverence, but Li Yen-p'ing's thought on quietude was of no small influence on Chu Hsi.

This learning of quietude was also accepted by the Confucians of Japan. It was especially among the Chu Hsi scholars at the end of the Bakufu and the beginning of the Meiji that the learning was established. For example, Kusumoto Tanzan focused upon it and regarded *seiza* realization as his credo. *Seiza* realization means the unifying of the mind in order to realize the Principle of Heaven by direct experience. "Realization" is not simply the accumulation of knowledge, not abstract or doctrinaire thought, but something that is whole and vital. *Seiza* realization is what Li Yen-p'ing took as a special characteristic of his learning. Kusumoto Tanzan also concerned himself with *seiza* realization, and by means of it he established a deep and subtle learning. I want to present in this chapter Tanzan's discussion of *seiza* realization.

123

According to Chu Hsi, the principle of people's common life is immanent within human nature. Thus the principle of all things is within one's nature, and one's nature contains the principle of all things. Since one's nature does not have an interior or an exterior, to seek our nature we must first seek the principle of things. The so-called investigation of things and exhaustion of principle are nothing more than simply exhausting the nature itself. If, however, one seeks only in the mind for the nature, regarding it as something that is internal, this becomes what in Zen Buddhism is called "looking into the nature and becoming the Buddha," or "pointing straight to the human mind." In this way one would lose the guiding principle of the common life of humankind and would have no hope of actually serving the world. However, nature is the substance of mind, and in turn mind is the ruler of the body and the spiritual life. Thus if one seeks only externally for the principle of things without the preservation and nourishment of the mind, there is the chance of inconsistency and incoherence in the unity of the nature. Thus mind must be preserved and nourished by means of abiding in reverence.

Chu Hsi spoke of both exhaustion of principle and abiding in reverence. This point of view was based upon Ch'eng I's teachings; however, in Chu Hsi exhaustion of principle becomes far more comprehensive and abiding in reverence deeper. Chu Hsi also emphasized the compatibility of the two. There is, however, a tendency in Chu Hsi's learning for exhaustion of principle to be first and abiding in reverence second. In addition, since it was the principle of the objective nature and the pure nature of principle that were emphasized, Chu Hsi regarded nature as principle rather than mind. The result of this is that there tends to be a lack of vital spirit to life. Wang Yang-ming of the Ming period instead took nature as mind and directly based principle on mind, considering mind as principle. This point of view has its origin in Lu Hsiang-shan and to some degree falls into a kind of subjective dogmatism, that is, dwelling in one's own emotions, which may cause a misunderstanding about the relation between one's own will and the Principle of Heaven.

Among the Confucians of the late Ming period, some believe in the Chu Hsi learning, some in the Wang Yang-ming learning, and some adopt or reject various aspects of the learning of Chu and Wang and blend them together. It was these individuals who in the hardships of their times added their own experiences to the learning of the nature and the mind and sought to bring a measure of solace to their generation. These Confucians again emitted a fresh splendor of teachings. However, during the Ch'ing period this kind of learning suffered from an oppressive government and followed the road of decline. Fortunately it was inherited by the Japanese Confucians at the end of the Bakufu and the beginning of the Meiji and thereby came to see another expansion.

At the time that Confucianism was first introduced into Japan it was considered to conform to the Japanese national character. There was little resistance, and it was accepted without hesitation. The Confucian K'ang Yu-wei (1858–1927), representing a school of revolutionary new thought in the final part of the Ch'ing period, was exiled in Japan, and it is said that he was surprised to find the deep level of penetration of Confucianism among the Japanese people. Confucianism in certain ways appeared to be more compatible with Japanese culture than with Chinese. It certainly was not greeted with the same questions that surrounded the introduction of Buddhism.

Late Ming thought transmitted to the Japanese Confucians was accompanied by the poignant experiences of the age and the rising of national consciousness. These Confucians believed in the Chu Hsi learning, or they believed in the Yang-ming learning but with a different point of view from earlier Confucians. They received the Chu Hsi learning or the Yang-ming learning through the great Confucians at the end of the Ming period, Kao P'an-lung, who was a neo-Chu Hsi scholar, and Liu Tsung-chou, who was a neo-Wang Yang-ming scholar. Kao and Liu are both tragic figures, who in the end sacrificed themselves for the nation in the disorder of the government and the deterioration of morality at the end of the Ming period. They tried to rescue the state by advocating the learning of the nature and the mind and emphasizing the role of personal experience. The sincerity of their dying for their country is well known.

Kao observed that the principle of the nature that the Chu Hsi learning focused upon combined in a subtle way with the spiritually vigorous mind, and he made it central to his teachings to unify this mind by *seiza* in order to realize principle. Although his emphasis was the learning of Chu Hsi, he took from Wang Yang-ming the learning that focused upon the spiritual life of the mind. Liu observed that Yang-ming's mind-learning, which regarded innate knowledge as the Principle of Heaven, ran the risk of trusting an empty perception and gave rise to the unfortunate effect of indulging the selfish will. He instead emphasized Principle of Heaven as the master of the mind and took "sincerity of intention" as a special characteristic of learning. He tried to eliminate the errors of the Yang-ming learning and thought that he would also be able to correct the errors of the Chu Hsi learning. In general it can be said that Kao is a Chu Hsi scholar through the Yang-ming learning and Liu is a Yang-ming scholar through the Chu Hsi learning. Kusumoto Tanzan's learning is a product of both of these men, but it is especially influenced by the learning of Kao.

The time when Tanzan most deeply aimed at the Confucian learning of the nature and the mind was in 1851 when he traveled to the school of Satō Issai in Edo. He was able to listen to discussions between the senior disciples of Issai, Yoshimura Shūyō and Ōhashi Totsuan. Up to that time Tanzan had been in Hirato and had been devoting himself to writing poetry and reciting the Classics. His study was almost entirely the recitation and memorization of the Classics. In a letter Tanzan wrote from Edo he said, "Up to now my study has been erroneous. Thus the poetry I have written has been frivolous and weak and has no merit whatsoever. But I have now been able to meet a good teacher and friends, and seeing my faults to this point, my learning has greatly changed." Tanzan, enlightened to the faults of his old learning, wrote an essay called *The Record of the Pavilion of Repentance (Kaidō ki)* expressing his aims. He showed it to Yoshimura Shūyō, and Shūyō encouraged him by giving him the *Discussion of the Pavilion of Repentance (Kaidō setsu)*.

It seems that Tanzan was more attracted to the study of Totsuan than to that of Shūyō. When Tanzan met Totsuan he found his learning deep and his practice noble. Deeply impressed, he said, "If I had not met this person, certainly my whole life would have passed in vain." Shūyō's learning emphasizes the learning of Yang-ming; Totsuan's learning in those days was between that of Kao and Liu and inclined a little toward Chu Hsi. Later Totsuan came to the point of emphasizing the Chu Hsi learning. In the same period Tanzan departed from the learning of Kao and came to praise the learning of Chu Hsi through the interpretation of Yamazaki Ansai. From about that time he began to feel that he was no longer satisfied with the learning of either Shūyō or Totsuan, and little by little he left them.

The learning of the nature and the mind, of Tanzan, considered *seiza* as the entryway, but this was because Tanzan believed in the learning of Kao through Totsuan. Tanzan regarded the most important point of learning to be the enlightenment to the original face of the mind by means of *seiza*. He wrote of his enlightenment in a two-volume work known as the *Record of Learning and Repeating (Gakushū roku)*. Reading this one can understand the broad outlines of Tanzan's teaching. At first the *Record of Learning and Repeating* was named *Record of Learning and Thought (Gakushi roku)*, but afterward its name was changed. It is not clear when this happened. The words "learning and repeating" are based upon a saying in the *Analects*, "To learn and then from time to time to repeat what has been learned, that is a delight."

In the opening paragraphs of the *Record of Learning and Repeating,* Tanzan referred to a phrase by Ch'eng Hao, "a breast full of commiseration," that is, "Heaven and earth are completely filled with the mind of commiseration. Therefore, for Mencius, when one sees a child about to fall into a well, or one sees the dragging of the sacrificial cow near the palace, one feels as painful as if one were oneself suffering the pain." Following this statement Tanzan makes the comment: "When I was practicing *seiza* I realized a little of the substance of the mind and I wrote down this phrase." From its occurrence in Mencius the mind of commiseration has been called the "beginning of goodness." Tanzan himself came to be enlightened to the goodness of the substance of the mind by means of *seiza.* He was not only enlightened in body and mind by means of *seiza,* but also enlightened to this mind filling all Heaven and earth.

Why was it that Ch'eng Hao said, "a breast full of commiseration"? According to Ch'eng Hao, what is called goodness is the productive will of the universe. Since the mind that produces all things is immanent in oneself, this is the way to nurture people. Thus for the person of goodness all things within society are within oneself. "A breast full of commiseration" was used as a result of his own experience that the productive will of the universe is immanent.

Ch'eng Hao, as we have seen previously in the *Discussion of Understanding Goodness,* felt that if one knows goodness of this kind, then Heaven, earth, and all things are completely of one mind and identical substance. Ch'eng Hao felt that if one were to come to truly respect one's life, then one must first come to understand the original nature of goodness. For Ch'eng Hao the four virtues of righteousness, propriety, wisdom, and faith are all complete within our nature; they are nothing more than looking at goodness from different perspectives. He advised people to preserve and nourish goodness with a sincere, introspective, and humble mind. Even if knowing it remains only theoretical, he still regarded the knowing of goodness as of the first importance. Ch'eng Hao by nature was capable of knowing the Way directly. This was based upon his own great inborn wisdom. Chu Hsi regarded Ch'eng Hao as having advanced knowledge and revered his learning, but he told his disciples that they must not follow the example of Ch'eng Hao so long as they did not have his ability. Ch'eng Hao, as has been previously mentioned, would sometimes practice *seiza,* though he did not base it upon Master Chou's regarding quietude as fundamental. Instead he regarded sincerity and reverence as the principles and emphasized the effort to penetrate both quietude and activity. This is the reason for his discussion of abiding in reverence.

What was Tanzan's conclusion about the Way? He died in 1884 at the age of fifty-six. While ill he wrote the expression: "I await Heaven's command to rest." This was his last writing and can be said to have stated the conclusion of his thought. According to my own teacher, Dr. Kusumoto Masatsugu, who was Tanzan's grandchild, what Tanzan called Heaven was the great love that returns to goodness. It is happiness, compassion, kindness, and peace, and it is the production of life. Therefore, for Tanzan substance was not different from the real world. He said, "Substance is function and function is substance." The establishment of the effort to "return to quietude" exists in this. There is no doubt that the phrase from the *Book of History,* "I await Heaven's command to rest," expresses Tanzan's final condition of resting himself. This is the very thing that supported the foundation of his life, covering politics, learning and poetry all through his life. Based upon this, the Way that Tanzan sought was nothing but the productive will of Heaven, that is, goodness, which rears things with compassion and love and harmonious force and rears them without any exhaustion. This is the penetrating way of Tanzan's politics, learning and poetry as well as his entire life. The characteristics of Tanzan's learning was a return to the original nature of humankind by first understanding the root itself through *seiza.* The words "return to quietude" transmit this idea well. Originally from Lao Tzu, Tanzan's use of these words is entirely different, since Lao Tzu neglected the way of the common life of humankind and returned to the Way of Heaven. Tanzan had a seal engraved with these two characters and always used them.

Rules for Returning in Seven

When Kusumoto Tanzan was in Edo he concentrated on the learning of *seiza* realization. He once made a trip to Matsushima with several friends, and although he was traveling, he never neglected his diligent study. This effort itself was not easy, but he felt that if there was even a single error, harmful effects could be easily produced. In other words, the attempt to obtain quietude itself is a source of agitation for the mind. If one tries to force the practice, then one will mistake its image for the attaining of truth. There is also a fear of sinking into the error of "assisting it to grow." This phrase, "assisting it to grow," is from Mencius. According to Mencius, if one grieves over the slow growth of corn and attempts to pull it up in order to speed up its growth, then it dies. It is the same with the study of the Way: assistance can do tremendous harm. "Assisting it to grow" is something that can harm the original nature by means of the intervention of human activity. If there is this "assisting it to grow," then the naturalness of the Principle of Heaven is lost. Tanzan feared this.

Part of Tanzan's *Matsushima Travel Journal (Matsushima kōki)* concerns this issue.

> 8th month, 20th day, very quiet. Though I practiced *seiza* very solemnly, my mind roamed and would not become settled. I thought that this must be because I was on a journey and so I greatly increased my introspective activity. However, since I was inexperienced in this kind of effort to settle the mind, whenever something would come up, my mind would again become agitated. What can be done? After a short time I thought that I must restrict the mind with greater energy and must not dissipate my vital force. And then when I practiced it, I was able to obtain a certain settlement of the mind. But then I suddenly became aware of a certain level of "assisting it to grow." Admonishing myself, the only thought that seemed appropriate was, "realization of the Principle of Heaven wherever one is."

This phrase "realization of the Principle of Heaven wherever one is," is from Chan Jo-shui, a school friend of Wang Yang-ming, who felt it to be essential to his own learning. Chan praised Ch'eng Hao's "realization of the Principle of Heaven," but added the words, "wherever one is." The reason for this is that if one realizes the Principle of Heaven in an active place, then the realization of it in a quiet place is simple. On the contrary, if one has obtained realization in a quiet place, it is of little use and it is difficult to avoid the agitation of the mind. It is very natural that Tanzan would have realized the harm of assisting growth in the effort of *seiza* realization, but he extended his thought to Chan's learning of "realization of the Principle of Heaven wherever one is."

In this way Tanzan's learning of realization matured step by step, and soon he came to understand that his effort must be both natural and beyond the limits of human behavior. For Tanzan the difficulty of learning in this period was equal to the acute practice recorded in Kao P'an-lung's *Recollection of the Toils of Learning,* which Tanzan at that point respected tremendously. I would like to introduce this writing: it is a very detailed account of Kao's self-realization and had a profound effect upon Tanzan's realization learning.

> In the autumn of 1594 I headed for Chieh-yang. When I looked within myself, in my mind principle and desire waged battle and my mind could obtain no peace. In Wu-lin I talked for several days with Lu Ku-ch'iao

and Wu Tzu-wang. One day Ku-ch'iao suddenly asked me, "What is the original substance like?" When I heard his words I was astonished and answered by saying, "Without sound, without smell," but in fact I had no true understanding and this came only from my mouth.

Later we crossed the river and that night the moon was bright as if it were purifying the world. I sat near the Liu-ho Tower; the scenery of the mountains and the Yangtse was beautiful. I drank with my friends and it was a most agreeable of times. Then suddenly this happiness diminished and I felt as if I were restrained in my mood. I exerted myself to rouse my spirits, but my mind did not accompany me. Late in the night after the others had gone I went on board the boat and increased my self introspection. I said to myself, "The scenery I saw today was beautiful, but what about my own mind?" Accordingly I investigated the foundation, and for the first time understood that not having seen anything of the Way, there was no use at all to the mind and body. I was driven on by this and thought, "If I do not understand this during this trip, then I shall not understand why I was born in this world."

The next day in the boat I arranged the mat and seriously set up rules and regulations as well as practicing what Chu Hsi called "half-day of *seiza,* half-day of study." When the mind would become unsettled during the practice of *seiza* I would consult the teachings of Master Ch'eng and Master Chu and practice one by one Ch'eng Hao's "sincerity and reverence," Master Chou's "regarding quietude as fundamental," Yang Shih's "viewing of pleasure, anger, sorrow, and joy when they are unmanifest," and Li Yen-p'ing's "sit in silence and purify the mind; realize for oneself the Principle of Heaven." In fact I kept these in front of me throughout the entire day. At night I did not undress and only when weary to the bone did I sleep. When I awoke from sleep I again practiced *seiza,* repeating and alternating these various rules. When the vital force of the mind was clear and peaceful, there was a feeling of filling all Heaven and earth, but this was only fleeting.

The trip lasted for two months and fortunately I was without normal involvements. The scenery was beautiful. My servant and I were mutually supportive and it was a very peaceful trip. At night I sipped wine. We stopped the boat at a green mountain and drifted to and fro beside a rushing stream. I practiced *seiza* on a rock. The refreshing sound of the stream flowing, the beautiful sound of the birds calling, the growth of trees and flourishing of the bamboo, although all these things pleased my mind, yet my mind was not attached to the setting. I passed by Ting-chou and traveled on by land. There was an inn and a small tower. To the front were mountains, to the rear a nearby rushing stream. I climbed it and was very happy. Since I held in my hand the collected works of the

Ch'eng brothers I opened it and saw that Ch'eng Hao had said, "In the midst of affairs and activities, and even in the midst of warfare, with a poor life joy still exists though water is my drink and a bent arm [my pillow]. The myriad changes all are caused by the conduct of the mind; in reality there is not a single affair. Accordingly I knew that life itself in reality was not a single thing, and thereupon a single thought which had so far been attached to me and had not separated from me now suddenly disappeared. At that moment, suddenly it felt as if a load of a hundred pounds had fallen to the ground from off my back. Then again like a flash of lightning I could see through the original substance, and following I was merged with the inexhaustible changes of the cosmos until there was no differentiation of Heaven and humankind or interior and exterior. At this point I saw that Heaven, earth, and the four directions were all my mind, the substance of the body was their field, and the square inch of space of the mind was their foundation. This is the spiritual and luminous character, but I do not know what to say of it. Ordinarily I despised scholars who discussed enlightenment with grand display, but the enlightenment at this time was something that was completely "ordinary." Accordingly I knew that the "ordinary" effort was significant for people.

In his *Agenda for Dwelling in the Mountains,* Kao demonstrates a daily schedule for dwelling in the mountains. Before the morning meal he lit incense and read the *Book of Changes.* After the morning meal he studied, and after the noonday meal he went out walking and humming. With the arising of an oppressive feeling he would shut his eyes and rest for a short time, sip tea, light incense, and after clearing the mind return to reading. As evening came on he could cease all of this and practice instead *seiza,* sitting until the length of a single stick of incense had burned out. When the evening sun set behind the mountains he went outside to view the clouds and also to take care of trees and shrubs. The evening meal was plain and simple; he would drink a little wine. Then when his countenance became as if gloriously drunk, he would wander at will. Before retiring he would again practice *seiza* and when he became sleepy, he would sleep. Such was his life.

This can be called his actual practice of what Chu Hsi referred to as "half-day of *seiza,* half-day of study." His extraordinary efforts with *seiza* are demonstrated by the many discussions of *seiza* even in his poetry. In the poem called "To Sing of Quiet-Sitting" (*Ching-tso yin*), we see that Kao loved practicing *seiza* in the mountains, by the water's edge, among the flowers, and under the trees.

What did Kao say in terms of the rules of *seiza*? Two essays address this question: *A Discussion of Quiet-Sitting,* and *A Later Discussion of Quiet-Sitting.* A *Discussion of Quiet-Sitting* speaks to this very directly.

In *seiza* even the least human activity must not be increased. It is to become quiet in an ordinary way from silence. The word "ordinary" is very significant and should not be passed over carelessly because it is the substance of human nature. When the substance of human nature is clear and pure and it has no single thing in it, this is called "ordinary." It is the naturalness of the Principle of Heaven. One must realize this for oneself and then one will obtain oneself. Do not forcefully remove false thoughts in quietude. When the true substance appears, false thoughts naturally subside. When the oppressive force arises again, do not force it and do not remove it. Actually, when the false thoughts become clear, the oppressive force will naturally become clear and the foundation of human nature will be realized. It is a return to the quietude of human nature, not an adding of intention or knowledge. If even a single thought is added, the original substance is lost.

When the transition from quietude to activity is an "ordinary" one, then activity is itself quiet and the time of quietude and activity as well as activity and quietude are the same. It is simply "ordinary." Therefore it can be said that it is neither quietude nor activity! It is only the scholar who has realized this through *seiza* practice, however, who can discuss the substance that is "neither activity nor quietude." If quietude produces results, then activity will certainly obtain true results. This is called reverence, this is called goodness, this is called sincerity.

According to this essay, if the effort of practicing *seiza* is natural, that is, not so much as even a little human effort is added, then as a matter of course one can be enlightened to the naturalness of the Principle of Heaven. Kao's word "ordinary" indicates nothing more than that both substance and effort must be natural. This direction of his thought was from the influence of Wang Yang-ming, who said that if effort is not from the strength of the naturalness of the original substance, then it is not true effort. The Yang-ming learning speaks of the unity of the original substance and the effort. He thought that true effort must be from the naturalness of the original substance, and to be enlightened to the original substance in the mind was the basis for discussion of the unity of the two. Among the Chu Hsi scholars at the end of the Ming period, many received this influence of the Yang-ming learning and spoke of the unity of the original substance and effort; however, they tended to place the emphasis upon the effort. Kao in his discussion of *seiza* emphasized the naturalness of the substance and therefore the naturalnesss of the effort and advocated the term "ordinary."

When the condition of "ordinary" is looked at closely, however, its achievement is extremely difficult. The reason is because it is the point of unity between the substance and the effort. In other words, while making effort one must also transcend effort. Accordingly, Kao thought that for the beginner it was better to have the effort of Chu Hsi's rigid model of abiding in reverence. This is discussed in Kao's *Later Discussion of Seiza*.

In the method of *seiza* the novice nourishes the nature of his mind by means of it and the beginner regards it as a way of becoming a novice. As a rule the mind of the beginner adheres to false thoughts and they do not know how to recognize the substance of the "ordinary." When they emphasize the "ordinary," the mind instead becomes scattered and dispersed. Therefore it is essential to unite the body and the mind and to consider this unity as fundamental. What is called unity is the substance of the "ordinary." When considering it fundamental an intention comes into play; however, this intention is not an intention to become attached to. If there is no attachment to the intention and in the mind there are no affairs, then it is unified. If there is attachment to an intention then there is no unification. Then how does one obtain the intention of being not attached to an intention? It is best to be well ordered and dignified in appearance. If that is the case, the mind will naturally be unified. Then when this effort has gradually matured it will finally become "ordinary." Therefore, regarding unity as fundamental is the completion of learning from beginning to the end.

What Kao considered to be the basis of regarding quietude as fundamental was the Ch'eng-Chu School description of reverence as "mastering unity without aims." This process, "mastering unity without aims," means to consider unity of first importance and make no strivings for things. It is a single-minded effort and, in the Ch'eng-Chu School, an ordered and dignified mind directed toward the Principle of Heaven. Originally, reverence was nothing other than a mind of propriety and provided the mind with a way to seek principle through the controlling of the selfishness of the mind. It is nothing but the mind becoming the original mind, that is, a return to humankind's true nature. This is the effort to nourish and preserve humankind's true nature.

This order and dignity were considered to extend to mind and body, interior and exterior. For Kusumoto Tanzan as well, the external appearance was ordered and dignified, and the interior mind was also ordered and dignified.

Order and dignity were said to include both interior and exterior. Long ago Confucius also discussed the importance of reverence saying, "In handling affairs, be reverent," "Cultivate reverence in the self," "Act with reverence in your duties and be honest," and others of this kind. This is simply common sense. A deeper philosophical meaning was provided by the Ch'eng-Chu School, and eventually it reached a unity of substance and effort.

What I want to speak of here is why the Ch'eng-Chu School did not advocate regarding of quietude as fundamental, but spoke instead of abiding in reverence. It was said by both Ch'eng and Chu that there was a bias toward quietude in Master Chou's regarding quietude as fundamental. When we speak of the substance of human nature in terms such as "quietude" and "activity," then I must say that it belongs to quietude. Even though I have said that it belongs to quietude, since it is human nature it includes both activity and quietude. In other words, quietude in terms of original substance is different from quietude in terms of temporality. However, quietude in terms of substance is not something that exists separately from activity and quietude in terms of temporality. Consequently, effort must include both activity and quietude. For that process nothing is equal to reverence, and it can be said that in comparison with the learning of Lu Hsiang-shan and Wang Yang-ming, Ch'eng and Chu did emphasize quietude.

The genesis of reverence from order and dignity was spoken of by Master Ch'eng, and Chu Hsi transmitted it. It is more than this, however, for Chu Hsi adopted the reverence spoken of by Master Ch'eng's disciples Yin T'un (1071–1142) and Hsieh Liang-tso (1050–1103). Yin T'un explained reverence as "the mind that is unified and does not allow a single thing." Hsieh Liang-tso said, "Always alert." "Always alert" means that the mind is always attentive and always observant. Let me put this in a simpler way. The mind is always clear and never obscure. Initially this expression came from Zen Buddhism, but in this context it is very different, suggesting a moral perception that is constantly clear. Chu Hsi understood the various interpretations of reverence, and of the three definitions it was the order and dignity that penetrated the other two. It is true that Tanzan emphasized Chu Hsi's abiding in reverence, but his special feature lies in emphasizing *seiza* as the root and trunk. Thus he said, "Reverence is order and dignity and the law of order and dignity is best seen in *seiza.*"

While in Edo, Tanzan followed the learning of the nature and mind emphasizing *seiza*. After he returned from Edo he was even more studious in this direction. He came to believe even more in Kao P'an-lung's learning, and he practiced Kao's *Rules for Returning in Seven* and was more and more sincere in his *seiza* realization. What follows is Kao's *Rules for Returning in Seven.*

What is called returning in seven is taken from the *Book of Changes*, which says, "On the seventh day comes return." [This is a statement in the hexagram of return in the *Book of Changes*. A single *yang* line is dropped off and is said to return again in seven days.] At the time that one is a little weary of activity, then one should immediately practice *seiza* for a seven-day period in order to settle the mind. Thereupon the body will be rested and nourished and the spirit clarified and the life vitality restored. On the first day rest both the body and the mind in a relaxed setting. If you want to sleep then sleep. Feel relaxed and at ease as much as possible and the vital force will become refreshed and the oppressive force will completely disappear. Then enter a hall, burn incense, and practice *seiza*. The rules of *seiza* are simply to arouse the mind to constant clarity and not permit the mind to be scattered by things. If the mind is not scattered by things, then the spirit will congeal naturally and will return to the original nature. At that time one must not employ any human effort, there must be no attachments and there must be no thought of producing results. However, for one who first practices *seiza*, since one does not know the method to get ahold of the mind, the person should try to master the great teachings of the sages and the worthies; then the person will proceed with it naturally.

When one has reached the third day of *seiza* then one is certain to reach the subtleties. After the fourth and fifth days one must be careful and avoid falling into laziness. After eating, walk slowly a little, do not indulge in wine or meat. When one does indulge in wine and meat the mind becomes more and more stirred up. When resting also do not take off one's clothes. At the time one wants to go to sleep, then go to bed: when one awakens, get up immediately. After seven days of this kind of practice then the spirit will be filled and there will be no illness.

Kao's *Rules for Returning in Seven* are most appropriate as rules for *seiza*.

Tanzan in the beginning adopted the learning of Liu Tsung-chou. Liu's learning, as Tanzan said, was based in Yang-ming's learning. However, the learning of Kao and Liu are closely related to each other. Thus Tanzan also said:

> In the Confucian learning at the end of the Ming period, I recommend the two scholars Kao P'an-lung and Liu Tsung-chou. Initially the two were very different, but in their later years and in their discussions of their enlightenment to the Way, they are in complete agreement with each other.

What Liu called human nature, as we have said earlier, is the ruling mind; strictly speaking, the ruling mind without a ruler. This is what Liu calls an "intention," and there was thought to be knowledge in this intention.

The understanding of human nature by Tanzan is very similar to this. Liu spoke figuratively of the rudder of a boat; Tanzan spoke of a compass. In the terminology of Zen Buddhism it is called "the old master." Tanzan first seeks to be enlightened to human nature. He sought this "old master who manifests the original face." In modern terms, it is the establishment of subjectivity. In terms of Tanzan, he felt that if he constantly acted in such a way as to seek subjectivity, then he would awaken as if from a dream and would return to life from the dead, all in a sudden flash with the subjectivity displaying its own distinctive character. Tanzan said that he was enlightened to his nature in this way and obtained a clue to the effort. He realized that regarding quietude as fundamental was the main principle. That is to say, when we divide the mind into substance and function, since the substance of the mind is quietude, if this substance of the mind is established by means of the effort of returning to quietude, then the function works of itself. Therefore Tanzan says that above all else it is important to establish the substance by means of a return to quietude.

This way of thinking is very compatible with the quietist branch of the Yang-ming School, and it is for this reason that Tanzan entertained the teachings of Nieh Pao and Lo Hung-hsien. However, it seems to me that Tanzan emphasized Chu Hsi's learning that took human nature as principle, and from the beginning he opposed Yang-ming's learning that considered mind as principle. Nevertheless, why did he adopt the discussion of this branch of the Yang-ming School? It was because the discussion of returning to quietude by Nieh and Lo considered quietude to be fundamental, and it had the possibility of returning Yang-ming's learning to the position of Chu Hsi. This was because the Chu Hsi learning originally explained the principle of nature as quiet when compared with the Yang-ming learning, which saw the principle of mind as active.

At the time that he practiced the *Rules for Returning in Seven,* Tanzan's learning was a kind of Chu Hsi learning, but he did not concentrate solely upon Chu Hsi. Later, however, he was involved with advanced research on the Chu Hsi learning and came to the conclusion that only Chu Hsi's learning was the orthodox teaching. In this respect he became slightly critical of Kao P'an-lung's learning. That is to say, in Kao's learning it was difficult to avoid the potential harm of being biased toward quietude, and eventually Tanzan adopted Chu Hsi's investigation of things and exhaustion of principle in order to avoid this. However, through Tanzan's serious attention to realization, he felt that the fundamental meaning of Chu Hsi's learning was to regard preservation and nourishment of the mind and nature as the root of the exhaustion of principle. He thought that it was simply not enough to be engrossed only in abiding in reverence and exhaustion of principle, or the parallel development of knowledge and action.

Since the Yang-ming learning, and the Lu Hsiang-shan learning that was its origin, take mind as principle, they bring about a practice overflowing in life's vital force and permit a person to have a vigorous moral belief. However, they lack the certainty and concrete knowledge to maintain in a rigorous way the mind and nature of the human being. They also lack the proper investigation into each principle in the human being's common life and the certitude and concreteness to realize it to the highest and purest ideal. There is thus a fear of sinking into a feeling of dogmatism and of creating hindrances in the accomplishment of service to the world. Since the Chu Hsi learning of Kao went through the learning of Yang-ming, it discerns the subtle aspect of mind as principle and realizes this, but it fails to investigate broadly concerning the principles of all things in the fashion of Chu Hsi. Tanzan said that Kao's learning was biased toward quietude because it neglected undertakings in the world on account of this weakness. Is this right? Probably Tanzan thought so. In what is called *seiza* realization, Kao and Tanzan had a very similar position because they reached the point of regarding the Chu Hsi learning as essential.

Seiza and the Exhaustion of Principle

Kusumoto Tanzan eventually considered preservation and nourishment of nature and mind as the foundation of his learning. This was the result of his practice of the learning of realization and also the influence of the Chu Hsi learning through the Yamazaki Ansai School. The Ansai School held an important position during the Tokugawa period, and its special contribution was to regard learning as not simply an issue of the accruing of knowledge. The orthodox lineage of the Ansai School was transmitted to Tanzan and his brother, Sekisui, and thus the Ansai learning gave forth its splendor because of these two at the end of the Bakufu and the beginning of the Meiji periods.

When Tanzan returned from Edo to Hirato he attempted to renovate the Confucian learning in Hirato by stressing the learning of nature and mind. It opposed the trends of the day, however, and for this reason was censored by the senior Confucians. As a result Tanzan returned to his native place, Hariojima in Sasebo. During this period he devoted himself to his research on Chu Hsi. He also built his hermitage, the Pavilion of the Toils of Learning, and taught his disciples. With the passage of the days, Tanzan engaged in the Chu

Hsi learning and came himself to see that it was the orthodox learning. At about the same time Ōhashi Totsuan of Edo also praised the Chu Hsi learning. The result was that these two individuals quite unexpectedly praised Chu Hsi. Nevertheless there was a difference between them. Tanzan's Chu Hsi learning, as we have already seen, was a learning that emphasized investigation of things and exhaustion of principle and that considered preservation and nourishment of mind and nature as the foundation. Totsuan, however, excelled in the analysis of principle, and although he too engaged in investigation of things and exhaustion of principle, he did not reach the point of considering preservation and nourishment of mind and nature as the foundation. According to Tanzan, when investigation of things and exhaustion of principle do not consider nourishment and the preservation of human nature and mind as the foundation, it is similar to Totsuan; it lacks what Chu Hsi called the consummate or final effort, and as a result it falls into worldly learning, aiming only at self-interest.

When Tanzan became familiar with the Ansai School he was about thirty-four years old. This was after he had heard of the learning from his younger brother, Sekisui, who had returned from Satō Issai in Edo. He had earlier inquired from a member of the Ansai School, Kaneko Sōzan (1785–1865); however, he did not pay any particular attention to the Ansai School itself. The teacher most revered by Tanzan was Tsukida Mōsai of Higo, who transmitted the Ansai School. In fact Tanzan's own acceptance of the Ansai learning was in large part due to Mōsai. In the beginning he had doubts about the learning of Mōsai, but some of his disciples had attended Mōsai's private school. Hearing of his character and learning and reading his books, he began to revere him. Tanzan himself did not have the opportunity to meet Mōsai during his lifetime though they corresponded. However, his younger brother, Sekisui, visited Mōsai, and Mōsai had great expectations of him.

Mōsai placed importance upon the preservation and nourishment of mind and nature and endeavored to seek for *seiza* realization. He considered the original Way to be in establishing the substance and acting upon the function. He also considered abiding in reverence and preservation and nourishment as important to the effort to establish the substance and took *seiza* as the root of abiding in reverence. When he was twenty-four years old he had traveled to Kyoto and followed the learning of Senju Kensai (1789–1859), and in spite of destitution, he applied himself with unyielding diligence and effort in the learning of realization. Suddenly one night he became aware of the true root of Heaven, earth, and all things. After he returned to Kyūshū, he cut off relations with all friends and earnestly investigated the true root of the Way, attempting to pursue it in the reading of books and things in general. He followed this course for about eight or nine years and gradually obtained a true enlightenment. At that point he said that he saw no contradictions between the books of the sages and the ways of the world.

Mōsai was a man of hard work and diligence, and we see evidence of this in his learning of *seiza* realization. It appears that in the beginning he still did not avoid human effort, and he struggled for several years but obtained no results. Accordingly, he doubled the effort, thinking he would get fairly good results. However, the more the effort was sincere, the more it was apparent that he was "assisting it to grow." Even with the effort relaxed, however, there still was no enlightenment. This was because the mind was not yet mature. For this condition nothing is better than to unify the mind and body and make the mind naturally reverential. He came to realize that the way most people try to reach the secret of the Great Way of the sages and worthies was like plowing the land without a plow or like crossing water without riding in a boat. Consequently, he took abiding in reverence, nourishment and preservation, and regarding quietude as fundamental as his foundation. Mōsai transmitted the orthodoxy of the Ansai learning. His realization of quietude and reverence passed through painstaking cultivation. Though he was obedient to the Chu Hsi learning that took the investigation of things and preservation and nourishment as its essential, Mōsai considered realization as fundamental because he felt keenly sorrowful about the attitude of Chu Hsi scholars who, though they verbally advocated the abiding in reverence and the exhausting of principle, did not put it into practice.

It is clear that Mōsai practiced what Chu Hsi said of the exhaustion of principle and the abiding in reverence. Tanzan, who paid close attention to realization, knew the learning of Mōsai and revered it. In Tanzan's *Record of Learning and Repeating* there is a paragraph devoted to his grief at the death of Mōsai. In it Tanzan said that his own learning, which focused upon Chu Hsi and in which he was able to rid himself of worldly concerns, was from what he had learned of nourishment and preservation in the Ansai School through Mōsai. This was expressed with a great deal of humility, and Tanzan keenly felt the importance of preservation and nourishment and realization even more through Mōsai. It is probably the case that he believed this to be the special character of the Chu Hsi learning.

What is the relation in Chu Hsi's practice of *seiza* between *seiza* and abiding in reverence? It is necessary to examine Chu Hsi's position in order to understand the *seiza* realization of Tanzan. When Chu Hsi was young he had no father, but when still young he received the teaching of Li Yen-p'ing who was a friend of his father. Yen-p'ing taught Chu Hsi that "The way of learning is not something that you give this or that theory about. It is only the realization of the Principle of Heaven by sitting in silence and purifying the mind." Yen-p'ing had been taught by his own teacher, Lo Ts'ung-yen: "Practice *seiza* and you will see the vital form of the unmanifest of pleasure, anger, sorrow, and joy." Yen-p'ing, however, taught Chu Hsi that it was in the unmanifest that the true ruler existed, that is, the vital form of the Principle of Heaven. Thus when one practices *seiza* and the mind is clarified, the mind returns to its original form. Thereupon it is understood as a perfect ruler. This ruler is the embodiment of the Principle of Heaven. It is said that this can be realized only in *seiza*. At the time that Chu Hsi was taught by Yen-p'ing he was still young. The result was that he could not take in everything that Yen-p'ing said. He endeavored, however, to master Yen-p'ing's teaching, raising questions over and over. The result was that he was able to understand through *seiza* the significance of the human mind possessing both the original pure nature as well as the material nature.

At this time in the court there was a faction for the new laws of Wang An-shih (1021–86), and because the policy was to appoint talent that was in retirement, Chu Hsi and other officials in retirement were given their orders. However, Chu Hsi did not consider it principled and pure to attend the court of the new laws, and as a result he declined it, considering instead the nourishment of the nature and the mind as the proper course of the gentleman.

However, Hu Hsien (1082–1162) came to serve in the court, but Chu Hsi was not content and wrote a sarcastic poem about it. Let us look at one or two verses from the poem.

Holding firm to the recluse life, resting in the empty valley,
Wind and moonlight over a river demand my attention.
Entrust floating clouds to stretch and whirl calmly,
Yet for ten thousand years the azure mountains are just azure.

A scholar by the name of Hu Hung saw this poem of Chu Hsi and felt that "it had substance, but it did not have function." That is, it was not an active work and instead sank into quietude. He said it was not adequate and warned Chu Hsi of this, writing a poem that suggested that true quietude had to be trained for in the midst of activity. The following is a verse from his poem.

The hermit is partial to the azure mountains' beauty,
This is because the azure of the azure mountains never grows old.
The clouds come out of the mountains and rain in Heaven and earth,
Having once been washed, the mountains are even more lovely.

Unlike Li Yen-p'ing, Hu Hung felt that since the substance of the unmanifest, that is, the Principle of Heaven, can only be seen functioning in the manifest mind, unless one understands the "subtle beginnings" of the Principle of Heaven in the manifest, it is impossible to nourish and preserve the mind. He thought that in preserving and nourishing the substance of the unmanifest solely through quietude, one would sink into the uselessness of Zen learning. Accordingly his first priority was the understanding of the "subtle beginnings," and only afterward was there preservation and nourishment of the unmanifest. For him the characteristic of learning was attention to the manifest.

When Chu Hsi saw Hu Hung's poem his mind was greatly moved and he personally visited his school, but time had passed and Hu Hung was no longer alive. Thus Chu Hsi heard Hu Hung's teaching from his disciple Chang Nan-hsien (1133–1180), and he himself followed the focus upon the manifest, that is, the understanding of the "subtle beginnings." However, he soon realized that this learning was deficient in what is called consummate effort. Based upon what Chu Hsi said, Hu focused upon the understanding of the "subtle beginnings" in the exhausting of the principle and paid little attention to the effort of preserving and nourishing. Because of this his mind was biased to activity and had no taste for the deep, concealed, and pure. Activity can be chaotic, and he was not able to see the deep form of serenity of the former sages and worthies. This is described in Chu Hsi's *Discussion of Personal Errors* (*Hui-wu shuo*).

"Subtle beginnings" for Chu Hsi is realized through preservation and nourishment. After all, the Principle of Heaven is something inherent in the human mind, and if the mind becomes darkened with worldly desires, it will become clear naturally. This is not something to be sought separately. The investigation of things and the exhaustion of principle does not go beyond clarifying what is itself naturally clear.

The effort of preservation and nourishment incorporates both activity and quietude. Therefore, as Master Ch'eng says, act in such a way that the mind by means of reverence will not be darkened by worldly desires. The result of this is the discernment of the Principle of Heaven and its realization. In that case, what is the consummate or final effort? It is simply abiding in reverence, and preservation and nourishment. For Chu Hsi the effort of preservation and nourishment must incorporate both activity and quietude, but what Master Chou called regarding quietude as fundamental has the same meaning. When only quietude is spoken of it is biased, and it is for this reason that Master Ch'eng did not speak of quietude, but of reverence instead. Therefore, although he spoke of the importance of *seiza*, he said, "Do not only pursue the effort solely in a quiet place. One must experience it in activity as well. The sages and worthies did not mean to teach only by practicing *seiza* and said it was important to use effort wherever one might be." Chu Hsi followed Master Ch'eng's abiding in reverence and considered the teaching regarding quietude as fundamental of Master Chou and Yen-p'ing as defective in its inclination toward quietude, especially the discussion by Yen-p'ing. This is an issue that continues with Chu Hsi until late in his life. Tanzan considered Chu Hsi's discussion of personal errors important, and said:

> Now of those who discuss the Sung learning, many lack what Chu Hsi called the consummate or final effort. Chu Hsi said, "Because I started the effort of the beginning scholar on the 'subtle beginnings,' the effort of preservation and nourishment does not appear in daily life and the ordinary mind is always inclined to activity. There is no taste of deep purity and when it appears in speech and conduct, the speech and conduct are also impatient and frivolous and the form of the former sages and worthies disappears." Thus one should be introspective.

Chu Hsi obviously had misgivings about Yen-p'ing's discussion of regarding quietude as fundamental, though, according to Tanzan, late in life he returned to Yen-p'ing.

For Chu Hsi, as we have seen previously, abiding in reverence and exhaustion of principle are regarded as mutually supporting and inseparable. In what follows, Tanzan discusses this.

> I recently discovered a concise and convenient method of learning involving two major methods, the mastering of reverence and the exhaustion of principle. The mastering of reverence incorporates both activity and quietude, and the effort to achieve it is not limited to one. For the beginner to get hold of the beginnings the method is *seiza*. The exhaustion of principle includes interior and exterior, and the effort may be of many kinds. For the beginner to get hold of a steadiness of character, the method should be study. Chu Hsi set up a routine for the sake of learning, saying, "Half-day of *seiza*, half-day of study." This is it.

The importance of study in Chu Hsi's understanding of the exhaustion of principle was a persistent theme for Tanzan, but it should not be forgotten that in study Chu Hsi himself insisted that *seiza* was still necessary.

> Formerly the scholar Ch'en Lieh agonized over his study because he had a bad memory. One day, however, he read what Mencius had said—"The way of learning is nothing other than seeking the mind that has

strayed"—and suddenly he was open to enlightenment. He had not been able to seek his own mind that had strayed; how was it possible to memorize what was written in books? Saying this, he shut his door and began the practice of *seiza* and sought the mind that had strayed for about a hundred days without any study. After that it reached the point that, no matter what he was reading, a single reading and he would not forget it.

In reading, first collect together mind and body, and quiet the mind a little. Then open a book and it will be effective. If the mind is driven toward external things and is chaotic, then the mind is completely separated from the Way. In this kind of situation one cannot read. There is no need for any explanation, just simply shut the gate and for a period of ten days to two weeks sit correctly. After that when one looks at books one will understand that what I say is not nonsense.

First of all, in learning *seiza* it is important to act in such a way as to cleanse and wash the dust of worldly ways by reading passages of the former sages and worthies in quietude. Then for the first time the effort will emerge in one's learning.

When I read nowadays and find that the spirit is dissipated, I reflect upon myself by practicing *seiza* and I gather together the effects. What about attempting this? Without a doubt one is quite sure to find it effective.

In addition to these statements Chu Hsi also said that though one studies, unless one unifies the spirit, study will have no flavor. He said that at times *seiza* will be more effective than study, and to some degree he dissuaded the disciples from looking at literature and advised them instead to practice *seiza*. However, Chu Hsi said that it was wrong to treat study and *seiza* as two different activities.

Dependent upon the individual, when *seiza* is practiced there can be two different approaches: on the one hand, there can be an elimination of thought; on the other hand, there can be thought of the Principle of the Way. However, don't think that there are actually two ways. Moreover, we must not say that the effort in *seiza* and study is any different. When preserving and nourishing the mind by *seiza*, it is particularly important to realize the Principle of the Way. This is called the true preservation and nourishment. However, it is not by arousing and encouraging the mind to sweep away evil and deluded thoughts by means of the Principle of the Way. Instead if one thinks only of the Principle of the Way, then naturally it will reach a point of not stirring evil thoughts. The fault of people at present is that *seiza* and reading become two rather than one, and as a result mistakes arise.

Chu Hsi says that one cannot dislike study and practice only *seiza,* grieving over the scattering of thoughts. Once peace of mind has been obtained, then one should return to the process of study. I want to cite Chu Hsi's caution about the seeking of quietude. One must not seek after quietude simply because one dislikes activity. *Seiza* does not mean seeking after only quietude by completely abandoning what one should do. Chu Hsi also distinguished between *seiza* and *zazen* as ways of concentration because the latter cuts off all thought, while the former does not bother itself with wasteful thought and becomes naturally settled and peaceful. *Seiza* also seeks an attentiveness. If there are matters to attend to, they are done, and when completed there is a return to a peaceful and settled mind. When the disciples complained that they could not make their minds quiet in spite of every effort because many miscellaneous thoughts came out while they were practicing *seiza* in their leisure time each day, Chu Hsi taught them Master Ch'eng's words:

> Since the mind is something that is originally alive, if one acts in such a way as to restrict it, it is unsatisfactory. It is good as long as it is not trifling with useless thought. If one acts in such a way as earnestly to seek quietude, instead one will be accompanied by abundant thoughts. Since it is already good, one should not bind oneself or act in haste, and then the mind naturally becomes quiet.

In addition, Chu Hsi answered two questions concerning the rules of *seiza:* "In *seiza* is it best to practice only *seiza* and be without examination and speculation?" Moreover, "In *seiza* it is good to discontinue useless and trivial thought: if this is so, will one nourish the mind and be at ease?" His answers: "In *seiza* don't restrain thought too much. It is best if you leave things as they are. If when sitting one closes the eyes, then thoughts will be produced." "It is of no use to get rid of all thought; unless there is actually evil thought it is all right."

Chu Hsi spoke of the importance of *seiza,* but it was not to exceed the effort of reverence even at times of quietude. This means that he did not consider it an especially essential feature of the effort of reverence. In a letter to his disciple Chang Hsia, he said:

> Ch'eng Hao advised people to practice *seiza,* but it was at the time that they were free from being engrossed in learning. At the time that there are no affairs one practices *seiza;* but when *seiza* becomes a special

effort, it is the *zazen* of Buddhism. If it is only the effort of reverence then it will naturally incorporate both activity and quietude and reach the point that effort will not stop.

The Ch'ing period scholar, Li Kuang-ti (1642–1718) said that reverence in Ch'eng and Chu was the total effort of activity and quietude and that it was not inclined to one or the other. He also said that Master Chou's regarding quietude as fundamental was something that hit the mark and, as a result, regarding quietude as fundamental in reverence became the foundation. The disciple of Yamazaki Ansai, Satō Naokata, discussed this, saying:

> Activity and quietude are the key to the natural Way of Heaven and by concentrating upon quietude to regulate activities, the scholar will truly cultivate this state. The followers of Lao Tzu and Buddhism have rejected activity and sought only quietude. This is an incomplete picture of the Way of Heaven. Most Confucians, on the other hand, act, but they do not understand the importance of regarding quietude as fundamental and therefore their activity is of little use. How is this sufficient to warrant the title scholar?

Based upon this he comes to interpret the Chu Hsi learning as something that considers quietude as fundamental.

The disciple of Naokata, Yanagawa Gōgi, collected together the discussion of *seiza* by Chu Hsi and wrote a book called *Collection of the Sayings of Chu Hsi on Quiet-Sitting*. In the epilogue he makes the following statement about the importance of *seiza:* "The absolute importance of the scholar's practicing quiet-sitting is like the necessity of a boat having a rudder." From this point of view, the Chu Hsi learning more and more comes to emphasize the effort of regarding quietude as fundamental. Because this trend entered into the learning of the Ansai School, Tsukida Mōsai also gave attention to *seiza,* and Tanzan no less than Mōsai gave it consideration. In this way it was felt that the learning of Chu Hsi approaches that of Li Yen-p'ing and Master Chou.

Originally because Chu Hsi searched extensively into the principle in humankind's common life, and it is a fundamental characteristic of Confucianism to make an ideal world, they thought it important not only to hold to the five virtues, that is, goodness, righteousness, propriety, wisdom, and faith—regarded as the fundamental code—but also to hold a broad knowledge. For Chu Hsi, unless this is the case, then even though there is concern about the world and a sense of humanity to think of people, one lacks a specific plan to realize this goal. In addition, it could even produce harmful effects against humanity. However, because Tanzan went through the learning of Kao P'an-lung and did not consider the broad learning to the extent of Chu Hsi, he expended real effort to bring together abiding in reverence and exhaustion of principle in the realization of the Principle of Heaven. This thought became more and more mature in his older age. Tanzan at the time that he was fifty-two said in a letter to his disciple Kaibu Shiki (1851–1927), "Today exhaust one principle, tomorrow another principle; when one continues this without stopping, the mind comes to a point where it is suddenly clear."

I would say that this is the result of his own realization of the subtle unity of the mind and principle and exhaustion of principle. Li Yen-p'ing said to Chu Hsi that if each principle is dissolved in the mind and the mind becomes clear, it still could not truly exhaust the principle. Tanzan's exhaustion of principle, however, is in fact what he practiced by himself of the teaching of Yen-p'ing. Tanzan studied Yen-p'ing and Master Chou and discussed the relation of abiding in reverence, and preservation and nourishment with the investigation of things and exhaustion of principle. He believed, however, in the Ansai learning, which said that preservation and nourishment include these. He also considered abiding in reverence by means of *seiza* as essential and regarded *seiza* realization as the final effort. Thus he said, "If the basic characteristic is already clear, when you meet with the affairs of the world, the greater part will be easily settled as if cutting with a sharp blade, and when you meet with various other affairs and handle them step by step they too will be settled with no trouble." Tanzan said, "Still water produces clarity," knowing that he had obtained clear knowledge by means of *seiza* and obtained wisdom that was deep and hidden to the extent that there remained no trace.

Seiza and Wisdom Stored

As Tanzan's learning of *seiza* realization matured in his later years, he discussed what is called the wisdom that is stored. According to Tanzan, Chu Hsi discussed it first based upon the *Hsi-tz'u chuan* commentary of the *Book of Changes* and Ansai then developed its general meaning. Since Tanzan was already familiar with the learning of the Ansai school, he came to understand the wisdom that is stored. The beginning of Tanzan's interest was after he had read an article by a disciple of Ansai, Miyake Shōsai (1662–1741), when he was thirty-six years old. The article said in part, "Knowledge is the dark place in the middle of the fire. It is the yin in the middle of the yang. All principle is stored in its darkness."

Chu Hsi made the following comments about stored wisdom.

Goodness is stored in the Four Beginnings [of Goodness]. Moreover wisdom is something that dwells at the endpoint of the Four Beginnings. Winter means "to lay up a store"; therefore its beginning is all creatures and its end is all creatures. Wisdom has the meaning of "to store" and also the sense of beginning and end. Thus in the Four Beginnings there is activity associated with the first three, the feeling of distress, of shame and disgrace, of deference to others. In wisdom there is nothing to be acted upon; it simply discerns what is right and wrong. This is the reason why it can be called "stored."

In this way wisdom is the endpoint of the Four Beginnings: goodness, righteousness, propriety, and wisdom. When it is compared to the four seasons—spring, summer, fall, and winter—wisdom corresponds to winter. Wisdom stores what is already gone, namely, past events, but it is also what knows the nature of the future. In this way Tanzan sees wisdom as corresponding to winter, and in terms of the virtues associated with the four seasons—that is, greatness, perseverance, cleverness, and constancy— wisdom is associated with constancy.

Tanzan says: "Wisdom belongs to winter and constancy. Its substance is calm and quiet, and it stores up what has gone before it. Its function moves in activity and possesses the subtle function of knowing what is to come. Thus wisdom is something that acts in the beginning and end of things." This clarifies what Chu Hsi said of stored wisdom. For Tanzan, the beginning of this discussion was in Chu Hsi's discussion of wisdom in the *Doctrine of the Mean* where he said that centrality was the origin of harmony and sincerity the true principle, as well as his discussion of the extension of knowledge. According to Tanzan, Ansai agreed with this, and from Tanzan's perspective this is the epitome of Confucian teachings even though very few Confucians of the Yüan and Ming periods knew anything at all about it.

The discussion of stored wisdom can be further extrapolated. Wisdom can be seen as the substance of the four virtues and therefore as the origin of the subtle function of principle as well as the storehouse of principle. Thus principle and wisdom are not different from each other, and therefore where there is stored wisdom there is subtle function. Thus to exhaust the principle of things is not to chase after external things. Chu Hsi said that if one practices the exhaustion of principle, in the end it is "suddenly penetrated" and one knows that it is only a single principle. From what has already been said, this kind of enlightenment is not mysterious.

There are some who say that principle is the way of things and righteousness is the way of affairs. They regard principle as external and righteousness as internal and thereby divide principle and righteousness into external and internal. Based upon what has already been said, it should not be divided into internal and external and it should be clear that it was originally a unity. Stored wisdom is boundless and empty, but in it there is included all existence. It is the totality of principle with no distinguishing characteristic, and within it there is a vigorous activity. Therefore it is the unity of existence and activity. In terms of the four seasons it is the moment of midnight of the winter solstice, and it corresponds to the point of time when quietude is completely exhausted and the subtle function is about to begin moving. In this fashion Tanzan regarded stored wisdom as the ultimate Way of humankind and the universe, that is, the Great Ultimate. Therefore, when it is said in the *Doctrine of the Mean* "The nature of the Mandate of Heaven"; in Lo Ts'ung-yen and Li Yen-p'ing, "Before the unmanifest"; and by Master Ch'eng, "Empty without a sign, everything has its form"—these were all seen as related to stored wisdom.

In Tanzan, as we have seen, among the four virtues wisdom is constancy and consists of the beginning and end of things. Since there is no wisdom that is separated from the mind, therefore in the extension of knowledge Tanzan emphasized the effort of reverence, which is the constancy of the mind. In reverence he placed emphasis upon regarding quietude as fundamental, which constantly unified mind and body. In this way the final effort of *seiza* realization was all the more necessary.

Dr. Kusumoto Masatsugu advocated Tanzan's expression, "There is no trace of stored wisdom. It is the extremity of quietude in the winter, yet without a distinguishing characteristic it is vigorous." He explained Tanzan's stored wisdom by saying that the deeper the wisdom of humankind, the less the trace that is left. It is exactly like the coming of winter. Everything is collected together in one place and becomes quiet. This is what is called the face of the human mind without a distinguishing characteristic, the absolute nature of the universe and the mind in which Heaven and earth produce all things. This quietude is filled with unlimited activity. The standpoint of the inner world becomes the standpoint of the external world. Conversely, when the conditions of the vigorous external world are supported by the effort of the constantly quiet inner world, its true meaning is known. Namely, for the first time it produces the common nature of life and returns to the mind, which gives birth to Heaven, earth, and all things. The cultivation of deep wisdom based upon *seiza* is nothing other than this.

Chu Hsi also discussed stored wisdom, as we have already mentioned. In Chu Hsi's discussion there are hints of this point of view here and there. For example, in his commentary on the *Great Learning,* he explained the phrase "illustrious virtue" by saying, "It is something that humankind obtains from Heaven, it is empty and luminous and is endowed with all principle and complies with all things." He also says in the *Questions on the Great Learning (Ta-hsüeh huo-wen),* "That kind of knowledge is the spirit of the mind, the subtlety of all principle and the ruler of all things." This may well be a discussion of stored wisdom. For Chu Hsi the "illustrious virtue" of the *Great Learning* is probably nothing other than stored wisdom. However, because knowledge of this kind is also covered over by material substance and human desires, the effort of abiding in reverence and investigation of things as well as exhaustion of principle was necessary. Abiding in reverence is the effort to preserve and nourish this knowledge, that is, it is the effort that activates and gives birth to it. The investigation of things and exhaustion of principle are the effort that exhausts the principle of things and reveals this knowledge. Chu Hsi regarded this knowledge as the illustrious virtue and the spiritual capacity of the mind, but he also saw the existing state of the mind of people of this world and employed his effort to that end. Therefore he reached the conclusion of not immediately focusing upon the perception of the mind as illustrious virtue and spiritual knowledge.

Wang Yang-ming, on the other hand, discussed the knowledge that Chu Hsi regarded as stored wisdom as something that was in conformity with the perception of the mind. Innate knowledge, which he took as the essence of his learning, was something of this kind. In this way Wang Yang-ming's discussion of innate knowledge was an expansion of Chu Hsi's discussion of stored wisdom. However, there are major differences between the two. Chu Hsi regarded this knowledge as of the nature, not the mind, but Yang-ming said it was the mind. For Chu Hsi, nature and mind were originally one, but he saw the mind as something where purity and impurity were mixed. Moreover, he separated the nature from the mind and tried to preserve the purity and the correctness of the nature. This is the reason that Chu Hsi emphasizes effort more than substance.

Wang Yang-ming regards human nature as the nature of the mind and said that there is no nature if it is separated from the mind. He speaks of human nature solely in terms of the mind. This is the reason that Yang-ming from beginning to end devoted himself to the mind itself. This is also the reason that he spoke of the extension of the innate knowledge. When based upon the Yang-ming learning, human nature is something dead and dried up. What he called innate knowledge is the sensitive perception that is itself the law of virtue, but it is something that unites into one the emotions of good and bad and makes good of good and bad of bad. This kind of learning of Yang-ming is said to have been a simple and easy thing.

Yang-ming, who regarded the learning of the innate knowledge as essential, did not speak in terms of regarding quietude as fundamental or of *seiza*. However, among his disciples some divided innate knowledge into the substance of quietude and the function of action, saying that not until the substance is established can the innate knowledge be expected to be completed in function. They also spoke of the establishment of the substance and the manifesting of the function as well as the return to quietude. This branch of learning was not the orthodoxy of the Yang-ming School, and they tended to combine Yang-ming thought with Chu Hsi learning. For example, Nieh Pao said:

> Stillness and feelings, activity and quietude, these are two things, but if feelings are not in accordance with stillness and activity not grounded in quietude, then they are completely false. Feelings are said to be produced from stillness and activity to be the way of the mind only when it is grounded in quietude.

He also said that innate knowledge is the mean of the unmanifest and therefore does not belong to perception. Perception is something that is influenced by innate knowledge, but innate knowledge produces perception naturally, and to regard perception as innate knowledge is a mistake.

Lo Hung-hsien also regarded the absolute principle of quietude as the highest good of the innate knowledge and said:

> Those who speak of innate knowledge all day long trifle with nothing more than mere perception. The spirit is swayed in accord with perception and on account of it there is no time for concentration and unification. Under these circumstances is there anyone who will not lose what Mencius called the mind of the child?

He spoke as well of the return to quietude. Although this one branch praised Yang-ming's discussion of innate knowledge, it also revered Chou Tun-i, Yang Shih, Lo Ts'ung-yen, and Li Yen-p'ing of the Sung period, and Ch'en Hsien-chang and others of the Ming period. They all utilized the principle of regarding quietude as fundamental and they accepted the learning of Ch'eng and Chu in terms of the standpoint of quietude. The discussion of the quietist branch became even more subtle in Wang Shih-huai (1522–1605), though this branch did not flourish to any degree. They sought to return to the quietistic thought of the Sung learning, which took Ch'eng and Chu as the models and opposed the active thought of Wang Yang-ming. Because of this, the views of this branch were disliked by other schools of the Yang-ming learning. However, their quietistic thought was adopted by Kao P'an-lung and other Chu Hsi scholars at the end of the Ming period and they are responsible for its preservation. Tanzan, who was inclined to the thought of Kao, accepted the thought of the quietist branch. He said, "There are two people among the disciples of Yang-ming—Nieh Pao and Lo Hung-hsien. They are said to be heretical Yang-ming followers, but in fact they are Yang-ming's meritorious retainers." The acceptance of the Sung and Ming learning of this kind made Tanzan more attentive to Chu Hsi's stored wisdom. It also created as the foundation of learning, realization through the consummate effort of *seiza*.

Chu Hsi discussed stored wisdom, but he did not regard knowledge as the center of human nature. The center for Chu Hsi of what he calls human nature is goodness. This is because goodness penetrates the four virtues: goodness, righteousness, propriety, and wisdom. Chu Hsi said, "Goodness is the foundation of goodness. Propriety is the externality of goodness. Righteousness is the regulation of goodness, and wisdom is the discernment of goodness." What is called goodness is the principle of the birth of things and the considerate mind. In comparing it to spring of the four seasons, Chu Hsi saw it as equivalent to goodness enveloping goodness, righteousness, propriety, and wisdom. "Spring is the birth of spring, summer the extension of spring, fall is the completion of spring, and winter is the storehouse of spring." Therefore Chu Hsi said that goodness enveloped knowledge, knowledge did not envelop goodness. It is perhaps because he thought that goodness held the broad mind that gives birth to all things in accordance with each respective principle and this was the origin of the Confucian spirit of unifying self and others, and that if only knowledge were to be utilized, then there was apt to be a fear of sinking into the selfishness of the Zen trifling with mind and knowledge. However, it is clear in the foregoing discussion of Chu Hsi that, although Chu Hsi spoke of goodness, he did not neglect knowledge, since it was considered a part of goodness.

Tanzan as a Chu Hsi scholar held the standpoint of Chu Hsi on the essentialness of goodness. This is clear in the commentary on Tanzan by Dr. Kusumoto Masatsugu. For what reason, however, did he pay attention to the stored wisdom of Chu Hsi and try to realize it by regarding quietude as fundamental based upon *seiza*? It is clear if one understands the successive progress of Tanzan's own Chu Hsi learning. Tanzan seriously adopted *seiza* realization, which came from the late Ming neo-Chu Hsi learning that had received the influence of the quietist branch of the Yang-ming School, and it was after that that he accepted the Chu Hsi learning of the Ansai School that focused upon abiding in reverence. As we have seen previously, however, he regarded *seiza* realization as the root of abiding in reverence. In a manner of speaking, Tanzan opposed the Yang-ming learning that regarded innate knowledge as the sole foundation and disregarded the investigation of things and the exhaustion of principle, but he was also a Chu Hsi scholar who was influenced by the discussion of the quietist branch of the Yang-ming School that regarded the substance of the innate knowledge as empty and quiet, and therefore emphasized straight and direct enlightenment to the substance by a return to quietude. I think that this is the reason that he paid particular attention to the stored wisdom of Chu Hsi and regarded its substance as the foundation of learning through *seiza* realization. It is also true of stored wisdom that if one forgets what Chu Hsi called the investigation of things and the exhaustion of principle, then it has an inclination toward the mind and knowledge of Lao Tzu and Chuang Tzu or possibly even Zen Buddhism.

Rules for *Seiza*

In 1861 Tanzan wrote a letter to Kōriki Sōseki and in this letter he gave his views on a number of points: the relationship between exhaustion of principle and abiding in reverence, the relationship between the *Elementary Learning* and the *Great Learning,* the meaning of the investigation of things and the extension of knowledge, the method of *seiza* practice as well as characteristics of the Ansai learning. If we look at what Tanzan called the rules of *seiza,* which he practiced constantly as the consummate effort, we can understand something more about this practice. I want to refer to these in what follows.

I have received your letter, which you sealed and sent at the beginning of this month. It is a matter of joy and congratulations that in this peaceful season, as you say, you are working very hard and your daily life is filled with contentment and happiness. In this season I am as well as ever and I have nothing worth saying. There is no need to have any concern about me. In the midst of spring I met you for a short time, something I had long cherished and it has been my greatest joy. I have heard that since that time you have been thoroughly engrossed in orthodox learning and just the other day you have expressed your opinion on this. Too happy to sleep, you say, as you revere and believe in the orthodox learning of

Confucius, Mencius, Ch'eng, and Chu. My congratulations are many and I hope that you make further effort. At any rate, the Mandate of Heaven prevails, development goes on, and goodness comes to the people. Though the mind is empty, it has a penetrating spirit and is endowed with all principles. Material desire, however, hinders me and I am repeatedly darkened, disturbed, and perplexed—and I don't know how to return to goodness. This is the same as in the case of the common people. However, [because humankind is like this], Confucius, Mencius, Ch'eng, and Chu established their honored teachings in order to turn the common people back to their original form of goodness. Summarizing their teachings, they consist of abiding in reverence and exhausting of principle, and these two must go hand in hand. This is what is called in the *Analects* "broad learning focused upon propriety," and in the *Doctrine of the Mean,* "revere the virtuous nature and also rely upon learning," and what Master Ch'eng spoke of as "the necessity of reverence in nourishment and the advancement of learning in the extension of knowledge." This was the theme that Chu Hsi revered through his life. If either of these were missing, then thorough training could not be achieved. Since Wang Yang-ming falls into a bias in his learning, he was criticized by men of knowledge.

For the people of the past who entered elementary school at the age of eight this effort of preservation and nourishment and abiding in reverence was fundamentally and purely established through the duties of the student. In later years, however, the teaching of the elementary school was abolished and consummate effort became poor. It was for this reason that Chu Hsi was concerned and wrote the *Elementary Learning.* In this book he clarified how the people of the past from childhood on were molded to a fundamental standard. Already an adult, he found it impossible to maintain control over the same effort in elementary and adult learning and he therefore brought forward the concept of reverence. [According to the *Doctrine of the Mean,*] "if a person can do it by one effort, he will do it with a hundred efforts; if a person can do it with a tenfold effort, he will do it with a thousand efforts." If this process of painstaking effort is not employed on reverence, it will be useless. The root will be neglected and what is intelligent will not be developed. In this there is nothing to correspond with "still water produces clarity."

Therefore, in terms of this effort for reverence, as is seen in detail in the *Questions on the Great Learning,* in anything, if the mind and body are not made quiet first, reverence will not be achieved. Originally what was called reverence incorporated both activity and quietude and it unified mind and body in all daily activities. To experience the taste of reverence and to realize what it is like, there is nothing better than to practice *seiza*. This is why Master Chou established [the principle of] regarding quietude as fundamental. *Seiza* is not the same as concentration through *zazen*.

In discussing *seiza*, Atobe Ryōken says:

"The way to practice *seiza* is to sit quietly, but not in a manner like *zazen*. *Zazen* is to sit with the legs folded, to see the tip of the nose, concentrate the mind below the navel and drive out thought. *Zazen* is to be practiced with a purpose. It is not something that is practiced whenever there is the time. As one fixes one or two sticks of incense and settles upon a time period of one or two hours, one becomes rigid, the mind becomes stiffened rather than smooth, and the mind and body become dead things. *Seiza* does not fix the limit or the time period; it can be practiced in the morning, in the evening, at night, after one encounters things, after one finishes something, when one has time to spare, when there is time between reading and writing, when there is nothing specific to do. With legs crossed or in any way that one likes, making the body straight, putting the hands together in one place, holding one's body relaxed, holding the mind like a smile and not stiffening the mind, one must sit relaxed.

"When one calms the mind, many thoughts will come out. It is wrong to try to get rid of these thoughts forcefully. In a way as if saying, go away, go away, let them go away slowly. If one calms one's mind, wasteful thoughts will stop of their own. If one pushes them away and gets rid of them forcefully, without fail others will continue to come out one after another.

"In the beginning there will be cases when one becomes drowsy. This is because the vital force of the mind has been calmed down. One has to be very careful about becoming drowsy. This is what Chu Hsi calls: 'Not achieving *seiza*, only gaining a nap.' Although various wasteful thoughts come out, this is only because the vital force of the mind is being calmed down. If one devotes oneself solely to *seiza*, then many things stop coming out. And a nap will not come out either! Of the sound of birds singing, the sound of wind blowing, the sound of rain falling, the sound of human voices nearby, they are like the sound of the bell that echoes to the mind. This is where there is perception in quietude. Thereafter when one becomes very quiet there is meaning in the sound of chopping wood, and one realizes the quietness of the mountain. The mind becomes serene and tranquil and then becomes clear. At first the eyes are restless, but when the mind becomes quiet they are not. One must think of what Chu Hsi calls: "After achieving nourishment, one finds oneself feeling at ease." Both mind and body become relaxed. When one is quiet without any wasteful thoughts we sometimes are reminded of the principles of the Classics, and if you take them out and taste them, you find them clear. After that one stops and becomes quiet again. Since the function of the mind is thinking, it is good to think what one should think, but when thinking has concluded itself, then stop, and one becomes calm. Meanwhile if someone comes from the outside, if a letter comes or if your wife or a servant asks you to do something, in compliance with the matter one finishes what should be done and then becomes quiet again.

"The moment that one recognizes this as the point of the unmanifest, it is already the manifest. The point of the unmanifest is before the voice of the bird or the sound of the wind echoes to the mind. If one recognizes that it is the sound of a bird or the wind, then it is the manifest. One must devote oneself to practicing *seiza* and know the taste of it, and the same is true of what we see. Birds flying, the wind moving leaves of trees is what we see naturally in our eyes in the midst of quietude and what echoes in our minds. If one wonders what they are, then that is the manifest. When one encounters things after practicing *seiza,* one does not have this same questioning mind. In turn, if one is agitated at things moving, then the true quietude is lost. There is the position of quietude and the position of activity. When one encounters things, it must be done with regard for quietude as fundamental. One must be careful to conduct daily activities more and more in quietude. If one does not lose the mind of *seiza* even for a little while, then the effort of regarding quietude as fundamental can be achieved. This is the part of which we say that reverence is the effort of quietude. It is also reverence that stops wasteful thoughts in *seiza*. The saying "Practice to awaken us from our slumber" is reverence with constant clarity. The taste of reverence cannot be known if it is not tried from the viewpoint of *seiza*. If it is tried in this way, then it is known well."

If you read this carefully, then you can understand much of the detail of the effort of *seiza*. Reverence is the way to establish the original mind and what is called the rightness of the mind. You must realize this and learn the whole of it. If you do so, then the unifying of mind and body, activity and quietude, going and stopping is achieved through reverence. *Seiza* is the point where one should make a consummate effort for the foundation of abiding in reverence and preservation and nourishment. Since you have taken pains to exhaust principle by reading books alone and have not experienced abiding in reverence and preservation and nourishment, it seems to me that you have not mastered well the principle of the Way, though I am sorry if I have conjectured this.

Chu Hsi instructed those engaged in only the exhaustion of principle to emphasize preservation and nourishment and those engaged in the preservation and nourishment alone to emphasize the exhaustion of principle. You must realize this consummate effort as the foundation and then move to the exhaustion of principle. It is similar to the completion of the cultivation of paddies and fields; only afterward are the seeds planted. This learning of investigation of things does not lie with persons of knowledge, for they attempt to exhaust all principles. If they were only to open their eyes, this would be the point at which "for the sages of past and present, the method is the same," for it is these two things meeting together. This is the teaching of the *Great Learning* and is understood implicitly through the transmission of the lineage of the famous worthies. If this is accomplished, the great work to rule the country and make the world at peace will go forth.

As far as the method of investigation of things and extension of knowledge is concerned, it is not unique. If one simply reads books of the sages and worthies, encounters things of the world, studies with friends, utilizes the mind and body, studies and investigates things one by one, even the creation of Heaven and earth and animals and plants, and investigates the natural principle of things, then after a long accumulation there will be a point of sudden enlightenment. It can be said that the exhaustion of principle is the exhaustion of the mind. In this all things originate in one root and the Great Ultimate as a unified body is surely made clear.

Let me put it this way: the principle of one mind is like the moon in the sky. The principles of all things are like the moon reflected in all rivers. The moons in all rivers are like the Great Ultimates with which each thing is endowed, and the moon in the sky is the one substance of the Great Ultimate. This Great Ultimate is what unifies the Great Ultimates of all things, and the principle of the one mind is what controls the principle of all things. Now one must see that there is nothing that one person's mind cannot know of the principle of all things in the world. Therefore unless the principles of all things are exhausted, it is impossible that the substance of the self is exhausted. Even though the principle of all things is exhausted, there is no increase or decrease in the substance of the mind itself. The moon in the sky is of course a single moon, but "this" and "that" mutually penetrate each other. Of course there is only this moon, and there is neither surplus nor deficiency. If one doesn't see the moon's reflection on all the rivers, merely the moon in the sky, then the subtle function of the whole is not exhausted. It is very difficult to express this in figures of speech. Persons of knowledge should understand implicitly. This is the great purpose of exhausting of principle. Anyway if one does not know the balance in our orthodox learning between abiding in reverence and the exhausting of principle, it is of no use. One must find out the taste of reverence from *seiza* and further consider both abiding and exhausting by means of Chu Hsi's *An Admonition on Reverence and Penance (Ching-chai chen)*. Furthermore, what constitutes the beginning of the learning and the end of it lies indeed in this one word "reverence." Although the foregoing is my opinion, you are studying the orthodox learning and I expect you to criticize it, since you kindly raised a question. In addition, in your letter you said that you have had doubts for many years. I want to hear from you by all means. This is the very reason why it is necessary to study together with friends. If you do not raise questions, then the substance of the mind is hindered one day. I want to express openly among friends these questions and exhaust the right and wrong of our discussion to the very end. Please be diligent and study hard.

As I have mentioned in the body of the letter, abiding in reverence and exhausting of principle are indeed the principles of the orthodox learning. Anyway, I have written it down in my own way, but I cannot convey it as I wish because I myself am not calm and because I have not understood it perfectly. The abiding in reverence and exhausting of principle doesn't mean that one abides in reverence today and exhausts principle tomorrow. Abiding in reverence is the foundation and goes first, but both reverence and exhausting of principle work together. If abiding in reverence is thoroughly complete, exhausting of principle becomes more and more precise, and if exhausting of principle advances, abiding in reverence will become sharper and sharper. You must understand this parallel advance well. If you have any slight doubt in the body of the letter or the postscript, don't hesitate to ask. This is the point of studying together with friends.

In our country, Ansai and three or four disciples knew the greater part of the orthodox learning of the Ch'eng-Chu School. I want to revive this orthodox study, which has been cut off since the school of Ansai. To advance orthodox learning, Ansai said, "The reason the sage established his teaching is because he wanted others to acknowledge the spirit of this mind, regarding quietude as the foundation of exhausting of principle and the subtle function of all principles. He also wanted people to recognize that the exhausting of principle is the effort to complete the mind in learning and study, thus nourishing both quietude and activity." How meaningful this is. Regulate ourselves in the morning, and in the evening earnestly realize it. Every time you notice something, please instruct me. I am looking forward to it. . . .

If one excludes the discussion of stored wisdom of his later years, one would be able to understand virtually the entirety of Tanzan's theories by means of this letter. Let me paraphrase in a simple manner the contents of this letter.

Though the human mind is empty, it is also spiritual. Within, it is endowed with all principles and this is something that is innate. However, people's minds in general are covered with material force and desires so that they do not know how to return to the original state. Accordingly the sages and worthies such as Confucius, Mencius, Master Ch'eng, and Chu Hsi gave various teachings for the sake of restoring the human mind to its original state. In short, this teaching is simply abiding in reverence and exhaustion of principle. Abiding in reverence and exhaustion of principle should advance together. When one lacks one of them, true cultivation becomes impossible. The learning of Wang Yang-ming was criticized in terms of this kind of bias.

Long ago, after people entered elementary school and cultivated their behavior and manners, they progressed to the root. In later times, however, this elementary education decayed. Thus, adults had to consider how to unify elementary and adult learning. After elementary education, one simply could not start again. Accordingly one must use the strength of ten thousand in preservation and nourishment and reverence. Otherwise the final effort will be crude and intelligence will not develop. If, however, preservation and nourishment are considered essential, naturally clear knowledge comes out. This is what is called "still water produces clarity."

Concerning the effort of reverence, Chu Hsi discusses it in detail in the *Questions on the Great Learning*, but it is something that one cannot practice if one does not first quiet and unify the body and the mind. Originally reverence is something that incorporates both activity and quietude and unifies body and mind in daily activity. To experience the taste of reverence nothing is better than *seiza*. Master Chou's quietude was also established in this same way. Although we speak of *seiza* it is not, however, like *zazen* or concentration practiced by the Zen School.

As far as the rules of *seiza* are concerned, the best discussion is that of Atobe Ryōken. According to him, *seiza* is not the sort of thing where the length of time is set, as in *zazen*, and one sits in the cross-legged position, congealing the mind strictly to a state of moribundity like the saying "The eyes look at the tip of the nose, the mind gathers below the navel, thought is destroyed." Instead *seiza* makes the mind quiet by not fixing the time, by having a composure of mind and body in leisure time so that mind and body are not stiffened, and by not forcefully driving away the wasteful thoughts. In this way one may get rid of them little by little. The same is true of perception. If thoughts arise, after they are settled make oneself quiet. If affairs arise, after they have been settled make oneself quiet. We must earnestly try to gain a taste of it by the practice of *seiza* in this way.

What is experienced in quietude is the unmanifest. When it is perceived, however, it is the manifest. When one practices *seiza* and also deals with worldly matters, if one manages things according to the movement of the mind as it is normally, then the original quietude is lost and quietude and activity become two. In these circumstances, one must take as the basic principle regarding of quietude as fundamental. That is to say, one aims to become quiet in daily life. Eventually nothing is separated from the effort of regarding quietude as fundamental. This is the reason why reverence is called the effort of quietude. At the time of *seiza*, reverence diminishes miscellaneous thought and reverence awakens one from sleep. The taste of reverence is something that is first understood when one practices *seiza*. These are the rules of *seiza* according to Atobe Ryōken.

Reverence is called both the ruler and the steadfastness of the mind, and when this is thoroughly understood the body and mind are unified. Eventually activity and quietude, going and stopping are all reverence and are unified. This is the consummate effort. Preservation and nourishment and exhaustion of principle must be practiced together. Otherwise preservation and nourishment are not true and exhaustion of principle is not sensitive. Accordingly Chu Hsi taught preservation and nourishment for the one who turned to exhaustion of principle. For the one who turned to nourishment and preservation, he taught exhaustion of principle. However, no matter what it is called, one must move to the exhaustion of principle after realizing the consummate, or final, effort. This is the same as sowing plants after the field has been plowed. Consequently the learning of the investigation of things and the exhaustion of principle is also not merely the seeking of broad knowledge, as the worldly Confucians would say. It is something that must pierce the original foundation of all things. One is able in fact from it to undertake the great feat of ordering the country and bringing peace to the world.

Although the terms "investigation of things" and "exhaustion of principle" are used, they have no special meaning. They are simply the reading of books by the sages and worthies, talking with friends, and in addition investigating things in Heaven and earth. It is just searching out the principle of nature, that is, the natural principle. When one accumulates effort of this kind, one steps into a sudden realization and thus exhausts the principle of all things. That is to say, one exhausts the essence of one's mind and finally comes to understand the one root of all things, that is, the one substance of the Great Ultimate. If one compares this principle of the one mind, that is, the substance of the mind, to the moon suspended in the heavenly firmament, the principle of all things is comparable to the moon reflecting on all rivers. The moon of all rivers, that is, the Great Ultimate with which each is endowed, is the moon of the whole firmament, that is, it is the one substance of the Great Ultimate, and the latter controls the former. Therefore the principle of the one mind, that is, the substance of the mind, is understood to be the one substance of the principle of all things. However, since the substance of the mind cannot be seen by the eyes and cannot be heard by the ears, if one does not exhaust the principle of all things, one will not be able to exhaust the substance of the mind. Since the principle and the substance of the mind are one, although one exhausts the principle of all things, it cannot but be concluded that there is neither increase nor decrease in the substance of the mind. It is exactly the same as saying that the moon suspended in the heavenly firmament and the moon reflected in all rivers is the same moon without any surplus or deficiency. However, if one doesn't see the moon in all the rivers, the subtle function of the whole of the moon of the heavenly firmament is not exhausted. This simply cannot be explained in language.

This is the general idea of the exhaustion of principle. In short, one must understand the relation of abiding in reverence and exhaustion of principle. It is not the relation that is referred to as today abiding in reverence, tomorrow the exhaustion of principle. The exhaustion of principle should be accomplished through the employment of abiding in reverence. When the effort of abiding in reverence progresses and the exhaustion of principle is refined, the exhaustion of principle progresses and the abiding of reverence is completed. One must understand this parallel development. However, reverence consists of the beginning and end of learning of the sage, and to know the taste of reverence there is nothing like *seiza*.

Yamazaki Ansai and three or four of his disciples transmitted the main purport of the learning of Ch'eng and Chu in Japan, and now is the time that we want to revive the learning that has been cut off since Yamazaki Ansai. Ansai describes the orthodox doctrine. He taught that in order to have people recognize the spirit of the mind, they must see that quietude of mind is the root of the exhaustion of principle, and the subtle function of all principles is stored in it. In addition, he also taught that the exhaustion of principle in the case of learning and study is the effort to complete the mind, and he taught that one must cultivate these two together. This is very true, and

I entirely agree with him. We must also be diligent in this manner morning and evening.

Based upon what has been presented above, one can both understand the general principle of the learning of Tanzan and see Tanzan's intention to teach *seiza*. The clear mind in *seiza* for Tanzan was deep and subtle and reached the point of realizing Heaven and earth and the basic root of all things. According to the transmission of Tsukida Mōsai, each time that Tanzan saw ashes of incense falling into the censer while practicing *seiza*, he felt something in his mind and realized that he and Heaven and earth as well as all things, were originally one body. In short, by means of *seiza* he realized the point of the creation of Heaven and earth and, based upon this, engaged in learning, wrote poetry, and served in government.

Around the second year of the Meiji, Tanzan laid down a daily schedule for private school students.

Daily Schedule

Chu Hsi said, "Establish a strict schedule but put one's thought at ease." This is his motto. Scholars should understand the meaning of this and should not neglect it.

Arise at 6:00 A.M., wash up, dress yourself properly, make your sights straight and sit strictly, burning one stick of incense. After that read the Classics, [read them] loudly until 8:00 A.M. and at 8:00 A.M. eat breakfast. After that sit at one's desk in the right posture, open and read the Classics. Cultivate the mind and think silently, penetrate righteousness and reason until 10:00 A.M.. At 10:00 A.M. open the philosophers' books and enjoy them quietly. Exhaust their intentions until noon.

After finishing lunch at noon, take a walk or stroll. Arrange your thoughts and practice *seiza* for the length of a single stick of incense. At times read a poem and sing with feeling, at other times read or write compositions. When their meaning is appropriate, you understand by yourself with composure and have the temperament of a Ts'eng Hsi. At 2:00 P.M. attend a lecture, and then until 6:00 P.M. turn to history with its transition of past and present, its trace of peace and war and its rise and fall.

After eating at 6:00 P.M. attend another lecture, and then take up the Classics or enjoy the philosophers, until you have settled yourself. Just at the time of going to bed sit with composure, reflect the right and wrong and gain and loss of what you have done during the day. Control miscellaneous thought keenly, cut off wasteful thought strictly, and return to the substance of emptiness and clearness. After that settle your hands and feet and go to sleep with composure. Even in your dreams you must experience the progress of your efforts.

Based upon this, Tanzan made up a daily schedule for the practice of *seiza* three times each day. The Confucian at the beginning of the Ch'ing period, Li Erh-ch'ü (1627–1705), also emphasized *seiza*. Three times a day, in the morning, noon, and evening, he would light a stick of incense and practice *seiza*. He named those incenses, morning incense, noon incense, and night incense. According to what he says, at dawn when one gets up the mind is still not attached to things and is pure, but with becoming active after getting up, the mind contacts external things and is easily distracted. Thus before anything else, it is essential to burn a stick of incense and practice *seiza*. By the time noon arrives, since it is easy to be encumbered by various things, practice a little *seiza* so that your purity will not be lost. At night we should reflect by means of *seiza* to see whether or not the mind of the day has been pure or not. Tanzan, it goes without saying, practiced *seiza* himself and it seems that he strictly enforced its training among his disciples. His instruction held as its goal *seiza* realization.

PART III
OKADA TAKEHIKO
IN DIALOGUE

MY LIFE

That I began the study of Confucianism is mainly dependent upon my ancestors and family as well as my teacher. I was born November 21, 1908. I don't really know much about my ancestors because my parents never talked of them at any length. My parents were people of few words. I have been told, however, that my ancestors, to my grandfather's generation, were medical doctors. Among them there were some who worked for the Himeji domain as official doctors. Some were both medical doctors and Confucians.

My own father, Okada Shigenari (1870–1935), was not a medical doctor. My father studied with Kameyama Umpei, the Harima sage.[1] Kameyama Umpei had studied at Shōheikō in Edo.[2] He wanted to become a disciple of Fujita Toko (1806–55), a member of the Mito School of Confucian studies, if not literally, at least in his thinking.[3] When Tokugawa Nariaki (1800–1860), feudal lord of the Mito domain, had opened an official school, Kodokan, in 1841, he asked Fujita Toko to write a draft work on the aims of the school. This work was known as *The Record of Kodokan (Kodokanki)*. In turn, Fujita Toko published a two-volume work *A Commentary to Kodokanki (Kodokanjutsugi)*, and Kameyama Umpei then wrote the two-volume *Notes on the Commentary on Kodokanjutsugi (Hyōchū Kodokanjutsugi)*, published in 1883.[4]

Kameyama Umpei considered himself to be a disciple of Satō Issai. He eventually became the teacher of the feudal lord of the Himeji domain. When my father studied with Kameyama Umpei, Kameyama had retired from official work for the feudal lord, moved to my hometown, and opened a private

165

Plate IV. Poem and Calligraphy by Okada.

Just Sitting

All things are united with the mind.
The mind is united with the self.
This self—what is it?
It is the person and it is not the person.

school.[5] He was frequently referred to as a sage by the townspeople, an indication of his warmth, modesty, and humility. According to my father, Kameyama was so thoughtful he would even look after the shoes of his disciples. After my father studied in Kameyama's private school, my father became a teacher in the elementary school in the village. A stone monument for Master Kameyama is located in the village. This monument was made possible by Kameyama's disciples such as my father.

My father is said to have respected and served his parents. It is even said that he carried his father on his back to a festival after his father was ill. My father also liked drinking *sake,* however, and would often drink until dawn when he had visitors. We were very poor, partially because of this. Speaking of my father's drinking, my mother, Taki (1870–1948), never complained about it. When he came home very drunk, my mother would sit and talk with him. On such occasions I often sat by them quietly. They did not mind.

My mother was from a wealthy family. She was a woman of culture and was very beautiful. After she married my father she worked very hard at home to earn money. She was wise and intelligent, though at times she seemed distant. She had a very rigid sense of discipline with her children, though I remember being scolded only once. Even when the finances of our house were so very low, my mother did not complain when my father's younger sister came to live with us, bringing her children with her.

My father was called the Shirahama sage by the village people. The village itself was named Shirahama. My father stopped working for the elementary school when I was nine and lived on a pension. He seemed to have a great degree of personal anguish within himself though I don't remember him ever showing any anger. He must have been heart-filled and kindly, though, for he continued to be called the Shirahama sage. He also taught the *Analects (Lun-yü)* of Confucius to the young people of the village. I may very well have been influenced by my father to study the Chinese Classics and particularly Confucianism. Compared with what I have learned from my parents, I am ashamed of how little education I have given my own children.

We were very poor and I myself started working in home-factories of craftsmen from when I was ten years old until I was fourteen, even though as a child I was physically weak. I earned a little wage and gave it all to my mother. When I did not work in the home-factories, I assisted my mother in her work. We were so poor that instead of eating fish, we had fishbones and skins.

While I did not touch textbooks at home, I did well at elementary school.[6] My parents never told me to study. I do wish, however, that they could have bought some books for me, but this was simply not possible. Before I was born my parents' house had burned down, and as a result there were few books of any kind. Then poverty made it impossible to buy any. In a way, not having books was also all right, because this gave me the free time to roam the mountains, rivers, and seashore. This experience led to an appreciation of nature, and this eventually resulted in my interest in the relationship between Japanese culture and the natural beauty of the land itself.[7]

I had one elder sister, two elder brothers, and one younger sister. My eldest brother, Yoshio, who was eight years my elder, influenced me in many ways as greatly as my parents did. He went to middle school and then found a job with the Sumitomo Zaibatsu in Osaka. Though he wanted very much to go to university, he gave up his education because he wanted to help our parents' financial situation. He was able, however, to combine school and work, studying to go to Kyoto University and working at the same time. In order to help the family financially, he worked as a private teacher at night. He continued to get along well with the management of the company, but then he came down with tuberculosis.

My brother worried about his parents as well as his brothers and sisters. I remember at times that I would find him reading books in English. Once I remember a biography of George Washington. Often we would go for walks together, and sometimes he would sing me songs in English. When I asked him questions about mathematics, he would solve my difficulties, explaining the problems to me at great length.

After I finished elementary school in 1921 I did not enter middle school for two years. This was because of the poverty of the family. The difficulty of entering middle school left me weak and sickly. Worrying about me, my brother took me to a specialist in Osaka. Even now I appreciate his kindness and consideration. It could be said that I have kept my brother Yoshio within my heart all these years.[8]

When I did enter middle school in 1923[9] my parents' finances were somewhat improved. This was because my father was working again. He had accepted a job in the accounting department of the village government. My eldest brother's tuberculosis had now become serious, however, and as a result he had to become a part-time worker.

I was quite happy until I became a second-year student in middle school, even though my family was poor and I was physically weak. I began to feel anguish myself, partly because I worried about my father. I had heard that in his position in the accounting office he himself had paid for the poor who could not afford the village tax. In addition, the village mayor had forced my father to spend village funds illegally upon the entertainment of governmental bureaucrats because the mayor had wanted to use such contacts to get investments. My father looked very depressed, and I asked him about such problems. But he did not want to talk about it and would say to me, "How can you be responsible saying such things?" I talked with my brother Yukio, who was four years my elder, about it but he had no sensitivity to it. My eldest brother was sick in Osaka, and so I could not talk with him about it. My mother and I went to an uncle of my father to ask for the money in order to compensate the village funds used for entertaining. He refused, which upset me very much and I determined never to borrow money again.

There was another matter that caused great anguish. This was the relationship between my father and my eldest brother. My brother, who was very dutiful, complained about our father's drinking. It was believed at that time that children whose parents drank would develop tuberculosis, and he asked our father to stop drinking. Of course, our father could not stop drinking. The relation between my father and eldest brother deteriorated. Seeing this relation I felt the pain and suffering of life.

This was also a time when the economy of Japan was worsening.[10] There were many leftists who led strikes, but as a middle school student I did not have enough information to form an opinion. It was not possible to obtain books on the subject, and so my own response was to increase my solitude and introvertedness.

Often I would go to Mt. Jinju located about five kilometers north of Shirahama village and overlooking the sea. I had heard that a Confucian had had his private school there. He was a senior minister of the Himeji domain.[11] The name Jinju (virtuous longevity) comes from a sentence from the *Analects,* "The virtuous are long-lived."[12] I always felt peaceful and calm there. Such behavior did not seem to be common among middle school students. When it would turn warm in June, I would swim every day in the sea. I was particularly fond of swimming, for it put me at a distance from other people, and I felt alone with the sea and the clouds.

After I finished my fourth year of middle school in 1927 I could not go to high school because of the poverty of my family even though most of my classmates went on.[13] I could not decide whether I should try to get a job even though, because of the recession, jobs were very difficult to obtain. The middle school I had gone to was a very good school, and most of the graduates went on to high school. I decided to take the entrance examination for Himeji High School, not knowing whether I would be able to go or not, and I passed it.[14] The school was located not far from our house, and I found that it would not be too expensive if I went without living in the dormitory, but continued to live at home. My father let me go, and I went there every day by bicycle, a distance of ten kilometers each way. I used to study in the library of the high school until 9:00 P.M. and then go home on my bicycle with the light from a candle to see the route.

With my own feelings of anguish because of my father, my eldest brother, and the worsening conditions, I began reading books on philosophy, in particular the philosopher Nishida Kitaro (1870–1945). These works were very difficult for me and I remember that I often spent several hours on a single page. At this time the family problems were becoming more and more serious. I also went to listen to a famous Christian priest, Ebina Danjo, preaching. But he disappointed me. What he said did not differ from the words of other priests, separating humankind from God and placing God in Heaven. This is one of the major reasons I have never been attracted to Christianity. I was in general disinterested in religion, with the exception of Zen Buddhism. I was interested in Zen Buddhism and had instruction in *zazen* from a professor at the high school who was acquainted with Zen. When I asked him the reason for the occurrence of problems and contradictions in society, he said it was necessary to look at such things very closely. In my mind I wanted to sort out what was right and what was wrong. To help me in my search I read not only philosophical works, but novels as well.

It was soon after I entered high school in 1928 that my eldest brother had to come to live with us. He had to give up his job because of his illness. He would often spit up blood, and at this point my father employed a nurse for him. He didn't speak to my parents at all and, fearing his own death, he devoted himself to reading many works on Buddhism. Now I wish I could have understood him better, but there was no opportunity.

While he was so ill, he married the nurse who was taking care of him. She must have had great sympathy for him. I respect her for marrying him even though she knew he was dying. Though my parents were on good terms with each other, my mother objected to the marriage, and my father approved it, probably because he felt it would make his son feel better. This marriage made my parents' relationship a little difficult, and this situation lasted until my brother's death.

Under such circumstances my sister-in-law must have had a very difficult time. The relationship between her and my mother was terrible. After she became pregnant my brother also treated her badly, but this was probably just because of his illness. Through most of it she was very patient. Eventually, however, her patience wore out and she tried to commit suicide. My mother was indifferent even to this, while my father worried a good deal about it. This resulted in an increased difficulty in the relationship of my parents with each other.

Under these circumstances I read constantly, visited with professors who had had Zen training, and meditated. My brother died when I was a second-year student in high school in 1929. His wife was still pregnant. She returned to her parents' home after my brother's death. I took her there and stayed for several days because of the beauty of the location. I had great sympathy for her. When she gave birth to a baby girl at her parents' home, my mother and I visited her. Later she visited us with her daughter. She later married again and I am afraid I lost track of her during the Second World War.

More and more I wanted to find a teacher of real humanity and wisdom. My family problems had given me insight into the often inconsistent behavior of my family members, and I wanted to find a real philosopher to be my teacher, one whose words and deeds matched. Completing the final year of high school in 1931, I had no money to go on to university. Though I wanted to go to either Tokyo University or Kyoto University, because of the poverty of my family it did not look promising. I had been hoping to study with Watsuji Tetsuro (1889–1960) at Tokyo University.[15] Watsuji had been a graduate of my own middle school and, as I learned, his ancestors had also had a similar background to my own in terms of the medical profession. My father and my brother Yukio objected to my further study, and in fact Yukio was even stronger in his opposition than my father.

I went to see the principal of the high school to ask him if he might have some clues as to a job for me. I hadn't done badly in high school, and the principal of the school thought it might be appropriate to obtain funds from someone else to send me to university. Though my brother was now dead, one of my brother's former superiors, Watanabe Kotohira, suggested I go to university with his support. Even with this support my father and brother objected. Eventually, however, they were persuaded and I was given approval. By that point it was too late to go to either Kyoto University or Tokyo University and so I chose Kyūshū University.[16] It was a good decision in terms of my health, for it was warmer than other places in Japan.

It was in 1931 that I met my teacher Dr. Kusumoto Masatsugu. When I met my teacher he was lecturing on the work *Instructions for Practical Living (Ch'uan-hsi lu)* by the Ming Neo-Confucian Wang Yang-ming. I was very impressed. I felt his personality was strong and excellent and his explanations were extremely good. This caused me to think that it was appropriate to study with a teacher who had both wisdom and a warm and strong personality, devoting my entire being and physical energy to him. I even put this in the form of a poem suggesting that I was longing to devote my life, soul and body, to such a person. It was similar to the Zen Master Dogen's love and longing for his own teacher Eisai (1141–1215). Dogen thought only of becoming a person like Eisai, devoting himself totally and completely. Very fortunately I was able myself to find such a person, my teacher Dr. Kusumoto. It seemed to me that it was extremely important to have a teacher with a very strong personality, probably because of my own personality and family background. Even now I continue to have the very same idea—wisdom and a warm and strong personality are inseparable.

At the university I had a part-time job in addition to the support given me by Watanabe Kotohira. I continued to send money home to my parents. When I returned home for my first vacation I discovered that my father had just returned home after being detained. He had been suspected of spending the village money illegally. This was very shocking to me as I knew him so well and I never suspected him. He was still very respected by the people in the village. But after this my parents went to Okayama to live with my brother Yukio, and my father died there in 1935, a very unhappy man. I brought my mother and younger sister to Fukuoka after I got a job there.

I met Mieko when I began my graduate study at the university, and this soon developed into marriage. I greatly enjoyed my life at the university during this period. I began the study of Sung dynasty Neo-Confucianiam under Dr. Kusumoto. At that time Dr. Kusumoto had just returned from study in Germany. He was very fond of German philosophy, and I enjoyed listening to him discuss it at great length. I myself enjoyed reading Kant and was particularly moved by Kant's categorical imperative. Dr. Kusumoto studied and analyzed Eastern thought in terms of Western ideas. I also used Western philosophical methodology in my studies and prepared my thesis on Sung Neo-Confucianism, dealing with issues of ontology. It was very well received, and it was recommended that I remain at the university. I had gone to university in 1931, was married to Mieko in the same year, and graduated in 1934. After graduation Dr. Kusumoto wanted me to stay on, and it was approved by the faculty in general.

In March of 1934, however, Dr. Kusumoto and I went on a trip to China, a trip which lasted for twenty days and took us to Tientsin and Beijing. I found when I returned that a job had been arranged for me. What happened was that the registrar's office at the university had arranged a teaching job for me in Jintsu Middle School in Toyama Prefecture on the west coast of Japan, and my mother had said Yes.[17] This led me to Toyama against my will as I felt I was abandoning my academic career. Because the weather in Toyama was particularly bad, the health of both my wife and I became worse and worse. In the end my wife came down with tuberculosis. She suffered from tuberculosis for several years and died in Fukuoka in 1941 after I had taken a job there teaching in Shuyukan Middle School.[18] She left me with two daughters.

When I met Dr. Kusumoto again, his way of studying had changed, a change that came about largely through his gradually deepening understanding of his own family background. He now focused primarily upon feeling and experience rather than strictly scholarly categories. For example, if you are studying the thinker Chu Hsi, you regard yourself as Chu Hsi and let Chu Hsi himself solve the problem of Chu Hsi. I felt that this kind of teaching simply couldn't be found in other teachers. It appealed to me greatly, particularly after the anguish of Toyama and the attention I had given to the practice of Zen meditation.

Now as I look back on it, there was a difference between Dr. Kusumoto and myself. This difference could be put in the following way. I consider that the study of Chinese thought is an even more personal and internal issue than Dr. Kusumoto found it. Dr. Kusumoto never expressed this idea as explicitly as I have. I have always thought that he had this kind of idea deep inside of himself. If Dr. Kusumoto were alive, I would ask him about this very point.

I married my present wife, Kimu, in Fukuoka on July 19, 1941. The grandfather of my present wife was a Confucian. While I was in Fukuoka I went to see my teacher, Dr. Kusumoto, once a week, wearing *hakama*[19] and reading the *Chronological Biography of Chu Hsi (Chu Tzu nien-p'u)*. I went with a young scholar who was studying Western philosophy. The learning of Dr. Kusumoto was able to incorporate both Eastern and Western materials. It was in 1943 that Dr. Kusumoto received an invitation to accept a position at Tokyo University. He did not accept the invitation and stayed at Kyūshū University. It was a matter of honor to him. The students at Tokyo University had launched a movement to get Dr. Kusumoto back to Tokyo University during the war years. I also recommended that he go to Tokyo, as the numbers of students at Kyūshū was limited.

We had to leave Fukuoka in 1943 because of my family problems. These problems concerned the bad relations between my present wife and the daughters of my deceased wife. We went to Nagasaki and then to Kumamoto where I taught at Nagasaki Normal School (1943–44) and then at Kumamoto Elementary Military School in 1945. After the end of the war we came back to Fukuoka and I again taught at Shuyukan Middle School from 1946 to 1949. In 1949 I began working at Kyūshū University. This was a period at which the suffering and anguish in the home setting were most extreme. I tried to overcome it by talking with my teacher, Dr. Kusumoto, training my students, and doing my research. This trouble lasted until I was fifty. Wang Yang-ming is believed to have said that the experiences of family affairs help us to understand the words of the sages. I agree with him, and it certainly applies in my case. In 1958, at the age of fifty, I became a full professor at Kyūshū University. In 1960 I received a doctorate of letters and in 1966 I was a visiting scholar at Columbia University in New York City for half a year.

My teacher, Dr. Kusumoto, had shown me a number of books by his grandfather, Kusumoto Tanzan.[20] I began to become interested in the study of Neo-Confucianism at the end of the Ming period. I had been working on a study of Wang Yang-ming and Lu Hsiang-shan, feeling there was something of worth to extract from their learning.[21] I was also interested in the study of Kao P'an-lung, especially his autobiography and his focus upon experiential knowledge in the process of the investigation of things as well as his practice of quiet-sitting.[22] I was also especially interested in Liu Tsung-chou's thought, in particular his suicide as an act of honor and conscience. I couldn't stop the tears when I read the lines expressing how he died.[23]

I was also very impressed with the books by Kusumoto Tanzan. A feeling of true reverence welled up within me when I read Kusumoto Tanzan's works. The general direction of Kusumoto Tanzan's thought may be summarized in the following way. To Kusumoto it was important to go back to the study of Chu Hsi after thoroughly studying the thought of the Ming period. My own theory of quiet-sitting has its roots here. I didn't know at the time how Kusumoto Tanzan was regarded as a thinker, and it was for this reason that I began studying his thought. What I found was that there were about ten Confucian scholars similar to Tanzan near the end of the Tokugawa period. All of these advocated this kind of study either of the Chu Hsi School or the Wang Yang-ming School, a study that was to be based upon inner experience. Those ten scholars had been largely ignored by scholars studying the history of Japanese philosophy, I suspect because their approach simply could not be understood. This was the reason I published my book on Kusumoto Tanzan, *The Life and Thought of Kusumoto Tanzan (Kusumoto Tanzan shōgai to shisō)*, using a great deal of information I was able to obtain from my own master, Dr. Kusumoto Masatsugu. After this I published the book on Neo-Confucian meditation and its relation to Buddhism, *Zazen to Seiza*.

Throughout this period I was still having major problems with my family, and I usually went to see my teacher once a week. I think I learned something by this contact, a transmission of heart to heart. I tried to teach students this way, and I often asked my students to come to my house to study and discuss books together. Those who followed me are now good scholars such as Professor Sato Hitochi at Hiroshima University and Professor Fukuda Shigeru at Kyūshū University.

Let me turn to the topic of the personality of my teacher. He always worried about my health because I was so weak. Whenever I talked with him about my family problems he listened very considerately. His personality had the humaneness of the famous Neo-Confucians Chou Tun-i and Ch'eng Hao.[24] I myself felt that I was in the warm breeze of spring when I was in his presence. I felt easy and carefree when I was returning home from my teacher's house, as the Ch'eng brothers reported when they left Chou Tun-i.[25] My teacher was physically very strong and this permitted him to study very hard. There was no way I could put anywhere near the time or energy into study because of my health. I certainly never worried about my teacher's health, and then suddenly he was diagnosed as having stomach cancer.[26] I feel so terribly sorry whenever I think about it, even now. He asked me at one point if after he was dead I would read the first chapter of the *Doctrine of the Mean* during the funeral service. And so, I read the first chapter of the *Doctrine of the Mean* and tears and sobs filled my eyes and face. I was even thinking of leaving Fukuoka, the place where I had devoted myself to my teacher who now had died. Before he died he gave me an ink stone as something to remember him by, an ink stone from the Sung dynasty. In addition, I also received pieces of calligraphy and many books belonging to Kusumoto Tanzan, my teacher's grandfather. This made me feel all the more committed to bringing Neo-Confucianism to society, for I was now a person who had had a great teacher who died. Because of this sense of responsibility, I organized the publication of a series of volumes on Neo-Confucianism.

When I recall all these people there really is no word with which I can thank them, my parents, my eldest brother, the person who supported me to go to university, and my teacher Dr. Kusumoto. Whenever I would complete a book I would express my gratitude to them by offering the book in front of their photograph or memorial tablet, burning incense and then pressing my hands together in prayer.

TAYLOR: In looking over your life, which particular events would you consider as critical turning points?

OKADA: Certainly what stands out most clearly was the meeting with my great teacher, Dr. Kusumoto Masatsugu, and reading the books of Kusumoto

Tanzan, grandfather of my own teacher. It was at that point that I felt I was in the tradition, that I was actually in the mainstream.

TAYLOR: Is it possible to say that, with the meeting of your teacher and the reading of the works of Kusumoto Tanzan, at that point your learning first truly began, learning in the sense of learning directed toward the goal of sagehood?[27]

OKADA: Yes, definitely, as for the first time I understood the meaning of Confucianism.

TAYLOR: From your own present perspective do you feel that in looking back over your life there has been a pattern and course of development that has stemmed from that initial point of learning?

OKADA: When I first began this learning, I could not have been conscious of any particular pattern or course of action. After I turned fifty, however, I was able to see something of this.

TAYLOR: In terms of the nature of learning itself, are life's crises an important part of motivation to proceed and persevere with learning, so that facing crisis and tragedy can push one on in learning?

OKADA: I have a basic principle upon which I act. This results in the fact that there is really no fear at any moment. If we understand the principle of the universe in silence, then no problem can confront us that will not be easily solved. The roots of my own ideas are of course Dr. Kusumoto Masatsugu and Kusumoto Tanzan. My teacher initially tried to use Western methods to understand Chinese thought. Gradually, however, he shifted away from this and adopted a method of his own background, a traditional Japanese way. This was demonstrated in his major volume on the history of Chinese thought, *Researches in Confucian Thought of the Sung and Ming Dynasties (Sō Min jidai Jugaku shisō no kenkyū)*.

TAYLOR: What is this traditional Japanese way?

OKADA: Its chief characteristic is an intellectual method with inner experiences.

TAYLOR: You have said that you studied Zen Buddhism at a certain point of your life. Was this formal study and practice, and were you seriously entertaining a Buddhist worldview?

OKADA: I tried to practice *zazen,* but I was not able to succeed in this practice because I could not give up my own Confucian point of view.

TAYLOR: In reviewing some of the material you have presented in terms of autobiographical reflection, you mention the Second World War only in passing. In light of the fact that most people of your generation consider the Second World War to have been one of the major events of their lives, I wonder what your own response to it was, especially considering you were living in Japan throughout the war years.

OKADA: I suppose in hindsight the war could not be helped, though I deeply regret its occurrence. I received my own draft call in 1931. It seemed inevitable that I would die if I had to go to war, given the weakness of my physical condition. I cannot deny that I was frightened to death. The thought of the Taoist philosopher Chuang Tzu calmed my heart, that one was to follow the ways of fate without hesitation.[28] After receiving my draft call, I visited my teacher's house. He said that fate was like a stone above your head, it became bigger and bigger if one tried to avoid it. I did want to devote myself to my country, and this is probably because of my Confucianism. I even studied the strategies of war. Real society is characterized by struggle and confrontation, and I felt this was an area that it was necessary to study just as earlier Confucians had done in their own generations. The issue of idealism is important but so too is the ability to deal with struggle in real society. In many ways, to develop idealism on the inside one must have the capacity of facing the struggle on the outside.

TAYLOR: Part of what I am interested in, in terms of autobiographical reflection, is the view you have presently of your life and its development. You have indicated that you are presently [in 1983] seventy-four years old. One of the first things that comes to my mind is Confucius' own autobiographical note in the *Analects*.[29] He says that at the age of seventy he could do whatever he wanted without fear of transgressing the right. What is your own present reaction to Confucius' comment?

OKADA: If you act according to the beliefs you have established through self-cultivation, then it is possible to be like this. However, such beliefs need to be flexible; they need to change with your age and to grow and develop.

TAYLOR: Do you feel that Confucius' own autobiographical note in the *Analects* becomes a model for all Confucians to view their own lives?

OKADA: Yes, I think it is, but I would still call myself a learner. When I look at other scholars, they seem to emphasize primarily the rational element of study rather than the inner experience. From this point of view, I feel very isolated. Even among my own disciples it seems hard to find people who would follow the idea of inner experience. It is important to realize, of course, that academic achievement is necessary even for inner experience itself. With the traditional examinations in China, if you didn't sit for the examination or didn't pass the examination, then while you might have deep learning experiences, what you can do with it is very limited.[30] In a sense not passing the examination meant that something was lacking in you, that you were not really good enough for self-cultivation. Of course, this applies only to the young; when you get older you shouldn't think this way. Myself for example, I look at it in this way. I seek the simple life and I forget all about academic achievement. Within me my heart is filled with the idea of the simple and pure life. By birth I am not a sociable person. I am not really suited to the social life. Yet I have a feeling of obligation and responsibility. It may seem that my own inner feeling of seeking for a quiet life stands in contrast to my feeling of obligation toward society. I don't really know whether it is a contradiction or not, but I say to myself that it is not!

KOTSUZA—JUST SITTING

Until now I have considered *seiza,* quiet-sitting, as the major form of self-cultivation, not unlike the role of *zazen* in the Zen schools of Buddhism in terms of its centrality to practice. Now, however, I think that sitting, just sitting, is of the utmost importance. The word *kotsuza,* just sitting, is the realization of this ideal. My former ideas of *seiza* have transformed themselves into the word *kotsuza.*

The inner nature of the mind will emerge and manifest itself if one just sits, that is, if one practices *kotsuza,* and nothing else. With *seiza* there can still be stimulation of ideas that can act as a hindrance to the realization of one's nature. With just sitting, the experience of the inner nature becomes manifest and there is true inner subjectivity (*naimen teki shūtaisei*). Quiet-sitting is the major method of cultivation adopted by Neo-Confucians. Activity, it seems, comes from quietude, but quietude itself does not come from activity. For activity to be correct and appropriate, it is necessary to understand quietude. Quietude itself of course means the quietness of the mind. The purpose in making the mind quiet is to cultivate the unmanifest nature of the mind.

To make one's mind quiet means to unify the mind, to draw it together, to make it whole. It has been said that it is important to have self-restraint, self-care, and self-fear and, furthermore, that watching oneself carefully when alone is of the utmost importance. To make one's mind quiet and whole there have been various methods adopted. For example, there are Zen Buddhist practices such as various forms of concentration and various special methods of breathing. To achieve quietude, however, you simply have to sit quietly. The stability of the body is essential to the creation of a mind of quietude. Even with the body stable, some of these special methods may be necessary, such as found in Zen Buddhist meditation. However, if you try to make your mind quiet, there will be activity. It is difficult to create that quietness. The primary essential is the stability of the body. When I was young I used to try to adopt some of these methods, but I found that when I was tired and just lay down, then I would gain a quiet mind. To sit at a desk or to lie down, these are appropriate activities to a quiet mind. If you just keep your body stable and quiet, something can come out of this. Essentially metaphysical activity and physical activity will become one, and the principle of things will be unified although its particularizations are diverse.

The existence of the body is both physical and metaphysical. This leads us to *kotsuza*. When there is a period of quietude, practice *kotsuza*. When there is activity, you need to instruct yourself in the principles of Confucian learning. These should include the investigation of things and the extension of knowledge, abiding in reverence, self-cultivation, and study. The philosopher Chu Hsi is of major importance in this respect. It might appear that *kotsuza* is different from these principles of Confucianism, but *kotsuza* is itself the ultimate form of a teaching such as abiding in reverence. Thus *kotsuza* is both the beginning and end of everything. Chu Hsi said, of course, that it was the investigation of principle that leads you to a sudden and total penetration of the unity of things. I don't agree with him in this respect. When you instruct other people, what is of the utmost importance is the cultivation of stillness. When you are able to cultivate this stillness, then in periods of activity, such activity itself becomes deep and profound. Something of this was involved when I changed the name of my study to Yuizean, from a word meaning "just this." Since that time I have felt that my mind has become deeper and more subjective and works spontaneously. This has led me to *kotsuza*.

In terms of educating others, one doesn't need to instruct in specific methods of concentration or the counting of breaths. Just let them sit quietly, nothing more than this. If I see someone who is distraught or in anguish, I suggest that he or she just sit quietly. I would say nothing more than that.

To phrase *kotsuza* in the categories of Western philosophy and logic makes the concept of *kotsuza* far too complicated. The essence of *kotsuza* is lost in this fashion. When I was young, I studied Western philosophy. The people I studied with told me it was important to be able to explain Eastern ideas in terms of Western culture. I feel now, however, that any analysis of Eastern thought using Western terms simply destroys the very essence of Eastern thought. It simply cannot be put into Western terms.

Part of my own learning when I was young included the writings of Henri Bergson. Bergson spoke frequently of "pure experience," an a priori category of experience. To explain such an experience is different from having the experience. The Japanese philosopher Nishida also discussed a priori experience. If you compare Nishida and Bergson, Nishida concentrated upon having an a priori experience whereas Bergson tried to explain the nature of such experiences. In the Eastern context, a practice and an experience are far more important than an explanation. Such practice and experience are the essence of learning.

I also studied Nietzsche when I was younger. Nietzsche, as I recall, attempted to explain the nature of self. He adopted a dialectical process of explanation but concluded that the self simply exists. I can't agree with this perspective in terms of an Eastern point of view. In Buddhism, for example, one does not explain the Buddha and then become the Buddha. Instead one focuses upon the realization of the Buddha nature. Only after such a realization can any "explanation" of what the Buddha is be given. Essence and process are entwined with each other.

At an earlier phase of my life I did try to explain Eastern thought in Western philosophical terms. I think now, however, that attempt was wrong. It may occasionally be necessary to use certain Western philosophical terms, but such terms never give the full explanation. It is not impossible to explain something of *kotsuza,* but frankly I prefer sitting with other people as an "explanation" of just sitting. And if an explanation is given, it is the simplest and briefest that is the best. For example, when one studies particular philosophers, one can understand something of them by looking over the major biographical events of their lives. We don't need to become lost in biographical detail. The simplest explanation is preferable, and it is the case that practice itself is always more important than explanations.

The scholars who study Neo-Confucianism try to analyze the philosophy, but it is not enough simply to understand the philosophy. For example, Chu Hsi advocated abiding in reverence, but it is far more important actually to practice abiding in reverence than to try to analyze it. For most of the scholars who study Chu Hsi, however, the analysis of Chu Hsi's thought is the study itself. This applies equally well to Confucius and the *Analects.* The scholars of the *Analects* are textual scholars, but I am not sure that Confucius even wanted people to read his writings. What is important is to practice Confucian ideals and contribute to the betterment of society. Those scholars who confine themselves to textual analysis of Chu Hsi's writings never think about the actual practice of Chu Hsi's ideas in society. Other people might think that I am one of those scholars who study the commentaries and texts of Chu Hsi or Wang Yang-ming, but in my mind such an approach is wrong. *Kotsuza* is a part of Chu Hsi and Wang Yang-ming. But I don't want to give an analysis of *kotsuza,* for the more that is explained, the less that is understood. I may sometime have to explain something about *kotsuza,* if I live long enough!

TAYLOR: The question that occurs to me is the relation between quiet-sitting, *seiza,* and just sitting, *kotsuza.* Is there a progression; does one begin with *seiza* and go on to *kotsuza*? Is there a sense that one of these is a beginning practice and one an advanced state of practice? Does the beginner start with *seiza*?

OKADA: *Kotsuza* should come first!

TAYLOR: If *kotsuza* comes first, how does that help the person who is trying to calm the mind; who is anxious and fearful and needs instruction on *how* to calm the mind? How does it help simply to say, "Just go and sit." Wouldn't it be better to start with breathing exercises, to get the person to the point where one can in fact settle the mind and then go on? I realize that philosophically or experientially it is important that *kotsuza* be first,[1] but in practice, and here we have the theory and practice dichotomy, doesn't the person necessitate some kind of instruction?

OKADA: I don't think so. Although there are times when a special method may be necessary for particular people, as far as I am concerned *kotsuza* is the most natural form of contemplation. In the beginning one might want to sit with one's spine straight and eyes shut, but the real problem in the beginning stages is developing the patience necessary.

TAYLOR: But don't you yourself feel there is an extraordinary difference between the initial fledgling stages of meditation and what you are discussing as *kotsuza*?

OKADA: Well, as I said earlier, activity comes from quietude, though there may be many steps in quietude itself. One advances according to age in some cases, or according to study in others. Take the example of a tree. One method is to start with the investigation of branches and leaves in order to come to understand the tree and its roots. On the other hand, you can go directly to the roots themselves. The investigation of the roots gives you an analysis of the tree including its branches and leaves. *Kotsuza* can be compared with the investigation of roots. It is simple and straightforward and goes to the heart of the matter.

TAYLOR: You say that *kotsuza* is "just sitting." Does this mean that it is sitting anywhere, anytime, or should it be done in one's study? In other words, rather than making a special practice out of it, is it in fact more the sense of the ordinariness of activity or the ordinariness of sitting that is the key to *kotsuza*?

OKADA: It doesn't matter where one practices *kotsuza*. In principle, wherever and whenever. In my particular case, I prefer my study, but I also practice it when I am lying down. It is also possible to practice *kotsuza* with other people.

TAYLOR: Kao P'an-lung uses a phrase in several of his essays on quiet-sitting, *p'ing-p'ing ch'ang-ch'ang* or just *p'ing-ch'ang*. Its meaning is "ordinariness" in the sense of the "ordinariness" of the Ultimate.[2] I wonder if what Kao P'an-lung means by this phrase is similar to what you have in mind in terms of *kotsuza*?

OKADA: Yes, for Kao P'an-lung *kotsuza* was to be anywhere and at anytime.

TAYLOR: Is *kotsuza*, like *seiza*, solidly in the tradition of the Chu Hsi School of Neo-Confucianism or does it provide an answer to Wang Yang-ming's critique of *seiza* as lacking in moral action by suggesting the possible activity of *kotsuza*?[3]

OKADA: *Kotsuza* remains within the context of the Chu Hsi School. In this sense it is simply a more subtle form of *seiza*.

TAYLOR: A number of contemplative traditions have suggested that the stilling of the mind is reasonably accessible in a quiet setting.[4] In other words, to practice meditation in a contemplative setting is itself almost redundant. For Zen masters such as Ta Hui and Dogen, the real test of meditation and its effectiveness in producing a quiet mind is the response of the quiet mind when placed in a setting of activity, or even turmoil and crisis. Does the mind remain unperturbed when faced with crisis?[5] If *kotsuza* ultimately is a practice to be undertaken in all settings, is the issue the same, is the primary concern to see that the quiet mind remains unperturbed?

OKADA: This same analysis applies to *kotsuza*. The state of activity and the state of quietude are ultimately the same state.

TAYLOR: If the state of quietude and that of activity are ultimately the same state, and the practice of *kotsuza* essentially perfects the transition between quietude and activity so that in the end there is no transition, is there an attitude or state of attentiveness to be retained in each moment?

OKADA: Yes.

TAYLOR: Do you feel that it is necessary that some sort of meditation should be a major part of the life of the modern person?

OKADA: I am of the opinion that some meditation like *seiza* or *kotsuza* is essential to modern society. This is the way one arrives at the original nature of the self. Every culture and people have some sort of means of meditation, but on the other hand, *seiza* and *kotsuza* are simple forms that could easily be adopted widely. Of course, each tradition is a conservative body; it has drawn perimeters around itself and won't easily accept things such as a form of meditation from another tradition.

TAYLOR: This raises a fascinating question. When one practices *seiza* or *kotsuza* and one is, let's say, a Christian or a Buddhist, is one still a Christian or a Buddhist in the context of the practice?

OKADA: When someone who is a Christian or a Buddhist practices *seiza* or *kotsuza,* that person may very well go beyond the boundaries of Christianity and Buddhism. This is because the worldview of *seiza* and *kotsuza* is a Confucian worldview. Thus the practice of *seiza* or *kotsuza* might lead the Christian or Buddhist to a different worldview, one that sees the primacy of humanity as itself ultimate.

TAYLOR: So what you are saying, if I understand you correctly, is that *seiza* and *kotsuza* may open the whole dimension of the Confucian religious world-view. It is not simply a practice that can be borrowed here and there in which the Christian remains Christian or the Buddhist remains Buddhist. The practice and the worldview in some sense cannot be separated.

OKADA: The Christian, the Buddhist, the Confucian, each has his own religious worldview. If the Christian or the Buddhist adopts the practices of *seiza* and *kotsuza,* then the person adopts a part of the Confucian view of the cosmos.[6] This specifically Confucian view focuses primarily upon the centrality of humanity. Other religions have various notions of gods and deities or an abstract "other," but Confucianism finds ultimate meaning in humanity itself. If Christian and Buddhist do adopt Confucian meditation practices, this role of humanity needs to be focused upon. It can be interpreted in terms of the love of God or the mind of the Buddha, but its central role cannot be minimized. This is a contribution that the Confucian worldview can make. This is not a form of syncretism but, rather, the recognition that Confucianism offers the meditation that focuses upon humanity and the ultimate meaning of humanity. And this point of view can make contributions to both Buddhism and Christianity.

THE NAMES OF MY STUDY

The study in my house has had different names at different times. I have given it the names Kominsai, Yuisean, and Shijinsha. These names reflect my own point of view just as my practice of quiet-sitting and its movement to *kotsuza* reflect my own learning. This is a topic I have not discussed with anyone, not even my own disciples.

When I had my small study built after moving from a town south of Fukuoka to my present address, I named my study Kominsai. My wife did not like the name Komin. She felt it was a little ostentatious. However, Komin reflected my point of view at that particular time. It means "to keep determination." It was understandable perhaps that my wife should criticize me for showing off a little. I might indeed have been a little egotistical at that time. The name Kominsai, in addition to being the name of my study, was the literary or style name I gave myself. This was in 1953 when I was forty-five years old. I was at the time working at Kyūshū University and life was difficult. It was only a few years after the end of the Second World War. I had lost many books because of the bombings during the war and had to spend a great deal of money to replace these books. Thus the circumstances of my life were very poor. There were no new clothes and what clothes we had were bought in second-hand shops. Poverty itself did not worry me. That was something I was familiar with from when I was a child. I had been physically weak really from birth on and had started working in factories when I was ten years of age as well as helping my mother with private work in the home. I worked in a factory before I went to school and after returning from school.

185

Sometimes this was very hard, particularly during the winter. I didn't eat polished rice, let alone fish, just bones and skin. Nevertheless, my heart was calm and stable in this setting—this is the word *komin*. Actually it has two meanings. It means "comfortable sleeping," the other, "to hold your determination." It is owing in large part to this environment of my childhood that the years of the Second World War and their aftermath did not overly concern me.

There was another motivation for the name Kominsai. After the Second World War there was much anguish in my family. This was something I wanted to overcome and that wish was also included in the name. I wanted some kind of transcendental metaphysical idea with which to cope with this anguish. I sought this kind of ideal in the writings of Chou Tun-i and Ch'eng Hao, preferring them to Chu Hsi and Ch'eng I. My own teacher, Dr. Kusumoto, praised highly the thoughts of Chou Tun-i and Ch'eng Hao and he probably influenced me to follow their teachings.

I couldn't at the same time deny my tendency to avoid reality by adopting the ideas of Chou Tun-i and Ch'eng Hao in order to overcome my anguish. During the Ming dynasty, Kao P'an-lung had said that only those understanding the real world could actually make a contribution to the state. I was of the opinion that perhaps my own anxiety for the name Komin was similar to this. However, though I have these tendencies to avoid anguish, my avoidance of reality was different from a Buddhist or Taoist approach.

However yet more circumstances for suffering and concern occurred in my family. I could not run away from this reality in my family life. I needed a specific and positive stance against such problems. This led me to the point of view that it was not enough to follow the teachings of the School of Mind, Lu Hsiang-shan and Wang Yang-ming. Their teachings might be acceptable for personal self-enlightenment, but they allowed one no strategy or method for dealing with the real problems that one faces. As I looked around me I realized that the world itself was engulfed in difficulties; China was going through its revolution, the Korean conflict was in progress, and Japan was having major problems concerning its own independence. Japanese universities were also seeing many conflicts. Such things forced one to face reality directly. I realized that we needed some basic principles for dealing with real society, with the conflicts of nations and the basic nature of humankind. This led me to begin the study of Chinese Legalist thought thinking that Confucianism would prove useless. But instead I came to realize the importance of Confucianism and in particular the Chu Hsi School of Confucian thought, especially as it is interpreted through the Tung-lin School of the late Ming dynasty. Without this approach, real problems could not be solved.

The Wang Yang-ming School simply doesn't give us any concrete method to face real problems. In order to face such problems, we need the investigation of things and the extension of knowledge, the major teachings of Chu Hsi. In order to apply these teachings one needs deep inner experience. It is such experience that leads one to the truth of the Principle of Heaven. If we compare the Chu Hsi School and the Tung-lin School, the Chu Hsi school advocates the Principle of Heaven, but it is put in a context of rationality. The Tung-lin School, on the other hand, says a great deal more about the inner experience, and thus their investigation of things and extension of knowledge are based upon an inner experience. It was the Tung-lin School that recommended the practice of quiet-sitting. This is an example of the extension of knowledge based upon inner experience. Chu Hsi, of course, discussed quiet-sitting and inner experience, but in terms of depth Chu Hsi did not reach the point of the Tung-lin School. My own point of view was to continue to emphasize quietude even in the study of Chu Hsi, considering essentially the Chu Hsi School and the Tung-lin School as a unified whole. Without that I would not be satisfied.

My own inner conflicts seemed to resolve themselves when I became sixty-five years old. At this stage of my life I reached a new understanding that the Principle of Heaven must be understood and then the problems of the world will be solved and this understanding must be through silent illumination. With this focus upon silent illumination I felt that the conflict between knowledge and inner experience had been solved. By silent illumination, I don't mean that I have reached some state of enlightenment where I have seen the oneness of all things. All I can say is that something came into my mind and it was Absolute, but I really can't say much about it. This led me to the second name for my study, Yuizean. *Yuize* means "just this." It is nothing more than "just this."

Recently, however, I have been thinking that even referring to "this" is saying too much. There should be no idea connected with it. It is just being together with others. It is the existence of each person each day. That is Absolute and that is all that there is. For this reason I gave my study its third name—Shijinsha. *Shijin* means just people in society, or just ordinary people and nothing more. In my heart I feel that this phrase, which comes from Liu Tsung-chou, is the proof of being human. I started using this new name in 1982 when I became seventy-three. By this name the metaphysical world becomes the practical world. The ultimate becomes the practical concept of *shijin*—just people, that is all. My own metaphysical world has been transformed into this concept of *shijin*—just people. I think in many ways that Eastern thought is always transforming the complicated object into a simple matter. The simpler the concept the deeper or more essential the point. This seems very different from the Western philosophical tradition. To me at least it is essential that people adopt the concept of simplicity. Consequently I have adopted this concept of *shijin*, just people, nothing more.

ON PRAYER

Confucians have always focused upon ancestor worship. This worship in turn is governed by propriety. There are various ways in which a reverential attitude may be shown; they vary through time and cultures alike. In China such reverential ways seem often elaborate or complex. In Japan, on the other hand, they are simple and straightforward.

In Christianity prayer is thought to involve a relationship with some "other," with something outside of yourself. In my own case, when I pray I might simply sit in front of my own teacher's photograph and give a report of what I am thinking about. For example, at present I have a visitor, Professor Taylor, and I have already reported to my teacher that we are having interviews. What happens in this case is that I feel I am with my teacher in my mind and that both my teacher and I are answering the questions posed by Professor Taylor. I had this same sense when I received an honorary degree from an institution in Taiwan[1] and I told the audience that it was my teacher who should be getting the degree, not myself. I have had similar feelings with my brother, my parents, even the trees and grasses of nature. In these cases it is the human aspect I think of first and foremost; it is not a god or the Buddha. It is the people who are with me who have a priority in my mind. This is simply the basic spirit of Confucianism. This focus upon the community of human beings is the very essence of being human. Once this is thoroughly established in the mind, one is peaceful. I have advocated quiet-sitting because this seemed the simplest way to establish this capacity of the mind.

189

TAYLOR: I wonder if you could distinguish between quiet-sitting and prayer.[2] In other words, if there are moments such as announcing to your teacher that I am interviewing you and these come under the category "prayer," can they be distinguished from the practice of quiet-sitting?

OKADA: Quiet-sitting means to sit quietly so that the mind might be protected from divergent and disparate thought. The purpose is for the mind to become whole and unified. If you begin to think about things, you must stop. Your mind must simply be allowed to go wherever it may. You do not consciously reject what comes out of your mind. You simply let it come out. If you must act, then you act. Through this means a quiet mind emerges.

TAYLOR: In terms of the relation between prayer and quiet-sitting, the description you have given of quiet-sitting would indicate that it is a process of sitting and stilling the mind, permitting the mind to express itself—whatever emerges—so that essentially thought continues to emerge of its own but will eventually quiet of its own, seemingly with no intentional activity. On the other hand, it would seem that the activity of addressing a former teacher is in fact a conscious activity and therefore by nature very different from quiet-sitting.

OKADA: In one sense there is a difference between quietude and activity, but within my mind they are the same. The distinction doesn't exist. Quietude or activity, they are both natural. In the same way a conscious addressing of my former teacher and the activity of quiet-sitting are both the same; they are both natural to my mind.

TAYLOR: If the conscious addressing of the teacher and the practice of quiet-sitting are the same in that they are natural in the same way as quietude and activity may be spoken of, can we at least look at the distinction as one between the manifest, *i-fa,* and unmanifest, *wei-fa,* capacities of the mind?

OKADA: Yes, such a distinction can be used as the basis of a discussion and explanation.[3]

ON DEATH

If those people whom I love, my wife, my parents or other relatives, die, then a deep grief arises in my heart, naturally. The law of the universe, however, is that those who are born will die; this we must believe. As a matter of fact those who have died still exist. They exist in my heart, and I shall never forget them. For example, when my teacher died, I suffered deeply and painfully. I want to think that when I myself die and go to an afterlife, I shall see my teacher again and I shall read books with him and study under him once again. Whether there actually is an afterlife or not, my teacher lives on in my heart. In a similar way my parents, my brothers and sisters, they all live on in my heart. And, of course, I remember my former wife every now and then, though I don't talk about it with my current wife!

In the Confucian tradition life and death are complementary to each other. The *Book of Changes* suggests this complementary nature, and most Confucians would think this way. Of course, over and above that, many would feel that the souls of the dead can continue to have a relationship with the living. For that reason, ancestor worship has played a major role.

From my own point of view, the relation of life and death is that of cause and effect. Because something is born, it will die. This is simply the law of the universe. Now if I know that I am going to die, then I would simply say I am following that principle. In my heart I would worry, of course, about my family, about society and the state. I guess too that I would be saying to the dead, "I'm coming to see you!" I would be thinking this way until my actual death. The actual question of the existence of an afterlife is unsolvable and endless. In my own heart I would entertain this particular question in the following way. If I have done something good or beneficial during my lifetime, then the people whom I have had contact with in the world might remember some small thing I have done or said and they might receive some small benefit from this. Even if it were true that there were an afterlife, my response would be nothing more than the hope that the living would derive some good, some benefit, from something I might have said or done.

The universe, of course, has a purpose and human beings exist in this universe with purpose. In fact the universe would be meaningless without human beings, since the universe exists together with the human mind; the human mind is a reflection of the mind of the universe.

ON THE GOODNESS OF HUMAN NATURE

Even now I believe in Mencius' basic theory of the goodness of human nature.[1] If we didn't believe in this ideal, how would it be possible to live together as human beings? The very concept of the survival of humanity and the world is directly tied to it. Without Mencius' idea you would not be able to trust even the person standing in front of you. This is truly the basic point that all humans are by nature good.

TAYLOR: Granted that the Confucian tradition has always focused upon the goodness of human nature, it still seems necessary to account for evil in human society. If all humans begin with the beginnings of goodness, then just exactly what accounts for the problem of evil?

OKADA: Evilness is selfishness in the human mind. Goodness, on the other hand, is what firmly exists in human nature itself.[2] The question that then arises, however, is, Which is more fundamental, evilness or goodness? When we look at the real world, it seems easy to agree with the concept that human beings are evil. This is particularly the case when you think in terms of societal problems or international affairs. With these kinds of conditions it almost appears necessary to accept the evilness of human nature. The same might be said in terms of the desires of children. Though there are such factors, the basic fact of the human community living together requires the recognition of the goodness of human nature. The real understanding of this goodness must itself be the product of a deep inner experience. The idea doesn't come from a rationalistic observation of human conduct. It must in

193

fact be considered in terms of religion itself. Thus, though there are many things that might lead us to a belief in the evilness of humans, we must accept the belief in the goodness of human nature. Without the belief, the world itself would not survive. Mencius' idea that all human beings are good is developed from a religious understanding of humankind. It is not on the basis of observation, but a firm belief in what must be the nature of humanity.

TAYLOR: It seems to me that one of the real challenges to this perspective of the goodness of human nature is that one finds oneself in situations where one essentially has to make a leap of faith. One has to base oneself upon that perspective, not knowing necessarily what the other person is going to do. Such a leap of faith, in religious terms, seems basic to the tradition itself.[3]

OKADA: I agree with you. However, in reality we cannot presuppose that everyone is going to act out of the goodness of their nature and we must have systems of control for evil actions.

TAYLOR: If we put this in a Christian framework, one might well say that the Quakers have always emphasized the ability to appeal to another's goodness—even if someone is pointing a gun to your head, you can still appeal to their inner sense of goodness, stemming from the basic Christian teaching of requiting evil with goodness. Is that in a sense the ultimate test of goodness?

OKADA: Personally, I don't agree with the response of the Quakers. Let me give an example. If someone has committed a very serious crime, then the person should be executed for that crime. The problem is that when you have to execute the person, you would do so while you were at the same time crying, crying and continuing to believe in the basic goodness of human nature. If you do not feel this act of execution in this very deep way, it really means that you do not believe in the goodness of human nature.

TAYLOR: But you would still go ahead with the execution?

OKADA: One cannot help it!

TAYLOR: So isn't it really the case that the Confucian position, and in turn its difference from a Quaker position, is summed up by Confucius himself when responding to someone who has asked if you should return goodness for evil, by asking if you return goodness for evil then what do you return for goodness?[4]

OKADA: That is right and I agree with Confucius in this passage, though there are also cases where flexibility is also needed. The Ch'eng brothers, for example, responded in different ways. The older Ch'eng brother had a sense of a magnanimous and compassionate heart and therefore was willing to forgive in certain cases of evil. The younger brother dealt with evil in a far more strict fashion. These two attitudes toward evil are typical ways of dealing with evil in society. In a sense everything is dependent upon our own ability as well as other people's resistance. If one has a magnanimous heart, one might be able to deal with situations of evil, but if not, then measures to eliminate the evil itself may be necessary. This seems the course of common day-to-day life. I can be magnanimous with person A but not with person B. Also I try to be more broad-minded with young people, and am far more strict with older people. These differing responses are all part of the complexity of one's own personality.

TAYLOR: One of the interesting points you have made, one rarely made in the literature, is the degree to which Mencius' principle of the goodness of human nature has to be an inner experience rather than a philosophical doctrine.[5] It would seem that for most studies of Confucian thought, Mencius is trying through analytic means to prove the goodness of human nature.

OKADA: As you say, there are many scholars who try to understand the goodness of human nature through rationalism. On the other hand, some try to consider the concept through their own inner experience. I try to understand the goodness of human nature through inner experience.

ART AND RELIGION

The philosophical and religious expressions of a particular historical period are closely related to the period's art. They are all part of the "atmosphere" of the period, and each helps to understand the other. If one grasps the meaning of the art, this provides an approach to the philosophy and religion. Thus, in the case of the thought of the Sung and Ming periods, it is essential to understand the art of these periods if the thought is to be fully comprehended. It works the other way as well, however. Art becomes understandable if the philosophy and religion are also understood. I myself am particularly interested in approaching the philosophy and religion *after* the understanding of the art. This has been my own approach to the thought of the Sung and Ming periods, and it was for this reason that I wrote *An Introduction to the Philosophy of the Sung and Ming Periods (Sō Min tetsugaku josetsu)*, which focuses upon the relation of art and thought. I realized that those people studying Sung and Ming thought lacked an understanding of the spirit of the age. They understood certain theoretical aspects of various philosophers, but even when it came to the difference between Sung and Ming thought, they were unable to grasp the difference. It seems to me that it is much easier if one considers first the differences in art between the Sung and Ming periods. Once the differences have been grasped, then the differences in thought are more readily approachable. Take painting, for example. In the Sung, there are painters who have a strong sense of the objective and the rational. In the Ming, on the other hand, there is a strong subjective quality and an expression of inner feelings. This suggests a distinction between the

196

Sung and Ming periods along the lines of the rationalistic and the subjective. This is a way of seeing the difference between the two greatest thinkers of these periods, Chu Hsi and Wang Yang-ming respectively. During the Sung, skill generally was considered more important than mind, while in the Ming, the reverse seems to be true. This is again basic to our understanding of the differences between Chu Hsi and Wang Yang-ming.

A similar difference can be seen in terms of ceramics. The prevalence of black-ink painting rather than color is equally applicable to the monotone coloring of Sung ceramics. The monotone color, like the black-ink painting, is an attempt to represent the ultimate form of color without simply negating it. Color appeals to one's sensations, but monotone color appeals to one's own inner state of mind. To understand the black ink paintings or the monotone color of ceramics, one must dig down deep within oneself. This tendency in ceramics corresponds to a change in the philosophical and religious climate of the time, which witnessed the arising of Neo-Confucianism. As we trace this development further, we can see that the continued development of the monotone ceramics during the Ming only further confirms the sense of the interior aspect of learning. In this sense, the T'ang dynasty with its bright display of colors appeals to the sensations, the Ch'ing with its display of skill and craft is not unlike its philosophical focus upon textual study. Both lack the depth of the self-reflective mode, seen in the Sung with what we might describe as a rational depth and in the Ming with its subjective depth.

TAYLOR: The discussion thus far has centered upon the relation between art and thought, whether philosophical or religious. I would like to ask you whether you feel that art itself can involve a religious or a philosophical depth.

OKADA: Art reveals the internal dimensions of the mind of the artist.

TAYLOR: In the West, Paul Tillich has suggested that the aesthetic experience of the artist can reveal the religious dimension itself.[1] Tillich would argue that great works of art potentially reveal religious dimension simply because of the depth to which the artists have gone into their own soul in order to express themselves.

OKADA: I would agree with this.

TAYLOR: Tillich's point is an interesting one because he seems to be suggesting, even from the point of view of a Christian theologian, that an artist can be religious through the aesthetic experience in the same way that someone else might be religious in terms of prayer or some other commonly recognized religious activity. For Tillich, art itself is one of the ways in which the depth dimension of human religiosity is revealed.

OKADA: I agree with this, and in East Asia I would like to see artists as the philosophical and religious leaders!

TAYLOR: Zen Buddhism and its relation to aesthetic experiences is a frequent topic of discussion. In the case of Zen painting, do we have the identification of a religious point of view with an artistic one?

OKADA: Zen painting is a good example of that point, though the same identity may be seen in the paintings of the Sung and Ming periods.

TAYLOR: Is there a Confucian equivalent to Zen painting in this respect?

OKADA: The Confucians were not as well known for their painting as they were for their calligraphy. It is through calligraphy that we can see their point of view.

TAYLOR: What does calligraphy reveal for a Confucian?

OKADA: Calligraphy shows mind and principle.

TAYLOR: Can one say that in looking at an example of calligraphy, one is engaging in the investigation of things to uncover mind or principle?

OKADA: Mind or principle may not appear from the calligraphy, but calligraphy does show the personality formed through the investigation of mind and principle by the calligrapher. The personality in this sense forms a wholeness with mind and principle, and the personality reveals its own internal dimension of mind and principle.

SCIENCE AND THE RESPECT FOR LIFE

I have a concern about the way in which science has developed. Its development has reached a point where it threatens the very existence of human life. The development of science should be for the benefit of the human community, but if there is a threat posed, then we need to be duly concerned about such developments. Nevertheless, we can't stop science and its development, for much of science is necessary for the human community. If we are going to make science totally responsive to the needs of the human community, we must let everyone—scientists and non-scientists alike—learn the importance of human life. In speaking of the importance of human life, it is essential to realize the importance of one's own life as well as the lives of others. We live in the same world together and mutual respect for life is a prerequisite. From my point of view Confucianism provides a suitable basis for this perspective. At the center of this perspective lies the Confucian idea of being in community with others. In short, one can live only by living in the company of others. In order to do this it is essential to follow the rules of society. The basis of Confucian ethics is to have consideration for the other person's heart. If we extend this concept, we can include all of nature.

TAYLOR: The late Chinese historian at the University of California (Berkeley), Joseph Levenson, has reflected that there was a very basic incompatibility between Confucianism and Western science and technology.[1] What is your reaction to this point of view?

OKADA: I don't agree with Professor Levenson's idea. To me Confucianism is compatible with the development of science. Once you understand the Chu

199

Hsi School you can see my point of view. Chu Hsi based himself upon respect for humanity and self-cultivation. He studied the arts and social sciences as well as natural sciences. To see the compatibility between Confucianism and science one must understand Chu Hsi's idea of "total substance and great functioning." According to that idea science benefits humanity, and humanity gives meaning to science. Chu Hsi's concept also suggests that human existence itself can be realized by science.

Chu Hsi's idea of the "total substance and great functioning" means several things. First, the human mind is moral, and second, all principles and laws of the natural world exist in the human mind. If we put this in a simple way, it would have to be said that we could not understand such laws or principles of nature *unless* they existed in the human mind. If this idea is not valid, then these principles and laws could never be known. This principle has been in large part ignored by people today, yet it is also the case that the very development of humanity itself can be understood by such principles and laws.

For Chu Hsi the very basis of such principles and laws was their ethical nature. Thus humanity itself must be understood in terms of ethics, and for this reason Chu Hsi spent all of his energies establishing human morality as the essence of Confucian teachings.

Let me put this in the framework of education in Japan—primary grades and junior high school. Before the Second World War we had a subject called self-cultivation. The education covered the following topics and in the following order: self-cultivation, Japanese literature, Chinese studies, history, social science, and natural science. This was a model of the Confucian educational system. If people in other cultures or even the Japanese now adopt the practice of self-cultivation and consider it the most important beginning point of education, then the contradiction between science and humanity will of its own disappear. In 1982 at the International Chu Hsi Conference in Hawaii I spoke with Tu Wei-ming.[2] He told me that he had been invited to go to Singapore to act as an adviser to the government of Singapore to establish Confucian education in the school system. We discussed several points about this subject, and I told him that the most important thing was the establishment of self-cultivation.

Ethics and Animals

TAYLOR: You have talked about the extraordinary importance of respect for human life and the degree to which science, and for that matter humanity if it is to survive, must reach toward the emergence of human respect. Therefore the degree to which science is based upon ethics is essentially the degree to which it is to be ultimately successful. My question concerns the degree to which ethics has been discussed primarily in terms of human life. I wonder about the degree to which a Confucian can speculate on the importance of not just human life, but of *all* life. In brief, do we have ethical responsibilities to *all* forms of life, not just human life?[3]

OKADA: Yes, I think we do. This idea of respect should be extended to all forms of life, animals and plants alike. The Confucian concept of being in community with other human beings can be extended to the community of life itself.

TAYLOR: From a Confucian perspective, humankind has the possibility of moral self-reflection and moral self-consciousness. The distinguishing mark of the human from an animal is moral self-consciousness and moral decision-making. Based upon the degree to which the human being is a moral decision-making individual, does the person have a moral responsibility for the safekeeping or the stewardship of other forms of life?[4]

OKADA: Because the Confucian ideal of forming one community with other human beings[5] should be extended to other forms of life, we do therefore have a moral responsibility for other forms of life. That all humankind has a heart of commiseration that cannot bear to see the suffering of others, such an idea should be applied to animals as well.

TAYLOR: An ethical concern of some consideration in the West is the issue of cruelty to animals. This is spoken of most frequently in terms of animal rights, suggesting that animals have ethical rights in some ways comparable to human rights. Of course, one of the major areas of concern for those who advocate animal rights is the use of animals for medical and scientific research. I wonder about the degree to which the extension of the heart of commiseration to all living things provides a foundation for a Confucian perspective on animal rights and the use of animals in research.[6]

OKADA: Of course, according to the heart of commiseration[7] we should not cause cruelty to animals. As regards the use of animals in medical or scientific research, here there are several interpretations. On the one hand, the use of animals appears to be necessary for the development of science. On the other hand, animals themselves could receive benefits from such research, for example, as regards a particular disease among animals. This is, however, a very difficult problem, for it is obvious that science requires animals and yet it is also the case that animals are caused much suffering because of this. Personally I think that the problem can be solved if we use the heart of commiseration. Let me put it this way: here in Japan we eat a lot of fish, and from time to time we have a memorial service for the fish that have been killed. If you think about the problem in this way, it might well be solved. Even when you have to kill animals it is necessary to have the heart of commiseration.

TAYLOR: In America and particularly in England where these questions are discussed at great length, there tend to be two positions taken with varying shades of meaning and interpretation. On the one hand are those who say that there should be no use at all, that no research, however well motivated, can justify the killing of animal life. On the other hand are those who say that even unlimited use of animals is justifiable because dealing with animals is not an ethical issue. It seems to me that what you are suggesting is a deep feeling of compassion through the heart of commiseration, recognizing that for the advancement of humanity and the advancement of science, animals must be used, but they must be used with care and respect for the life sacrificed.

OKADA: The two positions that you present are both extreme. The problem itself can be solved by the heart of commiseration. We must recognize that there are times when we need to differentiate humankind and animals. On the other hand, there are times when there should not be a difference drawn; humans and animals should be looked upon as the same. We should look upon individual situations with a heart of commiseration. This process of a case-by-case evaluation means that we need to be flexible and change if we feel the circumstances warrant.

Biomedical Ethics

TAYLOR: Continuing with the same issue of science and respect for life, let me pose some questions in the general area of biomedical ethics. I wonder first of all whether or not you would be in agreement that biomedical ethics is an important field precisely because it is saying that scientific and medical questions must also be governed by the ethical decision-making process.

OKADA: I would, and there are some very difficult problems in this area. If you take, for example, those people who have really been reduced to living vegetables, it is possible for them to go on "living" with the advancement of medical treatment, but the suffering that they cause their families is very extreme. It even reaches a point that the family members become seriously ill themselves under such circumstances. Such people, if they had a mind left, would surely say, don't worry about me anymore!

TAYLOR: You mean that the person would say that it is all right if you take my life?

OKADA: Yes. If patients are suffering from pain, then they might also say, please kill me; and I think under these circumstances it would be better to let them die.

TAYLOR: Suppose, however, as is the case is so many of these tragedies, that the person cannot say, then where does the ethical responsibility lie and how is the decision made?

OKADA: I don't think there is a simple single answer—it is good or it is bad! Such things are dependent upon the individual case and they are dependent as well upon the particular persons involved, the doctors, the family members, and the capacity of the ethical mind itself. We must rely upon the ethical mind, but we must also recognize that there are additional issues to be raised—economic consideration, social conditions, and so forth. There is no simple Yes or No. There is the famous story of the man who's sister-in-law almost drowned. According to Chinese tradition it is considered bad to hold a sister-in-law's hand and yet, given the circumstances, this man yielded and broke the tradition in order to save his sister-in-law. This is the sense in which rules are relative to context.

Abortion

TAYLOR: A very controversial issue in American life is the question of abortion. Once again extreme positions are posed. On the one hand, that all abortion is murder and no abortion should therefore be allowed under the law; on the other hand, that it is the undeniable and inalienable right of a woman to terminate an undesired pregnancy. From your point of view, where does the moral obligation lie? Does it lie with the unborn, assuming them their right to be born, or does it lie with the woman to determine for herself her own choice?

OKADA: These two solutions seem once again to me rather extreme. This issue also depends upon the context and the particulars of the case. Take, for example, the case of China. China is overpopulated and now each family is limited to only one child. If we were to bar abortion in China, the population would continue to grow and it would become a source of major problems for the entire country. So to control the size of the population may be part of human wisdom. We begin with contraception. But if that fails and the woman becomes pregnant, then we are faced with two issues: the rights of the un-born baby and the parents' ability to provide. I myself would accept the concept of abortion only when the parents cannot afford to provide for the child. I would not support abortion if the parents are seeking it only for their own selfish reason. Abortion is not preferable, but there are times when the birth of the baby is also a tragedy. In principle, if it is felt necessary, then contraception should be used. If the woman becomes pregnant, then the parents should accept the responsibility of the baby born to them and should carefully raise it. This is our fundamental purpose as human beings.

Technological Society

TAYLOR: Let me change the subject a little. Most of us would agree that we live in a technological society and in many ways in a technological world. One of the primary responses on the part of the individual to technological society is a sense of depersonalization. Tu Wei-ming has said that from his point of view one of the real challenges to the Confucian tradition is to be able to provide a method whereby one can live fully and authentically in technological society.[8] What is your feeling about this?

OKADA: I agree with Tu Wei-ming on this point. I also have my own ideas on how Confucians might play this role in technological society. The main purpose of Confucianism is to establish true humanity. No matter how far science has developed, the Confucian never loses sight of the development of humanity. Before any discussion of logic or rationality, the Confucian focuses upon the importance of subjectivity. In our day-to-day lives we distinguish what goes on within us from the outside world, but we become trapped by the outside world and in this way we lose our humanity. Given this situation we should try to control that external world, but in practice this is a very difficult thing to do. The important issue is to establish one's own inner subjectivity within the mind. It has seemed to me that with the increase in scientific knowledge, there has been a loss in the inner subjective capacity of the mind. Scientific knowledge stimulates the mind, but it also causes the loss of inner subjectivity within our minds. In order to retain our inner subjectivity and yet still accept scientific development, it is essential that we have some means to maintain our inner subjectivity. For that purpose, I consider the only method to be quiet-sitting. To me quiet-sitting is the only method to make our minds stable and to be able to establish inner subjectivity while science itself is continuing to develop.

TAYLOR: Do you see this problem of science and subjectivity eventually resolving itself in the future?

OKADA: This is a very difficult problem to solve. Inner subjectivity is certainly the only answer. It is in fact very simple; I would advocate that children as young as the age of two begin to practice quiet-sitting. Two-year-old children are old enough to begin quiet-sitting. By such a means we could firmly establish our inner subjectivity. In fact there is a preschool near my house where these little children practice quiet-sitting.

TAYLOR: If we begin learning forms of contemplative practice at these early ages, then would this create a significant change in the condition of the world?

OKADA: Of course, quiet-sitting is not the only thing that is needed, but it would play an important role.

TAYLOR: What else is needed besides quiet-sitting?

OKADA: The other major element is to teach children respect for human life, the life of others as well as their own. There is supposed to be such respect for human life, but often in this society people think only in terms of their selves, their own egotistic viewpoints, and they forget entirely about basic human respect.

TAYLOR: Will we be successful in this attempt to give a rebirth to human respect, or do we still face the grave danger of nuclear holocaust, the ultimate proof of technology gone mad?

OKADA: We are obligated to think that we shall triumph, even if we do not!

TAYLOR: Philosophers such as Bertrand Russell talk of what they call a kind of heroic fatalism. They mean by this that ultimately the universe is destined to no purpose, our own sun will die, the earth will freeze, and all life will be lost. They describe heroic fatalism as the attempt to continue on, even given few odds of ultimate survival. This is not an issue of soteriological transformation, only nonsurvival. From the Confucian view, are there grounds for optimism?

OKADA: I don't agree with this point of view. I still remember Confucius' own words, "We don't yet know about life,"[9] how could we thereby know what is going to happen in the future? It is obvious that everyone is born and everyone must die, but it seems ridiculous to think about death while we are still living. Humankind came to exist on this earth and it might disappear one day. That is a fact, and yet I am still opposed to thinking about the end of the world. The only point that might be useful is to raise the issue of the potential danger of the destruction of the world in order to make humanity realize the inherent importance of life itself. The nuclear threat has posed this as a real problem. To counter this we need to stress the importance of respect for human life more than the development of science. In practice, however, it does not develop itself in this way. This is regretful. Yet still we want to make that attempt to stress the importance of respect for life, especially to scientists and politicians.

Taylor: Confucians might very well play such a role in the Asian sphere, but it seems less likely in America or Europe. Is this an issue that Confucianism needs to address?

Okada: It is not important to discuss Confucianism per se. The important point is the issue of the common survival of humanity. We need to reach out to overcome differences and conflicts, to seek a oneness with others. This is the only means available. The West has focused upon analytic philosophy and science, the East upon the integration and wholeness of things. Both of these perspectives are indispensable. Until quite recently it seemed that the analytic Western model prevailed in the world. But we should not forget the Eastern method, the experience of the wholeness of things. Otherwise the Western analytic approach could bring about the destruction of human society. On the other hand, only to focus upon the Eastern model might result in the stopping of the scientific and technological development of civilization. Both are essential. Confucianism expresses this perspective, for it accepts the Western analytic model but also builds upon an Eastern model of the wholeness of things. To Confucianism, respect for human life and human dignity is the central issue.

Taylor: Is human dignity more important than life itself?

Okada: Human dignity cannot be separated from human life.

THE THREAT OF NUCLEAR WAR

The most central issue facing the human race today is the threat of nuclear war. A nuclear war would destroy the human race. We must address the issue of how to prevent such a war.

The leaders of the world are supposed to be addressing themselves to the prevention of nuclear war. Basically it seems to me that their approach is to take one of two possible alternatives. The first is a balance of power between the superpowers and the second is the seeking of peace by negotiation and the reduction of arms. I think that these two ideas should be considered simultaneously; otherwise we shall never have peace.

When one focuses upon individuals, they appear egotistical and self-centered. This is difficult to avoid. The result is that people struggle with each other. This is not only true of the individual himself or herself, but of society at large. Ethics is the basis for people living together in society. Between societies or nations, such egotistical and self-serving attitudes are even more dominant. One simply cannot advocate peace without recognizing this basic character of human nature and thus the character of human societies. This is a reality that we must face. Movements for world disarmament or the stopping of nuclear war can serve no useful purpose unless they are fully aware of the reality of human nature. Thus it is only reasonable to assume the importance of the balance of power of nations.

On the other hand, each nation should open its door to other people. In this sense the people of the world need to be in better communication with each other. People need to exchange ideas with each other. This level of communi-

207

cation has been prohibited by Communist regimes in the past, but we can encourage such countries to open their doors in the future. It is also important to have such communication among peoples of the free world as well. This is the way to bring about the realization of peace.

Each nation, each people has a different culture, a different tradition, and to understand other cultures it is imperative to communicate openly. If this communication is going to work, it is essential that each people not think of its own culture or its own tradition as absolute and right. There are differences between cultures; each nation has something distinct and unique. This distinctiveness and uniqueness should be respected to the utmost. Such respect is the most important point for the establishment of peace in the world.

Essentially this is a Confucian response to the world and its condition. According to other religions' point of view perhaps we should emphasize complete world disarmament. To me, however, this seems very idealistic. Of course, everyone strives for that point, but from the Confucian point of view we cannot think in those absolute categories of world disarmament in order to work for world peace. To the Confucian it is a practical matter. We begin at a very practical level, the establishment of the balance of power, and then afterward turn to a consideration of negotiation for disarmament. To the superpowers it is only a matter of struggle. I would insist that the only counter to this is a balance of power and then, once this is achieved, let the superpowers realize the degree to which nuclear war would bring about the total destruction of life—the end of the earth.

TAYLOR: In terms of this point of view, that it is necessary to deal with the real world, to face up to the real issues and not be an idealist, does this rest upon the basic Confucian view that human nature does need to be rectified and transformed, that egotistical motivation remains the primary problem, and that the problem of the superpowers is really only a reflection of the basic problem of human nature itself?

OKADA: These problems always stem from the nature of human nature. Each human being has in his or her nature two aspects, one is egoistic, the other moralistic. It is imperative that the moralistic become more dominant than the egoistic. When we consider the life of nations, the egoistic element seems in far greater magnitude than in the case of the individual. So in a sense the problem of the world is a far more serious and difficult one than that of the individual. This is the reason for the necessity of resolving this problem, a problem that must find its resolution in the balance of power followed by negotiation and disarmament.

TAYLOR: One of the classics of Confucian teachings, the *Great Learning,* suggests that ultimately political problems are actually problems in the development of the moral nature of the individual, the self-cultivation of the true nature. If self-cultivation is extensive and thorough, then these problems in the external environment will no longer have any basis. Can we say that this is still a viable point of view in terms of the magnitude of destruction possible with the threat of nuclear war?

OKADA: Even in this time, self-cultivation is still essential to the individual as it is spoken of in the *Great Learning.* One must be educated to the importance of self-cultivation, and if each individual in each country were to begin the practice of self-cultivation, then indeed we would have no further problem. That, of course, is our crisis! I think that Chu Hsi and Wang Yang-ming would agree with me on this. They would disagree between themselves on the nature of self-cultivation, but in terms of this world issue, they would agree!

WORLD RELIGIONS

In general I would have to say that religion serves a positive role in the world, but there are cases of harm as well. Most religions ask people to restrain human desires. Humankind has brought a lot of misery and strife upon itself through the attempt to satisfy its desires. The exercise of control by religions in this area of human desire could serve to reduce the level of turmoil in the world. In terms of the harmful aspects of religion, this can most easily be seen in the level of fanaticism that rejects the mutual respect for others and thus the goal of the survival of the whole human community. Such fanaticism breeds intolerance and violence against others.

In this respect I have tended to be critical of monotheistic traditions because of their tendency to reject other religious points of view. For example, there are many denominations of Christians in Japan. They reject other points of view, they even reject each other. Some forms of Christianity are very generous and broad-minded, but many remain very narrow-minded. Historically such attitudes have created strife and conflict. When we look at Eastern religions we might say that they too have in historical terms created conflicts, but compared with the case of the West, the severity and the magnitude are much much less. We might say that Western religions remain passionate in their pursuit, while Eastern points of view lack that quality of passion. We might put this in terms of quietude and activity. Where Western traditions in general terms tend toward activity, Eastern traditions tend to emphasize quietude. These are important characteristics to understand.

TAYLOR: Is it possible as you see it for religions of the world to become less intolerant? What is the feature of many of these religions that could be transformed to permit a greater capacity for tolerance?

OKADA: All that has to be emphasized is the true respect for human life.

TAYLOR: Why do you think it is that some religions seem so convinced of the necessity of proving to others the correctness of their point of view, while others do in fact seem more tolerant, more capable of living with different points of view? Do you think this is an issue inherent in the nature of religion, or is it an issue of the individual personalities that make up the religious community?

OKADA: Religions that are intolerant of other points of view portray certain human characteristics. Let's take Taoism and Zen Buddhism as an opposite example. Both Taoism and Zen Buddhism discuss the concept of emptiness. Emptiness means in very general terms two things; first, it focuses upon what is inclusive rather than exclusive and, second, it stresses the denial of human desires. These two aspects have been expressed in a variety of modes, but they both by their very nature gravitate against intolerance in religion.

TAYLOR: It would seem that the frequently encountered Eastern model of the religious life, which insists that different people should receive different teachings, is in certain ways clearly distinguishable from the Western monotheistic tradition's insistence upon uniform creedal expression. Perhaps that too increases the apparent sense of increased tolerance in the Eastern model.

OKADA: A person who has reached a higher stage of understanding has a greater level of tolerance, but I would stress again the significance of the Eastern ideas of emptiness and quietude. On the other hand, Eastern traditions also have their faults. Western traditions have shown a much greater interest in dealing with real problems in society. My own motivation for studying the Neo-Confucian tradition lay in my own feeling of the importance of facing real problems of the world while at the same time seeking individual self-cultivation. As far as the common person goes, it is essential to emphasize the importance of respect for human life. From my point of view that idea is a religious idea.

TAYLOR: Can we draw a distinction between a religious system and a religious value? In other words, you are emphasizing the religious nature of the respect for human life and yet there is not a tremendous amount of concern for a particular religious tradition or system.

OKADA: My ideas are probably not compatible with particular religious traditions or systems. We may very well need some particular tradition dependent upon a cultural context, but all we really need is perhaps an institute where we can meet to discuss world problems and spiritual problems. The focus needs to be self-cultivation. In fact my real idea is to establish academies such as one finds in Sung and Ming China where self-cultivation can be the main pursuit. Even humanities centers in universities could be used in this way, though they need to turn their attention toward the actual practice of self-cultivation. From the Sung worldview there was a recognition of the importance of respect for human life, and all education was oriented to that point of view. We must reestablish learning that recognizes the role of self-cultivation as it leads toward not just the accumulation of knowledge, but the inner subjective experience of humanity itself.

We don't really need to have Confucianism as Confucianism in the future. All we need is the respect for human life and human dignity. In this country—Japan—if we advocate Confucianism today, there is a very strong opposition; thus our focus must remain upon the issue of respect for human life and human dignity, not the name of the tradition. If the name itself disappears in the future, that is all right, just so long as the issue of human dignity remains. I could pose the question to someone, "What is more important to you, a distant god or humanity itself?" or "What is more important, a distant god or your parents?" Of course I am not Socrates, but I would still like to pose these kinds of questions!

NOTES

1. The Confucian Quest

1. *Mencius*, 6B:2.

2. W. T. deBary, *Sources of Chinese Tradition* (New York: Columbia University Press, 1960), p. 524.

3. For a translation and discussion of this text, see W. T. Chan, *A Source Book of Chinese Philosophy* (Princeton: Princeton University Press, 1963), pp. 84–94.

4. W. T. Chan, *Source Book*, p. 561.

5. W. T. deBary, *Chinese Tradition*, p. 532.

6. W. T. Chan, *Source Book*, p. 89.

7. This is a concept that Okada will focus upon in his interpretation of Chu Hsi and the practice of quiet-sitting. See chap. 2.

8. W. T. Chan, *Source Book*, p. 562. I have changed his translation from "seriousness" to "reverence."

9. Wach outlines four criteria for genuine religious experience; first, it must be a response to what is viewed as Absolute; second, it must be a total response; third, it must be intense; and fourth, it must issue forth into action. See Joachim Wach, *The Comparative Study of Religions* (New York: Columbia University Press, 1958), pp. 27–58.

10. See W. T. Chan, "Chu Hsi's Completion of Neo-Confucianism," *Études Song-Sung Studies: In Memoriam Étienne Balazs*, ed. Françoise Aubin (Paris: Mouton, 1973), pp. 59–90.

11. W. T. deBary, *Chinese Tradition*, p. 530.

12. *Mencius*, 2A:2.

13. W. T. Chan, *Source Book*, pp. 538–39. "Seriousness" has been changed to "reverence."

14. *Mencius*, 2A:2.

15. W. T. Chan, *Source Book*, p. 524. See Okada's rendering of this passage, *Zazen to Seiza*.

16. See translation and discussion of text in W. T. Chan, *Source Book*, pp. 84–94.

17. See W. T. Chan, trans., *Instructions for Practical Living and Other Neo-Confucian Writings by Wang Yang-ming* (New York: Columbia University Press, 1963), pp. 269–80.

18. Ibid., p. 279.

19. Ibid., pp. 279–80.

20. Ibid., p. 280.

21. This has been discussed by Tu Wei-ming. See Tu Wei-ming, *Humanity and Self-Cultivation: Essays in Confucian Thought* (Berkeley, Calif.: Asian Humanities Press, 1979), p. 149.

22. Instrumental in this respect is Okada's volume Ō-*Yomei to Minmatsu no jugaku (Wang Yang-ming and Late Ming Confucianism)* (Tokyo, 1970). For a general discussion, see Okada Takehiko, "The Chu Hsi and Wang Yang-ming Schools at the End of the Ming and Tokugawa Periods," *Philosophy East and West* 23, nos. 1–2 (January–April 1973): 139–62.

23. Note, e.g., W. T. deBary and Irene Bloom, eds., *Principle and Practicality: Essays in Neo-Confucianism and Practical Learning* (New York: Columbia University Press, 1979).

24. See W. T. deBary, "Introduction," *Self and Society in Ming Thought*, ed. W. T. deBary (New York: Columbia University Press, 1970), pp. 8ff.

25. See W. T. Chan, "The Ch'eng-Chu School of Early Ming," *Self and Society*, pp. 29–52.

26. Ibid., pp. 34–35.

27. Ibid., p. 36.

28. This is rectified in Tu Wei-ming, *Neo-Confucian Thought in Action: Wang Yang-ming's Youth (1472–1509)* (Berkeley: University of California Press, 1976), pp. 163ff.

29. See R. L. Taylor, *The Cultivation of Sagehood as a Religious Goal in Neo-Confucianism* (Missoula, Mont.: Scholar's Press, 1978), pp. 47–52, with an example of Kao's retention of the Ch'eng-Chu perspective.

30. Note Huang Tsung-hsi's assessment of Kao's position. See Huang Tsung-hsi, *Ming-ju hsüeh-an (Records of Learning of the Ming Confucians)* (Ssu-pu pei-yao ed.,), 58:18a–b.

31. Maruyama Masao, *Studies in the Intellectual History of Tokugawa Japan* (Princeton: Princeton University Press, 1975).

32. Of particular importance is deBary and Bloom, eds., *Principle and Practicality*. See also Peter Nosco, ed., *Confucianism and Tokugawa Culture* (Princeton: Princeton University Press, 1984); Richard Rubinger, *Private Academies of Tokugawa Japan* (Princeton: Princeton University Press, 1982); W. T. deBary, *The Liberal Tradition* (Hong Kong: Chinese University Press; New York: Columbia University Press, 1983).

33. Peter Nosco, "Introduction," *Confucianism and Tokugawa Culture*, pp. 7–8.

34. Ibid., p. 25.

35. W. T. deBary, "Introduction," *Principle and Practicality*, p. 18.

36. Nosco, "Introduction," pp. 3–26.

37. See W. T. deBary, "Sagehood as a Secular and Spiritual Ideal in Tokugawa Neo-Confucianism," *Principle and Practicality*, pp. 130–33.

38. Ibid., pp. 133–39. See also Irene Bloom, "On the 'Abstraction' of Ming Thought: Some Concrete Evidence from the Philosophy of Lo Ch'in-shun," *Principle and Practicality*, pp. 69–125.

39. W. T. deBary, "Introduction," *Principle and Practicality*, p. 21. For a study of Ishida Baigan, see Robert Bellah, *Tokugawa Religion: The Values of Pre-Industrial Japan* (Boston: Beacon Press, 1970).

40. For Okada's interpretation of Yamazaki Ansai, see Okada Takehiko, "Practical Learning in the Chu Hsi School: Yamazaki Ansai and Kaibara Ekken," *Principle and Practicality*, pp. 231–306. See also Okada Takehiko, "Neo-Confucian Thinkers in Nineteenth-Century Japan," *Confucianism and Tokugawa Culture*, pp. 215–50.

41. Yanagawa Gōgi, *Shushi seiza shusetsu*, 1717 ed., 12a–b.

42. Ibid., 1a–2b.

43. Okada, "Neo-Confucian Thinkers in Nineteenth-Century Japan," pp. 231–32.

44. Ibid., pp. 228, 235.

45. Satō Issai is also the teacher of Kameyama Umpei (1822–96), the teacher of Okada's

father. Thus the connection to Satō Issai for Okada is through both his teacher and his father.

46. A number of these issues are developed in chapter 6.

47. In addition to *Zazen to Seiza*, this is also detailed in Namba Yukio and Okada Takehiko, *Tsukida Mōsai Kusumoto Tanzan* (Tokyo, 1978) as well as Okada's own study of Kusumoto, *Kusumoto Tanzan shōgai to shisō (The Life and Thought of Kusumoto Tanzan)* (Fukuoka, 1959).

2. Centering the Self in Quiet-Sitting

1. Recent studies of quiet-sitting include W. T. deBary, "Neo-Confucian Cultivation and the Seventeenth-Century 'Enlightenment'," *The Unfolding of Neo-Confucianism*, ed. W. T. deBary (New York: Columbia University Press, 1975), pp. 170–72; R. L. Taylor, *The Cultivation of Sagehood as a Religious Goal in Neo-Confucianism* (Missoula, Mont.: Scholar's Press, 1978), and "Meditation in Ming Neo-Orthodoxy," *Journal of Chinese Philosophy* 6, no. 2 (June 1979): 149–82; Jacques Gernet, "Techniques de Recueillement, Religion et Philosophie: A Propos du *Jingzuo* Neo-Confuceen," *Bulletin de l'École Française d'Extrême-Orient* 69 (1981): 289–305.

2. Huang Tsung-hsi, *Sung-Yüan hsüeh-an (Records of Learning of the Sung and Yüan Confucians)* (Taipei, 1975), 10:64.

3. See, e.g., Alfred Forke, *Geschichte der neueren chinesischen Philosophie* (Hamburg, 1938), pp. 156–63.

4. See Gernet, "Techniques," particularly pp. 303–5, for a discussion of the question of Buddhist influence on Neo-Confucianism. I have discussed this question in "The Sudden/ Gradual Paradigm and Neo-Confucian Mind-Cultivation," *Philosophy East and West* 33, no. 1 (January 1983), particularly pp. 28–32, as well as "Subitist and Gradualist: A Simile for Neo-Confucian Learning," *Monumenta Serica* 36 (1984–86): 1–32.

5. Yanagawa, 1a–b, (*Chu Tzu yü-lei* [1880 ed.] 119:7a–b).

6. Yanagawa, 5b–6a, (*Chu Tzu yü-lei* 96:12a–b).

7. *Zazen to Seiza.*

8. For a summary of Chu Hsi's theory of mind, see Tang Chun-i, "The Development of the Concept of Moral Mind from Wang Yang-ming to Wang Chi," *Self and Society in Ming Thought*, ed. W. T. deBary (New York: Columbia University Press, 1970), pp. 93–97.

9. W. T. Chan, *A Source Book of Chinese Philosophy* (Princeton: Princeton University Press, 1963), p. 98.

10. *Sung-Yüan hsüeh-an*, 10:63.

11. *Sung-Yüan hsüeh-an*, 10:72.

12. A discussion of the influence of Hu Hung upon Chu Hsi may be found in Conrad Schirokauer, "Chu Hsi and Hu Hung," *Chu Hsi and Neo-Confucianism*, ed. W. T. Chan (Honolulu: University of Hawaii Press, 1986), pp. 480–502.

13. *Zazen to Seiza.*

14. *Mencius*, 6A:11.

15. Yanagawa, 4b (*Chu Tzu yü-lei* 11:2a).

16. Yanagawa, 4a (*Chu Tzu wen-chi* 63), in *Chu Tzu ta-ch'üan (Ssu-pu pei-yao* ed.) 63, 36b–37a.

17. Yanagawa, 1a (*Chu Tzu yü-lei* 12:11a–b).

18. Yanagawa, 10b (*Chu Tzu wen-chi* 42), in *Chu Tzu ta-ch'üan* 42, 2a.

19. Yanagawa, 10b (*Chu Tzu wen-chi* 42), in *Chu Tzu ta-ch'üan* 42, 2a.

20. Yanagawa, 2b–3a (*Chu Tzu yü-lei* 45:13a–b).

21. Yanagawa, 3a–3b (*Chu Tzu yü-lei* 12:17b).

22. Yanagawa, 7b (*Chu Tzu yü-lei* 12:16b).

23. Okada has referred to the importance of this principle in the "Dialogue" section below. See also Okada Takehiko, "Practical Learning in the Chu Hsi School," *Principle and Practicality: Essays in Neo-Confucianism and Practical Learning,* eds. W. T. deBary and Irene Bloom (New York: Columbia University Press, 1979) pp. 281–82, and Okada Takehiko, "Chu Hsi and Wisdom as Hidden and Stored," *Chu Hsi and Neo-Confucianism,* pp. 198–201. His own teacher also wrote on the subject. See Kusumoto Masatsuga, *Chūgoku tetsugaku kenkyū (Researches in Chinese Philosophy)* (Tokyo, 1975), pp. 353–91.

24. Yanagawa, 9a (*Chu Tzu yü-lei* 118:23a).

25. Yanagawa, 7a (*Chu Tzu yü-lei* 120:4a).

26. Yanagawa, 7a (*Chu Tzu yü-lei* 12:17b).

27. See W. T. Chan, "Chu Hsi's Completion of Neo-Confucianism," *Études Song-Sung Studies: In Memoriam Étienne Balazs,* ed. Françoise Aubin (Paris: Mouton, 1973).

28. For a discussion of the Diagram of the Great Ultimate, see W. T. Chan, *Source Book,* pp. 463–65.

29. Gernet has rendered this phrase "l'essentiel etait le calme," Gernet, "Techniques," p. 296.

30. See *Zazen to Seiza.* The *Chung-yung* suggests that the superior person settled himself in whatever circumstances he finds (*Chung-yung* 14). See W. T. Chan, *Source Book,* p. 101. The *Ta hsüeh* suggests that a point of rest must be found and that this is the foundation of stillness (*Ta-hsüeh* 2). See W. T. Chan, *Source Book,* p. 86.

31. For a partial translation, see Norman Waddell, "A Selection from the *Ts'ai-ken-t'an (Vegetable Root Discourses),*" *Eastern Buddhist* 2, no. 2 (November 1969): 88–98.

· 32. This is a reference to Chou Tun-i's cosmology and the first statement of his explanation of the Diagram of the Great Ultimate, which simply reads, "The Non-Ultimate and also the Great Ultimate." There have been many interpretations of this statement. Okada is taking the perspective that the Non-Ultimate is the foundation and is characterized by stillness.

33. Hexagram 24, *fu,* "return," is discussed in Richard Wilhelm, trans., *The I Ching or Book of Changes* (New York: Pantheon Books, 1964), Part I, pp. 103–6; Part II, pp. 144–49.

34. For Okada's more detailed study of Kao and the Tung-lin School, see his *Ō Yōmei to Minmatsu no jugaku (Wang Yang-ming and Late Ming Confucianism)* (Tokyo, 1970), pp. 409–38, and "Torin gaku" ("Tung-lin Learning") in Okada Takehiko, *Chūgoku shisō no genjitsu to risō (The Actuality and Ideal of Chinese Thought)* (Tokyo, 1984), pp. 507–89. See also Taylor, *Cultivation of Sagehood,* a study of Kao.

35. See Taylor, *Cultivation of Sagehood,* pp. 121–34, for a translation of this text. Also found in R. L. Taylor, "The Centered Self: Religious Autobiography in the Neo-Confucian Tradition," *History of Religions* 17, nos. 3–4 (February–May 1978): 266–83.

36. *Zazen to Seiza.*

37. Ibid.

38. See Taylor, *Cultivation of Sagehood,* pp. 195–97, for a translation of this text.

39. *Zazen to Seiza.*

40. These texts are also translated in Taylor, *Cultivation of Sagehood,* pp. 199–202, and analyzed in Taylor, "Meditation in Ming Neo-Orthodoxy," pp. 155–62.

41. *Zazen to Seiza.*

42. Ibid.

43. Ibid.

44. For a detailed study of Kusumoto Tanzan, see Okada, *Kusumoto Tanzan shōgai to shisō*

(The Life and Thought of Kusumoto Tanzan) (Fukuoka, 1959) and, with Yukio Namba, *Tsukida Mōsai Kusumoto Tanzan* (Tokyo, 1978). The final chapter of *Zazen to Seiza* is devoted to a selection of sayings from Tanzan but has not been included in this translation. There is also material in Okada Takehiko, "Neo-Confucian Thinkers in Nineteenth-Century Japan," *Confucianism and Tokugawa Culture,* ed. Peter Nosco (Princeton: Princeton University Press, 1984), pp. 215–50.

45. Beyond the discussion of storehouse wisdom in *Zazen to Seiza,* there is Okada's recent study "Chu Hsi and Wisdom as Hidden and Stored," *Chu Hsi and Neo-Confucianism* pp. 197–211. Note in particular pp. 202–4 for a discussion of Okada's interpretation of the role of Mencius in this theory.

46. Quoted in *Zazen to Seiza,* p. 159, but not included in the translation.

47. *Zazen to Seiza.*

48. Ibid.

49. Quoted in *Zazen to Seiza,* p. 151, but not included in the translation.

50. *Zazen to Seiza.*

51. Ibid.

52. Ibid.

53. Ibid.

54. Quoted in *Zazen to Seiza,* p. 155, but not included in the translation.

55. *Zazen to Seiza.*

56. "Dialogue."

57. Ibid.

3. Moral Action from a Contemplative Mode

1. This is indicated in the very structure of the *Great Learning,* representing the initial focus upon self-cultivation and the resultant capacity to act in the world.

2. Joachim Wach, *The Comparative Study of Religions* (New York: Columbia University Press, 1958), pp. 36–37.

3. William James states that it is the practice itself that confirms the religious point of view. William James, *The Varieties of Religious Experience* (New York: Penguin Books, 1982), p. 20.

4. This raises the question of whether strictly moral action is exclusive of religious action. Little and Twiss attempt to establish the difference between moral action guides (MAGs) and religious action guides (RAGs). D. Little and S. Twiss, Jr., "Basic Terms in the Study of Religious Ethics," *Religion and Morality: A Collection of Essays,* ed. G. Outka and J. Reeder, Jr. (Garden City, N. Y.: Doubleday Anchor Books, 1973). pp. 35–77. From my point of view, moral and religious questions are not separate within the Confucian tradition. It is, rather, a continuum of religio-ethical thinking and acting. For a response to the point of view that Hsün Tzu might be ethical but is not religious, see E. Machle, "Hsün-tzu as a Religious Philosopher," *Philosophy East and West* 26, no.4 (October 1976): 443–61.

5. *Zazen to Seiza.*

6. These criticisms of Buddhism are relevant to the discussion of Buddhist influence upon Neo-Confucianism. If this level of objection exists to Buddhism, then influences from Buddhism seem in need of rethinking. See Jacques Gernet, "Techniques de Recueillement, Religion et Philosophie," *Bulletin de l'École Française d'Extrême-Orient* 69 (1981): 303ff.

7. *Mencius,* 6A:2.

8. *Mencius,* 2A:6.

9. *Mencius,* 1A:1.

10. The *locus classicus* for this attitude is Confucius, who when he was asked about death indicated he did not yet understand life and therefore could not be expected to understand death. *Analects*, 11:11.

11. *Mencius*, 2A:6.

12. "Dialogue."

13. Ibid.

14. For these so-called "arguments" for goodness of human nature, see *Mencius*, 6A:1–4.

15. "Dialogue."

16. Ibid.

17. In response to a question from a disciple, Does one requite evil with goodness? Confucius answers by saying if you requite evil with goodness, then with what does one requite goodness? *Analects*, 14:36.

18. This is the general view, that Chu Hsi advocated a broad learning schema through the investigation of things and extension of knowledge that is not incompatible with the scientific method.

19. "Dialogue."

20. W. T. Stace, "Man against Darkness," reprinted in *Ways of Being Religious,* eds. F. Streng, C. Lloyd, Jr., and J. Allen (Englewood Cliffs, N. J.: Prentice-Hall, 1973), p. 339.

21. Clifford Geertz, "Religion as a Cultural System," *Reader in Comparative Religion: An Anthropological Approach,* 2nd edn., eds. W. Lessa and Evon Vogt (New York: Harper & Row, 1965), p. 211.

22. The literature in this field has expanded tremendously. See Tom Regan and Peter Singer, eds., *Animal Rights and Human Obligations* (Englewood Cliffs, N. J.: Prentice-Hall, 1976); Peter Singer, *Animal Liberation: A New Ethic for Our Treatment of Animals* (New York: Avon, 1975); Tom Regan, *The Case for Animal Rights* (Berkeley: University of California Press, 1985); and Tom Regan, ed., *Animal Sacrifices: Religious Perspectives on the Use of Animals in Science* (Philadelphia: Temple University Press, 1986), which contains R. L. Taylor, "Of Animals and Man: The Confucian Perspective," pp. 237–63.

23. *Analects*, 7:26, 10:12.

24. *Mencius*, 1A:7.

25. "Dialogue."

26. Ibid. "Heart of commiseration" is a reference to *Mencius*, 2A:6.

27. Ibid.

28. For a standard work informing the ethical issues surrounding these acts, see T. Beauchamp and J. Childress, *Principles of Biomedical Ethics* (New York: Oxford University Press, 1979). A strictly utilitarian approach is represented by Peter Singer, *Practical Ethics* (London: Cambridge University Press, 1979). A religious perspective is represented by J. Fletcher, *Morals and Medicine* (Boston: Beacon Press, 1960). See also Gerald Larue, *Euthanasia and Religion* (Los Angeles: Hemlock Society, 1985).

29. "Dialogue."

30. Ibid.

31. Ibid.

32. Ibid.

33. Ibid.

34. Ibid.

35. *Analects*, 11:11.

My Life
1. Harima—name of a province during the Tokugawa period.
2. Shōheikō was the official Tokugawa government school in Edo.
3. The Mito School followed Chu Hsi and found its model in a Chinese Ming dynasty loyalist, Chu Shun-shui (1600–1682), who settled in Japan in Mito. See Julia Ching, "The Practical Learning of Chu Shun-shui," *Principle and Practicality: Essays in Neo-Confucianism and Practical Learning,* eds. W. T. deBary and Irene Bloom (New York: Columbia University Press, 1979), pp. 189–230.
4. Okada's point is to show his family connection through Kameyama Umpei to Fujita Toko, a prominent member of the Mito School of Neo-Confucianism.
5. For a study of the private schools, *shijuka,* see Richard Rubinger, *Private Academies of Tokugawa Japan* (Princeton: Princeton University Press, 1982). For a general discussion of official schools in the same period, see R. P. Dore, *Education in Tokugawa Japan* (Berkeley: University of California Press, 1965).
6. Years of elementary school were 1915–21.
7. This is the beginning of Okada's interest in the relation of thought and aesthetics which culminates in the work *Sō Min tetsugaku josetsu (An Introduction to the Philosophy of the Sung and Ming Periods)* (Tokyo, 1977).
8. According to the family, he attended advanced elementary school, 1921–23.
9. He attended middle school, 1923–28. Middle school corresponds to contemporary high school.
10. The economic recession of 1920–25.
11. Senior minister or *karō* of the Himeji domain.
12. *Analects,* 6:21.
13. Okada is referring to the practice by the better students of taking examinations to enter high school in the fourth rather than fifth year of middle school, one year early.
14. He attended Himeji High School, 1928–31. High school under the old system is equivalent to college or undergraduate work.
15. Equivalent to modern graduate work.
16. He studied as a graduate student from 1931 to 1934.
17. He taught at Jintsu Middle School in Toyama, 1934–36.
18. Okada taught at Shuyukan Middle School in Fukuoka, 1938–42. After leaving Toyama he taught at Nobeoka Middle School in Miyazaki Prefecture, 1936–38, before going to Fukuoka.
19. *hakama*—man's formal attire composed of a divided skirt.
20. Okada does not specify which works of Kusumoto Tanzan he looked at. See Okada Takehiko, ed., *Kusumoto Tanzan Sekisui zenshu (The Collected Works of Kusumoto Tanzan and Kusumoto Sekisui)* (Fukuoka, 1980).
21. This work was first presented in his major volume *Ō Yomei to Minmatsu no jugaku (Wang Yang-ming and Late Ming Confucianism)* (Tokyo, 1970).
22. This was developed in *Zazen to Seiza.*
23. Liu Tsung-chou deliberately starved himself to death with the collapse of the Ming dynasty rather than serve under the Manchu rule of the Ch'ing period. See A. Hummel, *Eminent Chinese of the Ch'ing Period,* vol. 1 (Washington, D. C.: U. S. Government Printing Office,

1943–44), pp. 532–33.

24. This is referred to in *Zazen to Seiza*. See W. T. Chan, *Reflections on Things at Hand: The Neo-Confucian Anthology Compiled by Chu Hsi and Lü Tsu-chien* (New York: Columbia University Press, 1967), pp. 289–308, where this same kind of material is contained.

25. *Zazen to Seiza*.

26. He died in 1961.

27. See R. L. Taylor, *The Cultivation of Sagehood as a Religious Goal in Neo-Confucianism* (Missoula, Mont.: Scholar's Press, 1978), pp. 35–39; "The Centered Self: Religious Autobiography in the Neo-Confucian Tradition," *History of Religions* 17, nos. 3–4 (February–May 1978): 266–83; and "Journey into Self: The Autobiographical Reflections of Hu Chih," *History of Religions* 21, no. 4 (May 1982): 321–38, where this aspect of a critical turning point is developed.

28. The Taoist philosopher Chuang Tzu spoke often of death and of the degree to which it must be accepted as simply one more transformation of natural processes. See B. Watson, trans., *Chuang Tzu: Basic Writings* (New York: Columbia University Press, 1964), especially pp. 74, 81, 113.

29. *Analects*, 2:4.

30. This is one of Okada's major themes. Academic work is necessary, but at some critical point one's learning must be based on a deep and profound experience. This is the subjective dimension that he finds lacking in the way most Confucian studies are conducted.

Kotsuza—Just Sitting

1. In the sense that if it is other than primary, it is by nature divided from the ordinary, with which it is trying to demonstrate its essential unity.

2. See R. L. Taylor, "Meditation in Ming Neo-Orthodoxy," *Journal of Chinese Philosophy* 6, no. 2 (June 1979) pp. 172–74, where the implications of this notion are discussed.

3. The issue being raised is whether or not *kotsuza* answers, at least partially, some of Wang Yang-ming's critique of *seiza* as lacking in moral action, by suggesting that *kotsuza* is even closer to action by remaining free of a designation as a "method" of quietude.

4. The late Thomas Merton, a contemporary contemplative of the Cistercian Order, often spoke of this dilemma. See, e.g., his *Conjectures of a Guilty Bystander* (Garden City, N. Y.: Doubleday Image Books, 1965) or *Contemplation in a World of Action* (Garden City, N. Y.: Doubleday & Co., 1971).

5. Hakuin comments upon the necessity of carrying Zen practice into mundane affairs. See P. Yampolsky, *The Zen Master Hakuin: Selected Writings* (New York: Columbia University Press, 1971), pp. 58, 65, 69. Ta Hui says: "Usually (to meditate) you set your mind on a still concentration point, but you must be able to use it right in the midst of the hubbub. If you have no strength amidst commotion, after all its as if you never made any effort in stillness." In C. Cleary, trans., *Swampland Flowers: The Letters and Lectures of Zen Master Ta Hui* (New York: Grove Press, 1977), p. 28.

6. A very different view seems to be taken by Shunryu Suzuki, who argues *zazen* is a practice that has no relation to any particular religious tradition. See Shunryu Suzuki, *Zen Mind, Beginner's Mind* (New York: Weatherhill, 1970), p. 76.

On Prayer

1. In 1972 Okada received an honorary doctorate from *Chung-hua hsüeh-shu yüan* (China Academy), Yang-ming Shan, Taipei.

2. The question concerns the relationship between prayer and meditation. Okada's response is close to Happold's discussion of a continuum from prayer to meditation, not seeing them as rigidly distinct categories. F. C. Happold, *Prayer and Meditation: Their Nature and Practice* (Middlesex, England: Penguin Books, 1971), pp. 29–96.

3. In other words, while both have the same basic unity with a state of quietude, they differ in that the conscious addressing of the teacher is the activation of the mind and thus the manifest mind *i-fa*, rather than unmanifest, *wei-fa*.

On the Goodness of Human Nature

1. *Mencius*, 2A:6.

2. Okada's foundation is basic Confucian theory of goodness and evil. For a summation of this material, see W. T. Chan, "The Neo-Confucian Solution of the Problem of Evil," *Neo-Confucianism, etc.: Essays by Wing-tsit Chan*, ed. Charles Chen (Hanover, N. H.: Oriental Society, 1969), pp. 88–116.

3. The role of faith has been examined in an interesting way in Holmes Rolston III, *Religious Inquiry—Participation and Detachment* (New York: Philosophical Library, 1985), especially pp. 42–49.

4. *Analects*, 14:36.

5. A similar point is argued by Richard Robinson concerning the nature of the Four Noble Truths in Buddhism, not as "premises for a deductive system but enunciation of *gnosis* to be meditated upon until the hearer 'catches on' . . ." (Richard Robinson, *The Buddhist Religion* (Belmont, Calif.: Dickenson Publishing Co., 1970), p. 29.

Art and Religion

1. See the essay, "Religion as a Dimension in Men's Spiritual Life," in Paul Tillich, *Theology of Culture* (New York: Oxford University Press, 1964), pp. 3–9.

Science and the Respect for Life

1. See, e.g., Joseph Levenson, *Confucian China and Its Modern Fate: The Problem of Intellectual Continuity* (Berkeley: University of California Press, 1958), pp. 3–14.

2. At the International Conference on Chu Hsi, July 6–15, 1982, Honolulu, Hawaii. The proceedings from this conference have now been published. See W. T. Chan, ed., *Chu Hsi and Neo-Confucianism* (Honolulu: University of Hawaii Press, 1986).

3. Some of the literature on this question was reviewed in chapter 3. See in particular R. L. Taylor, "Of Animals and Men: The Confucian Perspective," *Animal Sacrifices: Religious Perspectives on the Use of Animals in Science*, ed. Tom Regan (Philadelphia: Temple University Press, 1986), pp. 239–63.

4. For a review of these various positions, see in particular Regan and Singer references cited in chap. 3, n. 22, above.

5. This is echoed in the text we have discussed earlier, the *Western Inscription* by Chang Tsai.

6. See the literature we have referred to earlier on animal rights and the use of animals in science.

7. *Mencius*, 2A:6.

8. From a conversation with Tu Wei-ming at the International Conference on Chu Hsi, July 6–15, 1982, Honolulu, Hawaii.

9. *Analects*, 11:11.

SELECTED BIBLIOGRAPHY OF OKADA'S WORKS

Works in Japanese

Chūgoku shisō no genjitsu to risō (The Actuality and Ideal of Chinese Thought). Tokyo, 1984.

Chūgoku to Chūgokujin (China and the Chinese). Tokyo, 1973.

Edo ki no jugaku (Confucian Learning of the Edo Period). Tokyo, 1982.

Ikeda Sōen sensai chosaku shu (The Collected Works of the Teacher Ikeda Soen), ed. Okada. Hyogo, 1981.

Kinsei kanseki so kan (Pre-Modern Chinese Classics Series), ed. Okada. Kyoto, 1972.

Kinsei kōki jukashū (Confucian Writings of the Late Modern Period). Tokyo, 1972.

Kusumoto Tanzan Sekisui zenshu (The Collected Works of Kusumoto Tanzan and Kusumoto Sekisui), ed. Okada. Fukuoka, 1980.

Kusumoto Tanzan shōgai to shisō (The Life and Thought of Kusumoto Tanzan). Fukuoka, 1959.

Ō Yōmei bunshū (Anthology of Wang Yang-ming), ed. Okada. Tokyo, 1970.

Ō Yōmei to Minmatsu no jugaku (Wang Yang-ming and Late Ming Confucianism). Tokyo, 1970.

Ryu Nendai bunshu (Anthology of Liu Nien-t'ai), ed. Okada. Tokyo, 1980.

Sō Min tetsugaku josetsu (An Introduction to the Philosophy of the Sung and Ming Periods). Tokyo, 1977.

Sōsho nihon no shisōka (Japanese Schools of Thought Series), ed. Okada. Tokyo, 1977.

Shushi gaku taikei (An Outline of the Learning of Chu Hsi). ed. Okada. 15 vols. Tokyo, 1974.

Tōyō no michi (The Eastern Way). 2 vols. Tokyo, 1969, 1976.

Tsukida Mōsai Kusumoto Tanzan (Tsukida Mōsai and Kusumoto Tansan) with Namba Yukio Tokyo, 1978.

Yōmei gaku no sekai (The World of [Wang] Yang-ming Studies), ed. Okada. Tokyo, 1986.

Yōmei gaku taikei (An Outline of the Learning of [Wang] Yang-ming), ed. Okada. 12 vols. Tokyo, 1971.

Zazen to Seiza (Buddhist and Confucian Meditation). Tokyo, 1972.

Works in English Translation

"The Chu Hsi and Wang Yang-ming Schools at the End of the Ming and Tokugawa Periods," *Philosophy East and West* 23, nos. 1–2 (January–April 1973): 139–62.

"Chu Hsi and Wisdom as Hidden and Stored," in *Chu Hsi and Neo-Confucianism*, ed. W. T. Chan (Honolulu: University of Hawaii Press, 1986), pp. 197–211.

"Neo-Confucian Thinkers in Nineteenth-Century Japan," in *Confucianism and Tokugawa Culture*, ed. Peter Nosco (Princeton: Princeton University Press, 1984), pp. 215–50.

"Practical Learning in the Chu Hsi School: Yamazaki Ansai and Kaibara Ekken," in *Principle and Practicality: Essays in Neo-Confucianism and Practical Learning*, eds. W. T. deBary and I. Bloom (New York: Columbia University Press, 1979), pp. 231–306.

"Trends of Neo-Confucianism in the Sung and Ming, The Tendency of Simplification in Theory and of Emphasizing Practice," *Acta Asiatica* 52 (1987), pp. 1–28.

"Wang Chi and the Rise of Existentialism," in *Self and Society in Ming Thought*, ed. W. T. deBary (New York: Columbia University Press, 1970), pp. 121–44.

INDEX

A Commentary to Kodokanki (*Kodokanjut-sugi*), 165
A Discussion of Quiet-Sitting (*Ching-tso shuo*), 47, 132
abiding in reverence (*chü-ching*), 17, 28, 33, 38, 42, 105–106, 115, 123–124, 128, 134, 136, 138–139, 141–142, 149, 152–153, 180–181; relation to *seiza*, 139–142, 155–161
aesthetic dimension: relation to religion, 197
Agenda for Dwelling in the Mountains (*Shan-chü k'o-ch'eng*), 45, 52, 131
An Admonition on Reverence and Penance (*Ching-chai chen*), 157
An Introduction to the Philosophy of the Sung and Ming Periods (*Sō Min tetsugaku josetsu*), 196
Analects (*Lun-yü*), 96, 126, 153, 167, 169, 177, 181
Atobe Ryōken, 50–51, 154–155, 158, 159

Bashō, 84
Bergson, Henri, 181
Book of Changes (*I Ching*), 84–86, 103, 113–114, 135, 146, 191; *fu* hexagram, 43, 46, 84–85
Book of History (*Shu Ching*), 128
Book of Poetry (*Shih Ching*), 106
Book or Rites (*Li Chi*), 14, 98
Buddhism. *See* Zen Buddhism
Buddhist and Confucian Meditation. See Zazen to seiza

Chan Jo-shui, 129
Chan, Wing-tsit, 42
Chang Chiu-ch'eng, 110
Chang Nan-hsien, 141

Chang Tsai, 14, 80, 103
Ch'en Hsien-chang, 150
Ch'en Pei-hsi, 110–111
Ch'eng-Chu School. *See* School of Principle
Ch'eng Hao, 19, 38, 45, 81, 100–101, 104, 106, 114–116, 118, 127, 129–131, 175; quiet-sitting, 34–36; *Discussion of Under-standing Goodness*, 102–103; Okada's preference for, 186
cheng-hsin. See rectification of the mind and heart
ch'eng-i. See sincerity of intention
Ch'eng I, 15–18, 42, 100–102, 104–106, 186; quiet-sitting, 34–35
chih-chih. See extension of knowledge
chih-ts'ang (Japanese: *chizō*) (wisdom stored), 49, 146–152
ching (quietude). *See* quietude
ching (reverence). *See* abiding in reverence
Ching-chai chen. See An Admonition on Reverence and Penance
ching-tso. See quiet-sitting
Ching-tso shuo. See A Discussion of Quiet-Sitting
Ching-tso shuo-huo. See Later Discussion of Quiet-Sitting
ch'iung-li. See exhaustion of principle
Chou Ju-teng, 122
Chou Tun-i, 17, 21, 34, 42, 123; regarding quietude as fundamental, 17, 33, 42–43, 51, 99–100, 105, 134, 141, 150; Okada's preference for, 186; personality, 175
Chronological Biography of Chu Hsi (*Chu Tzu nien-p'u*), 173
chü-ching. See abiding in reverence
chu-ching. See regarding quietude as funda-mental

225

Chu Hsi, 15–17, 22, 27, 33–35, 42, 63, 110–111, 115–116, 153–155, 174, 182, 186; Four Beginnings, 49–50, 147; Gradual Learning, 121; half-day quiet-sitting, half-day study, 18, 37, 45, 52, 130–131; quiet-sitting, 36–41, 123–124, 127, 130, 133–134, 136, 138–147, 149; science, 200; stored wisdom, 151. *See also* investigation of things, exhaustion of principle and School of Principle

Chu Hsi and Wang Yang-ming: difference through art, 196–197; relation with Okada, 209; relation to *kotsuza*, 54, 182

Chu Tzu nien-p'u. See Chronological Biography of Chu Hsi

Ch'uan-hsi lu. See Instructions for Practical Living

ch'üan-t'i ta-yung. See "total substance and great functioning"

Chuang Tzu, 90–93, 96, 99, 103, 109, 177

Chung-yung. See Doctrine of the Mean

Classic of Combat (Tosen kyo), 88

Claudel, Paul, 84

Collection of Sayings of Chu Hsi on Quiet-Sitting (Shushi seiza shusetsu), 27, 145

Confucian attitudes: abortion, 67–69, 203–204; art and religion, 196–198; biomedical ethics, 67–69, 202–203; concept of evil, 193–194; critique of Zen Buddhism, 9, 59, 106–117; death, 61, 72–73, 205; ethical obligations to animals, 66–67, 200–202; goal of sagehood, 13–14; meditation, 123–162, 179–184; prayer, 189–190; science and subjectivity, 204; technological society, 204–206; world religions, 71–72, 210–212. *See also* Okada Takehiko

Confucian enlightenment experience, 14, 45, 131, 136, 138–139, 156, 187

Confucianism: as a living tradition, 7–8; studied only as history, 10, 181–182; Okada's own study, 167. *See also* religion

Confucius, 96–97, 134

critique of Zen Buddhism, 59, 106–117

cultivation of the person (*hsiu-shen*), 15

deBary, Wm. Theodore, 7; burden of culture, 22; Mandarin/Bakufu orthodoxies, 25

death: grief, 191; of teacher, 175; of first wife, 175; no thought of, 205; no view of afterlife, 72–73, 191–192; related to ethics, 202–203

Discussion of the Pavilion of Repentance (Kaidō setsu), 126

Discussion of Personal Errors (Hui-wu shuo), 141

Discussion of Understanding Goodness (Shih-jen p'ien), 102–103, 127

Doctrine of the Mean (Chung-yung), 36, 43, 79, 98, 106, 147–148, 153; at teacher's funderal, 175

Dogen, 120, 172, 183

Eisai, 172

Elementary Learning (Hsiao-hsüeh), 27, 152–153

exhaustion of principle (*ch'iung-li*), 16, 22–25, 33, 38, 42, 105, 112, 124, 136–146, 149, 152–153, 156–161

extension of knowledge (*chih-chih*), 15–16, 20, 22–25, 33, 105, 112, 124, 152–153, 156, 180, 187

Four Beginnings, 49, 107, 147

Fu-ch'i kuei. See Rules for Returning in Seven

Fujita Toko, 165

Fujiwara Seika, 25–26

Fukuda Shigeru, 175

Gakushi roku. See Record of Learning and Thought

Gakushū roku. See Record of Learning and Repeating

Geertz, Clifford, 65

goodness (*jen*), 19, 50, 66, 97, 102–103, 107–108, 114, 127, 147, 151

Great Learning (Ta-hsüeh), 14–16, 20, 23, 27, 33, 43, 71, 79, 149, 156

Great Ultimate (*T'ai-chi*), 43, 99, 148, 156, 160

Hakuin, 82, 120

Han Fei-tzu, 87–88, 103–104

Hayashi Razan, 25–26, 28–29

Heaven. *See T'ien*

Ho-tung School, 22

Hsi-ming. See Western Inscription

Hsiao-hsüeh. See Elementary Learning

Hsieh Liang-tso, 134

Hsin-hsin ming. See Mind of Faith Inscription

Hsin-hsüeh. See School of Mind

hsiu-shen. See cultivation of the person

Hsüeh Hsüan, 22

Hu Chü-jen, 22–23
Hu Hsien, 140
Hu Hung, 37, 140–141
Huang Shan-ku, 100
Hui Neng, 120
Hui-wu shuo. See Discussion of Personal Errors
humaneness. *See* goodness
Hung Chih, 120

I Ching. See Book of Changes
i-fa (manifest [mind]), 36
i-nien. See singleness of thought
idealism, 87, 94, 97, 108
innate knowing (*liang-chih*), 20
Instructions for Practical Living (*Ch'uan-hsi lu*), 171
investigation of things (*ko-wu*), 15–16, 20, 22, 33, 112, 124, 136, 138, 141, 149, 152–153, 156, 159, 180, 187
Ishida Baigan, 26

jen. See goodness
jitsugaku. See practical learning

Kaibu Shiki, 146
Kaidō ki. See The Record of the Pavilion of Repentance
Kaidō setsu. See Discussion of the Pavilion of Repentance
Kao P'an-lung, 23, 25, 29, 31, 129–137, 174, 186; neo-Chu Hsi scholar, 125; *p'ing-ch'ang* (ordinariness), 183; relation to *kotsuza*, 183; quiet-sitting, 44–48, 56–57, 128–137
Kameyama Umpei, 165, 167
Kaneko Sōzan, 138
Kang Yü-wei, 125
Kant, 172
Kimon School, 26
ko-wu. See investigation of things
Kominsai, 185–187
Kōriki Sōseki, 50, 152
kotsuza (just sitting), 52–55, 57–59, 179–184; exclusive Confucian practice, 184; "Just Sitting" (a poem), 166; *naimen teki shūtaisei* (true inner subjectivity), 179; relation to *seiza*, 179, 182; relation to *zazen*, 180
Kuei-ku Tzu, 87–88, 103

K'un-hsüeh chi. See Recollections of the Toils of Learning
kung-fu. See moral action
Kusumoto Masatsugu, 29, 128, 148, 151, 186; interpretation of *Western Inscription*, 103–104; Okada meeting and studying under, 171–176
Kusumoto Sekisui, 28, 30
Kusumoto Tanzan, 9, 28–30, 116, 151, 174–176; daily schedule, 161–162; method of *seiza*, 50, 152–161; *seiza* realization, 48, 50, 123, 125–128, 133, 135–137, 145, 147–148; wisdom stored, 49–50, 146–152
Kusumoto Tanzan shōgai to shisō. See The Life and Thought of Kusumoto Tanzan

Lao Tzu, 99, 103, 109, 128; connection to Legalism, 88–89; transcendentalism, 90–91
Later Discussion of Quiet-Sitting (*Ching-tso shuo-huo*), 48, 133
Legalism (*fa-chia*), 44, 86–89. *See also* Han Fei-tzu, Kuei-ku Tzu, Shang Yang, Shen Pu-hai, Sun Tzu and Wu Tzu
Levenson, Joseph, 199
li. See principle
Li Chi. See Book of Rites
Li Erh-ch'ü, 162
Li-hsüeh. See School of Principle
Li Kuang-ti, 145
Li Yen-p'ing, 34, 36–39, 45, 115, 119, 123, 130, 139–140, 142, 145–146, 150
liang-chih. See innate knowing
Lieh Tzu, 93
Liu Tsung-chou, 29–30, 49, 116–117, 125, 174
Lo Ch'in-shun, 26
Lo Hung-hsien, 21, 30, 49, 136, 150–151
Lo Ts'ung-yen, 34, 37, 115, 119, 123, 140, 150
Lu Fu-t'ing, 119
Lu Hsiang-shan, 18, 110, 137, 174, 186
Lu-Wang School. *See* School of Mind

Mao Tse-tung, 86
Maruyama Masao, 24
Matsushima kōki. See Matsushima Travel Journal
Matsushima Travel Journal (*Matsushima kōki*), 129
Meditation Hymn (*Zazen wasan*), 82

Mencius, 18–19, 38, 66–67, 127; human nature, 60–61, 193–195; King Hsüan and the cow, 107; theory of sagehood, 13
Mind of Faith Inscription (Hsin-hsin ming), 82
Miyake Shōsai, 146
Mo Tzu, 91
Mokushō Zen, 119–120
moral action (*kung-fu*), 21, 183

nature, world of: as Absolute Truth, 83–84; as quiet, 84–86. *See also T'ien li* (Principle of Heaven)
Nieh Pao, 21, 30, 49, 136, 150–151
Nietzsche, 181
Nishida Kitaro, 170–181
Non-Ultimate (*wu-chi*), 43
Nosco, Peter, 25
Notes on the Commentary on Kodokanjutsugi (Hyōchū Kodokanjutsugi), 165
nuclear war, 70–71, 205, 207–209

Ogyū Sorai, 89
Ōhashi Totsuan, 28–29, 126, 138
Okada Shigenari, 165
Okada Takehiko: abortion, 67–69, 203–204; art and religion, 196–198; as living Confucian, 7–8; attitudes on death, 70, 72–73, 191–192; biomedical ethics, 67–69, 202–203; ethics and animals, 66–67, 200–202; human nature, 60–63, 193–195; humanistic spirit, 77; life, 165–178; nuclear war, 70–71, 207–209; prayer, 189–190; technological society, 69–70, 204–206; science and human values, 63–67, 199–200; world religions, 71–72; 210–212. *See also* quiet-sitting, Zen Buddhism
On Calming the Nature (Ting-hsing shu), 80
Ōta Zensai, 88
Ou-yang Hsiu, 110

pan-jih ching-tso pan-jih tu shu (a half-day quiet-sitting, a half-day study), 18, 37, 45, 52, 130–131
practical learning (*jitsugaku*), 25
prayer: example of Okada, 175; relation to meditation, 190; use by Okada, 189
principle (*li*), 13, 15–18, 20, 22–25, 49, 104–105, 108, 138, 146–147, 156
Principle of Heaven. *See T'ien-li*

Questions on the Great Learning (Ta-hsüeh huo-wen), 149, 158
quiet-sitting (*ching-tso, seiza*), 9, 17, 27–28, 52–55, 77–83; and Ch'eng Hao, 35–36, 101; and Ch'eng I, 35, 101; and Chu Hsi, 36–41; and exhaustion of principle, 137–146; and Kao P'an-lung, 44–48, 128–137; and Kusumoto Tanzan, 48–52, 123–126; and moral action, 56–59; and wisdom stored, 146–152; breath control, 33; critique by Confucians, 117–122; critique of Zen Buddhism, 56, 106–117; exclusive Confucian practice, 184; origins, 34–36; relation to *zazen*, 50, 77–78, 82, 94, 117, 144–145, 154; rules for practice, 128–137, 152–162; *seiza* realization, 48, 138–139, 146, 152, 162; *seiza* to *kotsuza*, 52–55, 179–184; stilling the mind, 43, 78–83; technological society, 204–205. *See also* Zen Buddhism
quietude (*ching*): idealist use, 94–106; Legalist use, 86–89; of nature, 83–86; Okada's interpretation, 42–44, 83–93; problem of excessive, 17, 34; relation to reverence, 98–106; reassessed by Chou Tun-i, 41–44; transcendentalist use, 89–93

realism. *See* Legalism
Recollections of the Toils of Learning (K'un-hsüeh chi), 44–45, 129
Record of Learning and Repeating (Gakushū roku), 126–127, 139
Record of Learning and Thought (Gakushi roku), 126
Records of Learning of the Sung and Yüan Confucians (Sung-Yüan hsüeh-an), 34
rectification of the mind and heart (*cheng-hsin*), 15
regarding quietude as fundamental (*chu-ching*), 17, 28, 33, 38, 42–43, 51, 99–100, 105–106, 134, 141, 148, 150
religion: Confucianism as, 57–59; future of Confucian, 212; intolerance of Western, 210–211; real problems faced by Western, 211
Researches in Confucian Thought of the Sung and Ming Dynasties (Sō Min jidai Jugaku shisō no kenkyū), 176
reverence (*ching*). *See* abiding in reverence (*chü-ching*)

Rinzai Zen, 119. *See also* Zen Buddhism
Rules for Returning in Seven (*Fu-ch'i kuei*), 45–46, 52, 134–136

sagehood: as a realizable goal, 13; for Okada, 176
Saikontan. See Vegetable Root Discourses
Sato Hitochi, 175
Satō Issai, 29–30, 126, 138, 165
Satō Naokata, 27–28, 145
School of Mind, 18–21; Kusumoto Tanzan's relation to, 29–30, 136–137; opposition to mediation, 21, 117–122; quietist branch, 21, 24, 136, 150
School of Principle, 15–18, 21–26, 36; during Tokugawa, 24–28; late Ming, 21–24; Kusumoto Tanzan's tradition, 28–30, 123–128, 137–139, 146–162
science: need for humanistic development, 63–66, 199–200; relation to inner subjectivity, 204. *See also* Confucian attitudes
self-cultivation: School of Mind approach, 18–21; School of Principle approach, 15–18
Seng Ts'an, 82
Senju Kensai, 138
Settling Obstinacy (Ting-wan). See Western Inscription
Shan-chü k'o-ch'eng. See Agenda for Dwelling in the Mountains
Shang Yang, 87
Shen Pu-hai, 87
Shih Chieh, 109
Shih Ching. See Book of Poetry
Shih-jen p'ien. See Discussion of Understanding Goodness
Shijinsha, 187–188
Shushi seiza shusetsu. See Collection of the Sayings of Chu Hsi on Quiet-Sitting
sincerity of intention (*ch'eng-i*), 15, 125
singleness of thought (*i-nien*), 40
Sō Min jidai Jugaku shisō no kenkyū. See Researches in Confucian Thought of the Sung and Ming Dynasties
Sō Min tetsugaku josetsu. See An Introduction to the Philosophy of the Sung and Ming Periods
Stace, W. T., 64–65
Sun Tzu, 87–89, 103
Sung-Yüan hsüeh-an. See Records of Learning of the Sung and Yüan Confucians

Ta-hsüeh. See Great Learning
Ta-hsüeh huo-wen. See Questions on the Great Learning
Ta Hui, 120, 183
The Classic of Control (Wo-ch'i ching), 88
The Life and Thought of Kusumoto Tanzan (Kusumoto Tanzan shōgai to shisō), 174
The Record of Kodokan (Kodokanki), 165
The Record of the Pavilion of Repentance (Kaidō ki), 126
t'i and *yung* (substance and function), 37, 98–99, 113, 128, 136, 138, 140, 150
T'ien (Heaven): as Absolute Truth, 13, 83
T'ien-li (Principle of Heaven), 37, 104, 110, 118–119, 124–125, 132, 140; as Absolute Truth, 13; directly experienced, 14, 37, 123, 129; as nature, 83–86
Tillich, Paul, 197–198
Ting-hsing shu. See On Calming the Nature
Tokugawa Nariaki, 165
Tōsen kyo. See Classic of Combat
total substance and great functioning (*ch'üan-t'i ta-yung*), 16, 40, 63, 200
transcendentalism, 89–93
Tsukida Mōsai, 29–30, 138, 145, 161
Ts'ung-jen School, 22
Tu Wei-ming, 200, 204
Tung-lin School, 23, 44, 187. *See also* Kao P'an-lung

Vegetable Root Discourses (Saikontan), 43, 81–82, 106

Wach, Joachim, 17, 57–58
Wang An-shih, 140
Wang Chi, 121
Wang Hsin-min, 81
Wang Ken, 121
Wang Shih-huai, 150
Wang Yang-ming, 18, 20–21, 108–109, 115–120, 124–125, 129, 132, 149–150, 153, 171, 174, 182; existentialism, 121; objection to *seiza*, 117–119; Okada's rejection, 186; sudden learning, 121
Wang Yang-ming School, 18–21, 29–30. *See also* School of Mind
Watsuji Tetsuro, 171
wei-fa (umanifest [mind]), 36
Western Inscription (Hsi-ming), 14, 26, 103–104

Wo-ch'i ching. See The Classic of Control
World War II, 176–177, 185
Wu Tzu, 87
Wu Yü-pi, 22–23

Yamazaki Ansai, 26–28, 30, 126, 137–138, 146, 157, 160
Yanagawa Gōgi, 27, 145
Yang Shih, 45, 96, 123, 130, 150
Yi T'oegae, 25–26
Yin T'un, 134
Yoshimura Shūyō, 29, 126
Yuizean, 187

Zazen to seiza, 31, 35, 37, 42–44, 48, 52, 59–60; polemical nature of, 9; technical yet personal nature of, 9–10; when written, 174
Zazen wasan. See Meditation Hymn
Zen Buddhism, 8–9, 99–100, 111; critique of, 59, 106–117; Okada's practice of, 170–171, 176; quietude can lead to, 17, 34, 100, 105; relation to *kotsuza,* 180, *seiza* and *zazen,* 50, 77–78, 82, 94, 117, 144–145, 154
Zen painting, 198